Qualitative Research Approaches for Psychotherapy

Qualitative Research Approaches for Psychotherapy offers the reader a range of current qualitative research approaches congruent with the values and practices of psychotherapy itself: experience-based, reflective, contextualized, and critical.

This volume contains 14 compelling, challenging new essays from authors in both the Northern and Southern hemispheres, writing from a range of theoretical and cultural perspectives. The book covers both established and emerging approaches to qualitative research in this field, beginning with case study, ending with post-qualitative, and with hermeneutic, reflexive, psychosocial, Talanoa, queer, feminist, critical race theory, heuristic, grounded theory, authoethnographic, poetic and collaborative writing approaches in between. These chapters introduce and explore the complexity of the specific research approach, its assumptions, challenges, ethics, and potentials, including examples from the authors' own research, therapeutic practice, and life. The book is not a 'how to' guide to methods but, rather, a stimulus for psychotherapy researchers to think and feel their way differently into their research endeavours.

This book will be an invaluable resource to postgraduate students, practitioners, and established researchers in psychotherapy who are undertaking (or considering) qualitative research for their projects. It will also appeal to course tutors and trainers looking for a volume around which to structure a qualitative research methods course.

Keith Tudor is Professor of Psychotherapy at Auckland University of Technology (AUT), Aotearoa New Zealand, where he is also Co-Lead of the AUT Group for Research in the Psychological Therapies. He is the editor of *Claude Steiner, Emotional Activist* (2020), and the author of *Conscience and Critic* (2017), both published by Routledge.

Jonathan Wyatt is Professor of Qualitative Inquiry and a Co-Director of the Centre for Creative-Relational Inquiry at the University of Edinburgh, UK. His book, *Therapy, Stand-up, and the Gesture of Writing: Towards Creative-Relational Inquiry*, published by Routledge, won the 2020 ICQI Book Award.

Qualitative Research Approaches for Psychotherapy

Reflexivity, Methodology, and Criticality

Edited by
Keith Tudor and Jonathan Wyatt

LONDON AND NEW YORK

Designed cover image: Tess Wyatt

First published 2023
by Routledge
4 Park Square, Milton Park, Abingdon, Oxon OX14 4RN

and by Routledge
605 Third Avenue, New York, NY 10158

Routledge is an imprint of the Taylor & Francis Group, an informa business

© 2023 selection and editorial matter, Keith Tudor and Jonathan Wyatt; individual chapters, the contributors

The rights of Keith Tudor and Jonathan Wyatt to be identified as the author[s] of the editorial material, and of the authors for their individual chapters, has been asserted in accordance with sections 77 and 78 of the Copyright, Designs and Patents Act 1988.

All rights reserved. No part of this book may be reprinted or reproduced or utilised in any form or by any electronic, mechanical, or other means, now known or hereafter invented, including photocopying and recording, or in any information storage or retrieval system, without permission in writing from the publishers.

Trademark notice: Product or corporate names may be trademarks or registered trademarks, and are used only for identification and explanation without intent to infringe.

ISBN: 978-1-032-24946-9 (hbk)
ISBN: 978-1-032-24948-3 (pbk)
ISBN: 978-1-003-28085-9 (ebk)

DOI: 10.4324/9781003280859

Typeset in Bembo
by Taylor & Francis Books

Contents

List of illustrations	vii
Contributor Biographies	viii

Introduction   1
KEITH TUDOR AND JONATHAN WYATT

1 Into the thick of it: Troubling case studies and researching close to therapeutic practice   3
LIZ BONDI

2 Hermeneutic phenomenology: Exploring and making meaning of lived experience in psychotherapy research   15
KERRY THOMAS-ANTTILA AND MARGOT SOLOMON

3 Using performative meta-reflexivity in psychotherapy research   31
JACQUELINE KAREN ANDREA SERRA UNDURRAGA

4 A psychosocial coming into play: Researching authenticity in therapy, the academy, and friendship   45
NINI FANG, ANNE PIRRIE, AND PETER REDMAN

5 Feminist research in psychotherapy: The strange case of the United Kingdom's 'hostile environment' policy   58
EMILY LE COUTEUR

6 Critical race theory: A methodology for research in psychotherapy   72
DIVINE CHARURA AND SONYA CLYBURN

7 Pasifika research methodologies and psychotherapy   87
JULIA IOANE AND ATHENA TAPU TU'ITAHI

8 Queering psychotherapy research: Collaborative autoethnography and fossicking   102
TRISH THOMPSON AND DANIEL X. HARRIS

vi *Contents*

9 Critical heuristics in psychotherapy research: From 'I-who-feels' to
   'We-who-care—and act'   115
   KEITH TUDOR

10 Keeping it real: Grounded theory for a profession on the brink   133
    ELIZABETH DAY

11 Researching from the inside: Using autoethnography to produce
    ethical research from within psychotherapy practice   149
    SARAH HELPS

12 (Re)searching poetically: Poetic inquiry in psychotherapy   163
    EMMA GREEN

13 Putting ourselves in the picture: Phototherapy, collaborative
    writing, and psychotherapy research   176
    JANE SPEEDY AND JONATHAN WYATT

14 From post-qualitative inquiry towards creative-relational inquiry in
    (and beyond) the education/training of therapists   193
    FIONA MURRAY

15 Re-searching research: Reflections on contributions to qualitative
    and post-qualitative research   208
    KEITH TUDOR AND JONATHAN WYATT

    Index   219

Illustrations

Figures

3.1	Reflexivities as productive ways of relating	32
9.1	The four quadrants of knowledge systems (Wilber, 1997)	122
9.2	The four quadrants of Wilber's (1997) knowledge systems applied to heuristic research enquiry	124
13.1	Jane at seven years old (photograph: Francis Frith)	179
13.2	Jonathan at six or seven	180
13.3	Jane at 17 years old (photograph: Michael Speedy)	181
13.4	Jonathan, aged 17 (photograph: Carolyn Markey)	182
13.5	Jane at 66 (photograph: Sarah Hall)	184
13.6	Jonathan at 60 (photograph: Tess Wyatt)	184
13.7	Chris and Jane	187

Table

3.1	Example of four conceptualisations of subjectivity and their impact on the use of reflexivity and its productions	33

Contributor Biographies

Liz Bondi is a psychodynamic practitioner in private practice with strong links to a voluntary sector counselling service in Edinburgh, Scotland. She is also Honorary Professorial Fellow at the University of Edinburgh, where she previously contributed to counsellor education. She has published extensively, with recent co-edited books including *Practitioner Research in Counselling and Psychotherapy: The Power of Examples* (Palgrave Macmillan, 2016) and *Making Spaces: Putting Psychoanalytic Thinking to Work* (Karnac, 2014).

Divine Charura is a Professor of Counselling Psychology at York St John University, England. He is a counselling psychologist and registered as a practitioner psychologist in the United Kingdom. Divine is also an Honorary Fellow of the United Kingdom Council for Psychotherapy (UKCP) and an adult psychotherapist. As a psychologist, psychotherapist, and researcher, his work focuses on psychotraumatology and the impact of trauma across the lifespan. Divine has co-authored a number of books in psychology and psychotherapy.

Sonya Clyburn is an Associate Professor in the counselling program at The Chicago School of Professional Psychology. She is a licensed clinical psychologist. Dr Clyburn has been practicing clinical psychology for over 15 years and has a private practice. Dr Clyburn is a certified trainer, professor, consultant, evaluator, life coach, and victim advocate. She also coordinates the Crisis Intervention Management Team and supervises pre-doctoral students and psychiatric residents.

Elizabeth Day is Head of Department of Psychotherapy & Counselling at Auckland University of Technology, where she conducts and supervises research, and teaches in the Master of Psychotherapy programme. She publishes on field theory, mindfulness, gender and sexuality identity, and the philosophical bases of psychotherapy, telepsychotherapy, and professional practice, and co-edited the book Psychotherapy and Counselling: Reflections on Practice (Oxford University Press, 2015). Her professional service includes research committee chair and member of the Psychotherapy & Counselling Federation of Australia, and editorial board member of Psychotherapy & Counselling Journal of Australia.

Contributor Biographies ix

Nini Fang is a Lecturer in Counselling and Psychotherapy at the University of Edinburgh, UK. She has published extensively in the fields of psychosocial studies and creative, qualitative inquiry concerning the lived domains of the other. She is an Associate Director for the Centre for Creative-Relational Inquiry and also sits on the Executive Board for the Association for Psychosocial Studies and the Editorial Board for New Associations (British Psychoanalytic Council).

Emma Green is a psychotherapist living and working in Tāmaki Makaurau/ Auckland, Aotearoa New Zealand. She taught in the Department of Psychotherapy & Counselling at Auckland University of Technology. She now works exclusively in private practice. Her research interests include culture, gender and sexuality, critical whiteness, transformational social change, feminist theory, and psychotherapy including Jungian theory. She has a special interest in qualitative methodologies that attend to different ways of knowing.

Daniel X. Harris is Associate Dean, Research & Innovation in the School of Education, RMIT University (Melbourne, Australia), an Australian Research Council Future Fellow, and Co-Director of Creative Agency research lab: www.creativeresearchhub.com. Harris is editor of the book series Creativity, Education and the Arts (Palgrave), and has authored over 100 articles/book chapters, 19 books, as well as plays, films, and spoken-word performances. Their research focuses on creativity studies, cultural, sexual, and gender diversities, and performance and activism.

Sarah Helps is a consultant clinical psychologist and systemic psychotherapist at King's College Hospital, London, UK, and lecturer at King's College London, UK. Her research interests involve examining systemic, relational, and leadership practices using autoethnographic, conversation analytic, and other qualitative methodologies. She held academic, clinical, and leadership positions at the Tavistock Clinic in London until 2021 and has worked widely across London and the South-East. She is editor of the Journal of Family Therapy.

Julia Ioane is Samoan, born and raised in Aotearoa New Zealand. She is a pracademic with a small psychology practice as a clinical psychologist, and is an Associate Professor in Clinical Psychology at Massey University, Auckland. Julia continues to advocate for Indigenous/Pasifika knowledge to be embedded with the curriculum, methodologies, research practice, and frameworks. She also prioritises teaching psychology that is inclusive of the diverse and collective communities she and her colleagues serve in Aotearoa New Zealand.

Emily le Couteur is a counselling psychologist in professional training at the University of Manchester in North-West England, interested in feminist and critical theory, and a proponent of furthering a politicised, social justice agenda in counselling psychology and beyond conducive to the disruption

x Contributor Biographies

of systemic oppression. She currently works with a homeless outreach team in Manchester and is writing her thesis—a qualitative exploration into the lives of single women experiencing homelessness.

Fiona Murray is a practicing counsellor and a lecturer in Counselling and Psychotherapy and Applied Social Sciences at the University of Edinburgh, Scotland. She is also a Co-Director of the Centre for Creative-Relational Inquiry.

Anne Pirrie is Reader in Education at the University of the West of Scotland. Her monograph Virtue and the Quiet Art of Scholarship: Reclaiming the University (Routledge, 2019) offers a fresh and unorthodox perspective on what it means to be a 'good knower' in a higher education environment dominated by the market order.

Peter Redman is a Senior Lecturer in Sociology at the Open University, England. He is a member of the Association for Psychosocial Studies, and a former editor of the journal *Psychoanalysis, Culture & Society* and Palgrave's 'Studies in the Psychosocial' book series.

Jacqueline Karen Andrea Serra Undurraga is a lecturer in Counselling and Psychotherapy at the University of Edinburgh. In previous research, Karen has worked on re-conceptualising narcissism from a relational and embodied perspective and thought about the ways of using existential phenomenology in humanistic psychotherapy. She then worked on reflexivity, proposing the concepts of diffractive reflexivity and performative meta-reflexivity. Karen is currently working on the intersection between postcolonial/decolonial perspectives, posthumanist theories, and psychotherapy.

Margot Solomon retired in 2020 from 26 years teaching on the Master of Psychotherapy in the Department of Psychotherapy & Counselling, Auckland University of Technology. She has a passion for research methodologies that are a fit for psychotherapy, especially hermeneutic phenomenology and heuristic self-study, and continues to work as a psychoanalytic and group analytic psychotherapist in private practice. She is a member of Group Analysis International, New Zealand Association of Psychotherapy, Australian Association of Group Psychotherapy, and International Association of Relational Psychoanalytic Psychotherapy.

Jane Speedy is Professor Emeritus in education at the University of Bristol, UK, and she also has a studio practice as a fine artist (a painter). She is best known for her work in the field of collaborative writing as inquiry: her latest book is *Artful Collaborative Inquiry: Making and Writing Creative, Qualitative Research* (Routledge, 2022), edited with Davina Kirkpatrick, Sue Porter, and Jonathan Wyatt.

Athena Tapu Tu'itahi is a psychotherapist, who is registered with both the Psychotherapists Board of Aotearoa New Zealand and the Accident

Compensation Commission, and a lecturer at Auckland University of Technology. She has experience working in Pasifika mental health services at Auckland and Waitematā District Health Boards and Adolescent and Children mental health services. She has worked in the community at Auckland City Mission—Te Whare Hīnātore and at St Vinnies Charitable Trust, as well as community wellbeing programmes such as Dressed in Confidence.

Kerry Thomas–Anttila, PhD, MHSc (Psychotherapy) (Hons), MA (Hons), is a Senior Lecturer and Programme Leader of the Master of Psychotherapy in the Department of Psychotherapy and Counselling, Auckland University of Technology. She teaches, researches, and supervises in the Department and also works as a psychoanalytic psychotherapist in private practice.

Trish Thompson (she/her) is a clinical counsellor, psychotherapist, and supervisor in private practice in Melbourne, Australia. She works with individuals, couples, and groups, and has also worked with community organisations, notably with the LGBTQI+ community. She has taught in counselling training programmes and has a strong interest in mentoring counsellors in early career, particularly through group supervision, combining reflective practice with creative and artistic collaborations. She has contributed articles to Psychotherapy & Counselling Today and Psychotherapy.net.

Introduction

Keith Tudor and Jonathan Wyatt

We are delighted to welcome you, the reader, to this book on qualitative research in psychotherapy.

The book comprises 14 chapters on different forms of or approaches to qualitative research as used in or applied to researching psychotherapy. While we focus on research into the practice of psychotherapy, we are aware that, for practitioners in different countries, there is considerable overlap between the practice and discipline of psychotherapy and that of counselling and of clinical and counselling psychology and we are delighted that the contributors to this volume represent these different disciplines of the psychological therapies. We are also delighted that ours has been a collaboration, primarily between our two universities—those of Auckland University of Technology (AUT) in Aotearoa New Zealand (with five colleagues contributing four chapters) and the University of Edinburgh (UoE) in Scotland (with five colleagues contributing five chapters), together with another four authors from elsewhere who are affiliated with the Centre for Creative-Relational Inquiry at the UoE—and we hope that this marks the beginning of further exchange and future collaborations between us. In a final chapter, we offer our own reflections on the contributions and the volume as a whole.

We have placed the chapters in an order (one ordering of many possible). The ordering is, on the one hand, to some extent suggestive of a historicity, the book beginning with case study and ending with post-qualitative and beyond. This nod to historicity is tentative and 'soft', each chapter's approach, whatever its traditions, being located in the now, the present of undertaking psychotherapy research. On the other hand, the ordering arguably takes the reader from a focus upon the intimate (the therapeutic encounter itself) into a focus on the explicitly sociopolitical, and onto a foregrounding of the creative and literary. There are overlaps aplenty between these, hence our decision not to have book sections.

Norman Denzin, who has made a considerable contribution to the qualitative revolution in research (see Denzin & Lincoln, 2005), suggests that qualitative research methods have moved to the mainstream (Denzin, 2009, 2010). While we agree with this with regard to the social sciences as a whole, we think this does not yet apply to the psychological therapies, at least from the

DOI: 10.4324/9781003280859-1

2 Introduction

point of view of therapists and researchers. There is, however, still some way to go for this particular revolution to reach the palaces of policy-makers who largely ignore the practice of psychotherapy and the vaults of funders who, for the main, don't support research in psychotherapy. We hope that, in some small way, this volume (along with others, including two recent volumes edited by Bager-Charleson & McBeath, 2020, 2022) helps this larger progressive project.

We thank all our contributors for being part of this project with us from start to finish. We are grateful for their commitment, patience, and outstanding work. Jonathan thanks Tess, present as always; and Keith, for being such a thoughtful, generous collaborator. Keith thanks Jonathan, for these same qualities—as we acknowledge in the reflective chapter which closes the book, it's been a delightful and easy collaboration. Keith also thanks his colleagues at AUT—Elizabeth, Emma, Kerry, and Margot—for their positive response to the invitation to be involved in this project; and, lastly and firstly, Louise for her support of his writing—and editing—habit! Finally, we both thank Angie Strachan for her fine editorial assistance and colleagues at Routledge—Hannah Shakespeare, Lucy Kennedy, and Matt Bickerton—for seeing this book through its production.

References

Bager-Charleson, S., & McBeath, A. (Eds.). (2020). *Enjoying research in counselling and psychotherapy: Qualitative, quantitative and mixed methods research.* Springer.

Bager-Charleson, S., & McBeath, A. (Eds.). (2022). *Supporting research in counselling and psychotherapy: Qualitative, quantitative and mixed methods research.* Springer.

Denzin, N. K. (2009). *Qualitative inquiry under fire: Toward a new paradigm dialogue.* Left Coast Press.

Denzin, N. K. (2010). Moments, mixed methods, and paradigm dialogs. *Qualitative Inquiry, 16*(6), 419–427. https://doi.org/10.1177/1077800410364608

Denzin, N. K., & Lincoln, Y. S. (2005). Introduction: The discipline and practice of qualitative research. In N. K. Denzin & Y. S. Lincoln (Eds.), *The handbook of qualitative research* (3rd ed., pp. 1–32). Sage.

1 Into the thick of it

Troubling case studies and researching close to therapeutic practice

Liz Bondi

Case study research is a widely cited qualitative methodology for exploring therapeutic practice, but what is meant by a case study is open to question and full of contention, which this chapter explores. Drawing on discussions of case study research from across the social sciences as well as the field of psychotherapy, I trouble the concept of the 'case' and open up questions about the focus and framing of 'case studies'. Using examples, I explore the power of 'thick description' and unique particularities in conveying important qualities of practice to a range of audiences.

★★★★

Beginnings

It is 3pm and, as expected, the buzzer goes. I release the main door to let Jessica onto the stair and I open the front door of the first-floor flat, which is home to my consulting room. We have not met before or even spoken on the phone; she is coming here today following a brief email exchange initiated by her enquiry about seeing me in my capacity as a psychotherapist. I have offered a meeting at this time, conveyed some basic information about where to find me and my fee, and let her know that I do not have a waiting room, requesting that she arrive as close as possible to the appointed time. In so doing I have begun to establish the frame for our therapeutic relationship, echoing Freud's (1913) recommendations for the beginning of treatment about meeting at a fixed time and place for an agreed fee. I hear Jessica close the main door behind her and then her footsteps, light and precise on the stairs. Soon a smartly dressed, petite young woman reaches the landing, sees me at the open door and smiles shyly. I welcome her in and gesture her to cross the small hallway of the flat to the open door of my consulting room. As she enters, I ask her to take a seat on the sofa. Following her into the room, I close the door firmly and take my seat. I notice what I take to be a hesitation in the way she looks around the room and I think perhaps that I register a sense of her fragility as well as her uncertainty. Then I say, 'so you found me'. Reflecting on this later, I realise that I want to let her hear the sound of my voice again and I want to give both of us a chance to stay in, rather than rush past, this moment at the very beginning. My

DOI: 10.4324/9781003280859-2

4   *Liz Bondi*

> *choice of words, I also come to realise, is full of hope, conveying the possibility that not only has she found her way to my address but that at an unconscious level she might also have found someone she is looking for (Gordon, 2009). Jessica responds to my statement by saying that she likes this part of the city. Perhaps she is also meeting my hopefulness with her own.*

I began my academic career in the early 1980s in the field of human geography, and, as I worked out the focus and approach I would adopt in my doctoral research, I swiftly assumed that it would entail focusing on a particular example, the case in question being both a place (a city) and a process (consultation on a plan to reorganise school provision). Place-based examples were (and remain) very common in my original field, with an interest in the specific and the particular, being an aspect of what might be called a geographical sensibility. While there was also a thriving field of quantitative geography, qualitative research was equally if not more well-established, accompanied by extensive engagement with methodological debates evident in the wider social sciences. When I trained as a counsellor in the mid-1990s I was soon immersed in a form of clinical practice that valued the personal, the subjective, and the particular in another way and from another perspective. However, I was very much at home epistemologically, in the sense of understanding valuable forms of knowing and knowledge to be steeped in these qualities. It was, therefore, both bemusing and shocking to discover that discussions of research in counselling and psychotherapy seemed to be bedevilled by antagonism with, and sometimes disrespect for, methodologies that did not conform to normative expectations of medical science, characterised by objectivity and detachment, and remote from the profound particularity of clinical encounters. It was a relief to turn to thinkers like Michael Rustin (1997) making connections between epistemological debates in the social sciences with which I was familiar, and clinical research in counselling, psychotherapy, and psychoanalysis. Echoing the influential ethnographic engagement of French philosopher Bruno Latour (1983; Latour & Woolgar, 1979) with the generation of knowledge in and through the laboratory, Rustin (1997, 2001) considered whether, and if so how, the consulting room might be the clinician's equivalent. On this understanding, clinical practice is integral to generating knowledge—that is research—entailing intensive and systematic investigation, which is a typical definition of research (Bondi & Fewell, 2016, 2017).

The consulting room is where the majority of practitioners work, encountering their clients or patients as individuals, couples, families, or groups. These encounters are deeply personal and utterly dependent on the subjectivity of those involved. Developing new knowledge or understanding for both practitioners and those who consult them takes place through the subjective experience of the participants. In the extract above, my account of the very beginning of my therapeutic work with Jessica relies heavily on my embodied, subjective experience of meeting her in person for the first time, in a way that I hope is recognisable to others, and which draws attention to details, which

Into the thick of it   5

might go unremarked, but which, once noticed, carry meanings that matter. It illustrates how I began to observe, think about, and reflect upon my experience of Jessica. I would argue that these processes of observation, description, thought, and reflection lie at the core of any and all qualitative research. Put another way, although not usually formulated as such, clinical practice can be understood as a form of research, the most significant difference being that, in clinical practice, the privacy and confidentiality of the clients or patients is paramount. Consequently, clinical practice is never put directly into wider circulation, whereas transmission to a wider audience is usually a requirement, or at least an expectation, of research (Bondi, 2013). I return later in this chapter to the issues of privacy and confidentiality in relation to Jessica and clinical research more generally.

On the idea of a 'case'

Within a few seconds of Jessica's arrival, I am setting the scene, letting her know that we have 50 minutes, that I would like to hear from her about what has brought her here today, that I may ask a few questions along the way, that she may have questions she wishes to ask of me and that before we finish we will talk about the practicalities. Here I adapt one of Freud's (1913) recommendations, which included the 'fundamental rule' requiring the analysand to say everything that comes into her mind without censorship and, in his words, 'never leave anything out because, for some reason or other, it is unpleasant to tell it' (Freud, 1913 , p. 135). I do not state this as a requirement of those who come to see me and I never present it as a rule, although, depending upon the feel of the work, I may, in due course, invite the kind of free association or the recounting of dreams that Freud theorised as pathways to the unconscious. Like Freud I listen for unconscious communications in what a person says, and, influenced by more overtly relational approaches to psychotherapy, I am equally interested in how a person's way of being with themselves and others makes its presence felt wordlessly in our relationship. If I am asked, as I often am, 'what should I talk about?', I might say 'whatever you like' or I might make more specific invitations or open up for exploration what lies behind the question, depending on the form and level of anxiety I sense in the person asking the question. In British psychoanalyst Winnicott's (1965) lovely phrase, I want to offer a 'facilitating environment', through which the therapeutic relationship is an integral part of the setting and provides a crucible in which internal distress and unconscious conflicts can be explored and perhaps transformed.

When practitioners write about work with their clients or patients, for example as part of their training programmes, for clinical seminars, or for publication, the language of the 'case' is widely used. But what is a 'case'? At one level a case is an 'instance' or an 'example': this is how dictionaries define the term. But in particular settings or fields, the 'case' has acquired more specific meanings. For example, a 'legal case' refers to the idea of a dispute between parties that is subject to a legal process. Of particular relevance to the field of

6   *Liz Bondi*

counselling and psychotherapy is that psychoanalysis itself emerged through 'case histories', beginning with the jointly authored collection *Studies in Hysteria* (Freud & Breuer, 1895/2004), and evolving through Freud's long essays concerned with single 'cases' (Dora [Freud, 1905/2006], Little Hans [Freud, 1909/2002a], the Rat Man [Freud, 1909/2002d], the Schreber case [Freud, 1911/2002c], and the Wolf Man [Freud, 1918/2002b]), as well as numerous brief clinical vignettes illustrating arguments made in other essays. In his efforts to secure scientific status for himself and for the field of psychoanalysis, Freud aimed to generate theory from his clinical experience. However, he found that he couldn't get away from telling rich and detailed stories about his intensive clinical work with individual patients:

> I myself still find it strange that the case histories I write read like novellas and lack, so to speak, the serious stamp of science. I have to console myself with the thought that the nature of the object rather than my own personal preference is clearly responsible for this; ... in the study of hysteria ... an in-depth portrayal of the workings of the inner life, such as one expects to be given by novelists and poets ... allow[s] me to gain a kind of insight into the course of an hysteria.
>
> (Freud & Breuer, 1895/2004, pp. 164–165)

It was on the basis of case histories of this kind, shared by Freud and his colleagues (initially in the Wednesday Psychological Society, which became the Vienna Psychoanalytic Society), that he developed the theory and practice of psychoanalysis. As psychoanalysis developed as a body of theory, Freud's followers also showed in their case histories how they were applying his ideas in their clinical practice. In the second extract from my work with Jessica, I do much the same thing, locating myself within a tradition initiated by Freud and further shaped by subsequent theorists including D. W. Winnicott.

In my experience as therapist, supervisor, and trainer, when practitioners in training are asked to write a 'case study', a 'case report', or a 'case history', they sometimes become anxious, imagining something is expected of them for which they have no training or experience. The framing of their clinical experience as a 'case' seems to evoke something alien. There are good reasons for this. According to Michel Foucault (1977), the clinical sciences created a concept of the case as 'an individual as he may be described, judged, measured, compared with others, in his very individuality' (p. 191). As John Forrester (2017) observes, this 'idea of the case appears to be closely linked with the ... idea of the compilation of a dossier' (p. 12). Emphasising the de-humanising consequences of this, he quotes from Graham Greene's (1971) novel *Heart of the Matter*: 'when something became a case it no longer seemed to concern a human being: there was no shame or suffering in a case' (p. 193).

On this account, the objectification associated with medical sciences has infected the idea of the 'case' in counselling and psychotherapy as much as it has devalued the knowledge generated through rich, reflective description. For

Into the thick of it 7

example, in his survey of case study research in counselling and psychotherapy, John McLeod (2010) defines a case in counselling and psychotherapy as 'some kind of treatment episode in which a person (or family group) receives help from a therapist' (p. 11). His reference to 'some kind of treatment episode' reifies—makes a material or concrete thing or object—what is a richly subjective process. If, to pick up on Graham Greene's words, 'there is no shame or suffering in a case', the very idea of a case has become far removed from—perhaps diametrically opposed to—essential features of therapeutic practice. Of course, this is not what those running training programmes intend when they ask students to write 'case studies', but it does help to illuminate the uncertainty and alienation provoked by such requests in those whose training has been asking them to engage personally and to make use of the flow and the details of their subjective experience of being with their clients or patients.

From general knowledge claims to thick description

As I speak to Jessica of the therapeutic frame, she meets my gaze, perhaps reading my face, as well as my voice and my posture, for indications of the qualities of this stranger into whose presence she has stepped. As I fall silent, she drops her gaze and I have a sense of her gathering herself to speak, which she does after a short pause. I am interested in her story and I am interested in how she tells it, noticing the softness of her voice, the way she seems to fade into momentary silences before gathering herself again, taking a breath and continuing her telling with renewed strength in her voice. I begin to have a sense of her rhythms of speech and silence (Carroll, 2005). I am aware of focusing intensely on what Jessica is saying, noticing both a stillness in my flesh and a sensation that feels to me something like a quivering anticipation in my skin, waiting to see what registers. There is something about this that is familiar from my experience of other first sessions, but there are also qualities that are very particular. When I first meet a new client, I am acutely aware of two sensate bodies coming into contact, not skin-to-skin but oriented towards each other in a private space. As a practitioner, I register not only a story but a flesh-and-blood person, feeling the impress of the other's presence on my psyche-soma (Winnicott, 1954).

Scientific knowledge is often understood as knowledge that makes universal claims about its subject matter. In his scientific aspirations, Freud sought to do this, for example, by developing general statements about the human psyche from his and his colleagues' clinical experience. This approach to generating knowledge treats the case history or case study instrumentally. Engaged with instrumentally, a case is not treated as valuable in and of itself but as something that can serve another purpose – for example, to be combined with others in order to make more general statements, perhaps about a 'class' of 'cases' (as in inductive reasoning), or to test the validity of such general statements (as in deductive reasoning). This instrumental treatment of cases contributes to the alienation that may be evoked in practitioners by the idea of case studies. But there are other ways of understanding and thinking with cases. Writing about

8 *Liz Bondi*

in-depth case study research in the social sciences, Bent Flyvbjerg (2001, 2006) identifies common misunderstandings of the approach. Central to his argument is a critique of the widespread assumption that the most valuable form of knowledge consists of general or universal truth claims, which are often understood as the hallmark of science. He explains that such statements necessarily exclude all reference to or consideration of particular contexts. He argues that, contrary to commonly held assumptions, context-independent knowledge is often 'thin' and lacking in real value, whereas statements that do not claim generality but instead provide contextually rich description have the potential to carry much deeper insight. This is, I think, one reason why Freud, despite his scientific aspirations, found himself writing case histories in a form that reminded him of novellas. It is also why readers are often so drawn to illustrative examples in texts about counselling and psychotherapy, and it informs the approach I have adopted in the extracts about my work with Jessica.

The idea of 'thick description' as a contextually rich account of processes and observations was introduced by the philosopher Gilbert Ryle (1971) and popularised by the anthropologist Clifford Geertz (1973), who sought to convey the complexity of cultural life in the communities he studied. This perspective is taken up by educational philosopher Joseph Dunne (2005), who makes an impassioned plea for the insightfulness and knowledge-generating power of in-depth cases or examples, which

> in their deep embeddedness in a particular milieu … renounce the generalising ambitions of wider-gauge research, … [and] when they are well done—which, among other things, will require a keenly reflective awareness of their 'point of view'—possess what might be called epiphanic power: they disclose an exemplary significance in the setting they depict so that it proves capable of illuminating other settings—without the need for rerouting through abstract generalities and, indeed, with greatest potential effect for those most deeply in the throes of the very particularity of another setting.
>
> (p. 386)

According to this perspective, richly, or thickly, descriptive and reflective accounts of practice speak directly to other practitioners immersed in their own particular clinical settings and experiences. Despite himself, I think this is what Freud was often doing in his case studies: he only needed one Anna O to begin to elaborate his concept of transference and he needed only one Little Hans to start formulating his theory of the Oedipal complex.

Understanding in-depth cases or examples as intrinsically valuable, and potentially epiphanic or transformative, enables and supports research that is close to practice. How practitioners do this and where their focus lies cannot be decided externally: we each make our own, contextually specific decisions about how to write about practice.

Being deeply involved

As I write about my sensate experience of the first few minutes of my therapeutic work with Jessica, a memory surfaces that comes from over 20 years ago when I began my training. My peers and I worked in small groups, practising with each other under the gaze of a video-recorder. Reviewing one of my sessions in a small group, a fellow student described her sense that I seemed somehow to extend myself from my body in my chair to also gently encircle the person to whom I was listening. I came to understand what she sensed as a kind of receptivity that is embodied in my voice, my posture, my gaze, my idiomatic way of being in space-time with another (Bollas, 1987; Orbach, 1999). This wasn't and isn't a technique or an act: it comes from a deep desire to listen, attune, and attend to the other. It comes at least in part from what I have done, consciously and unconsciously, with my early struggles about being received as I longed to be received.

I grew up with four other siblings, all born within 10 years of each other. I recall my mother sometimes finding the noise, the clamour, the hubbub, intolerable. She might request that we 'pipe down' in a voice that had a superficial air of calmness about it. These words now seem very ordinary and neutral, but her tone of voice, her face, her bodily bearing conveyed to me something far from calm and far more emotionally laden. She framed my childhood world, her presence utterly familiar and taken-for-granted. And it is her unworded embodied communication preceding and surrounding that 'pipe down' that calls to me across the decades. I still sense what I understand to have been her exhaustion, her exasperation, and something like distressed perplexity about how she had ended up being mother to five such lively children so keen on exercising their voices and their lungs. Her words 'pipe down' seem to me to say very much less than what she conveyed through other means. At the time, I had no words for what I perceived, but I absorbed a sense that she needed me to restrain myself and to protect her from my ebullience. I received her words less as a request or conscious instruction and more, to draw on Merleau-Ponty (2012), as 'an event that grasp[ed] my body' (p. 244).

Sitting in my consulting room with Jessica I have a sense of a tension that she too embodies between exuberance and self-restraint. I notice it in her gestures and her voice. Although it reminds me of a tension that I know in myself, it is also utterly different. Jessica necessarily expresses her idiom in the way she is in this space with me (Bollas, 1987). I understand my responsibility right now to be to receive this without intruding or making demands of her (any more than I can avoid).

I have described the therapeutic relationship as a crucible in which therapeutic work is done. Understood in this way, the subjective experience of the practitioner is integral to how she/he/they are able to learn about the internal world of the client or patient. It is also actively involved in processes of therapeutic change, which may happen at least in part through the internal processing undertaken by the practitioner. Conceptualising this process in terms of the countertransference, Christopher Bollas (1987) writes that 'in order to find the patient we must look for him [or her or them] within ourselves. This

10 *Liz Bondi*

process inevitably points to the fact that there are two "patients" within the session' (p. 202). As a consequence of 'working with, rather than against the countertransference [the practitioner] must be prepared on occasion to become situationally ill' (p. 204). This experience of becoming 'situationally ill' often becomes apparent in supervision, perhaps signalled by the supervisee requesting help to think about a troubling or perplexing experience, or by the supervisor saying something like 'can we think about this in terms of the countertransference?'

Writing about one's practice almost invariably extends thinking and insight, as I have illustrated in my account of beginning my work with Jessica. Practitioners researching close to practice are therefore likely to use writing as a method of enquiry (Richardson & St. Pierre, 2005). This often entails reflecting deeply about ourselves, perhaps including our own personal histories, along with our vulnerabilities and frailties, at least as much as those of our clients or patients. Given that therapeutic practice requires of its practitioners intimate engagement with our own subjective experience, it is inevitable that writing about it is deeply involving and is likely to precipitate new insights and discoveries, which may be interesting and stimulating but which may also be disturbing and exposing. On the one hand, writing enables us to share our discoveries and reflections on practice more widely with others; on the other hand, this wider sharing is fraught with questions and difficulties for practitioners and their clients or patients.

Integrity and consent

Jessica arrived in my consulting room as a well-prepared, conscientious, competent adult client able to tell a personal story that conveys salient facts clearly. At this level, she knows why she has come and what she wants from coming to see me. I meet and respond to this part of her, interested in her, moved by her story, and already warming to her as a person. But there is another kind of meeting too: inarticulate, ill-defined, embodied, sensory, affective, often unconscious, largely eluding my attempts to describe it. Neither Jessica nor I could prepare for this meeting consciously, and yet it is crucial to the possibility of our working together therapeutically.

When Freud (1905/2006) published his 'Fragment of an Analysis of Hysteria (Dora)', he was aware of the risk of inflicting personal damage on his former patient. He outlined three reasons why he felt that he had acted in a way that provided her with sufficient protection: he had delayed publication until four years after the end of his work with her; he had published in a specialist journal, which he assumed would only be read by a narrow, professionally qualified audience; and he had omitted names or other details that could lead readers to identify her.

Much has changed in the years since Freud made these claims, changes that have made it much harder for practitioners to publish material that might compromise or contravene the privacy and confidentiality of the consulting room, and that might be recognisable to clients or patients, even if they have

Into the thick of it 11

considered another safeguard to which Freud did not refer, namely, seeking explicit permission. Freud's defence that he published in a specialist journal with a limited readership may have appeared to be a reasonable and understandable claim in 1905, but we now know that there is never any guarantee that the circulation of a publication will remain limited. Freud's work has generated huge interest and a vastly wider circulation than he anticipated; today, anything put into the public domain can 'go viral'. Likewise, the pseudonym 'Dora' did not prevent the real identity of Freud's patient becoming known. Freud acknowledged that his former patient would recognise herself if she came across his paper, but he assumed that by delaying publication he could be confident that her interest in her own distress would have faded. Such an assumption now seems careless and naïve at best and would certainly contravene ethical requirements to maintain confidentiality and to do no harm.

Seeking informed consent from current or former clients or patients to write and/or to publish case studies has become a possibility but is also always fraught (Bridges, 2010; Sperry & Pies, 2010). In medical, psychological, and social research, researchers are expected to seek consent at outset, with participants retaining the right to withdraw at any time. In psychotherapy, this changes the nature of the contract between practitioner and client or patient from the very start. In view of this, psychotherapists sometimes seek consent during or after the end of a period of therapeutic work, whether for training purposes or with research ethics approval. In all these circumstances, the process of seeking consent engages the conscious, competent adult in the client or patient. Practitioners may seek to acknowledge and perhaps explore with their clients or patients some of the complexities that arise from the inevitable presence of other parts that are less available to a process of informed consent, but however extensively this is discussed, it seems implausible that consent can ever be fully informed since we cannot know in advance about unanticipated impacts and nor can we fully grasp even those impacts we have anticipated. It is also inevitable that the very process of requesting permission introduces into the therapeutic work something that changes its frame: for both parties, an imaginary external audience is introduced. While it may be possible to explore this therapeutically, the purpose of the work is irrevocably changed. This is the case even if the work has been completed and retrospective consent is sought (McLeod, 2010; Polden, 1998).

The case histories published by Freud and his colleagues focused very much on their patients, referring to themselves in quite limited ways, although Freud's authorial voice is often strong and makes available a good deal about his thinking. However, the move away from Freud's original drive theory, with its model of the practitioner as remaining separate and detached, towards avowedly relational approaches, within and beyond psychoanalysis, position practitioners as deeply immersed in the therapeutic process. Consequently, researching close to practice inevitably brings the internal experience of practitioners firmly into view. Indeed, I have emphasised and illustrated that what we come to know in therapeutic practice is learned through our subjective

12 *Liz Bondi*

awareness, and I have drawn attention to the idea that what arises within our subjective experience and how we respond to it is often integral to the therapeutic effect of the work we do. Something that might still be called a 'case study' is therefore now likely to be at least as much about the practitioner's internal world, including our own personal histories, struggles, disturbances, and vulnerabilities, as it is about our client's or patient's story of themselves and their distress. This transfers some of the risks associated with disclosure away from the client or patient and towards the practitioner.

When writing for publication about myself and my internal experience I need to be attentive to the potential impacts on past, current, and future clients as well as on myself and others close to me. In my account of starting my work with Jessica, I disclose autobiographical information (notably about being one of five children) and about how I remember experiencing my mother. Although she is no longer alive, I am not released from responsibility towards her memory, including other people's memories of her. I have tried to be clear about the particularity and subjectivity of my experience but others, especially my siblings, might feel very differently and might therefore consider that I misrepresent the mother who was as important to each of them as to me. In relation to clients, one of my concerns is about disrupting the frame by arousing curiosity about me away from the scene of the therapeutic work, making it less obviously available for exploration. In one way or another, something comparable is probably true for all practitioners today because of the accessibility of so much personal information on the internet. We have to make our own judgements, therefore, about what we decide to put into the public domain, judgements which have to bear with the inevitable uncertainties of life.

In the case study material included in this chapter, I have drawn directly and as honestly as I can on my own experience. My consulting room really is in a first-floor flat accessed via a buzzer at street level. However, Jessica is a fiction, albeit one inspired by real first meetings with real people. This has become a common approach among practitioners writing in ways designed to communicate effectively and realistically about what happens in psychotherapy without infringing on the need for privacy and confidentiality (Grosz, 2014; Orbach, 1999, 2016). The risk is loss of authenticity and of clients or patients becoming hazy figures overshadowed by the more fully described presence of the author/practitioner. On the other hand, this approach enables the 'feel' of the practice of therapy from the practitioner's perspective to be conveyed with liveliness, genuineness, and integrity.

In conclusion

Whether my account of beginning my therapeutic work with Jessica constitutes a case study depends upon what is meant by the term 'case study'. Because of its associations with the dossier and the objectification of what happens in therapeutic practice, I am not comfortable with the term, although I also lapse

Into the thick of it 13

back into it in the hope of illustrating something that might be recognisable as having some affinity to the concept while retaining qualities that honour the richly immersive, subjective, and embodied nature of the work. I have also illustrated how in-depth exploration of a brief moment, in this instance the first few minutes of meeting a new client, might prove to be illuminating and enriching in a way that is very different from more traditionally understood case studies, which typically focus on a session, series of sessions, or complete period of therapeutic work with a client or patient and in so doing tend to create more perceptual distance between the practitioner and the person or people consulting them.

In writing about 'case studies' I have attempted to navigate between the opposing pulls of wanting to step back in order to trouble some of the issues at stake and of showing what it might mean to research close to practice. For Freud, psychoanalysis was research and could not be otherwise. I would like to reclaim that view for therapeutic practice today, with richly descriptive and reflective writing being what allows and enables the strange magic of the consulting room to be offered in another form to a wider audience, subject, of course, to careful consideration of the safeguards required by and for its participants.

References

Bollas, C. (1987). *The shadow of the object*. Free Association Books.
Bondi, L. (2013). Research and therapy: Generating meaning and feeling gaps. *Qualitative Inquiry*, *19*(1), 9–19. https://doi.org/10.1177/107780041246297
Bondi, L., & Fewell, J. (Eds). (2016). *Practitioner research in counselling and psychotherapy*. Palgrave.
Bondi, L., & Fewell, J. (2017). Getting personal: A feminist argument for research aligned to therapeutic practice. *Counselling and Psychotherapy Research*, *17*(2), 113–122. https://doi.org/10.1002/capr.12102
Bridges, N. A. (2010). Clinical writing about clients: Seeking consent and negotiating the impact on clients and their treatment. *Counseling and Values*, *54*(2), 103–116. https://doi.org/10.1002/j.2161-007X.2010.tb00009.x
Carroll, R. (2005). Rhythm, reorientation, reversal: Deep reorganisation of the self in psychotherapy. In J. Ryan (Ed.), *How does psychotherapy work?* (pp. 85–112). Taylor and Francis.
Dunne, J. (2005). An intricate fabric: Understanding the rationality of practice. *Pedagogy, Culture and Society*, *13*(3), 367–389. https://doi.org/10.1080/14681360500200234
Flyvbjerg, B. (2001). *Making social science matter*. Cambridge University Press.
Flyvbjerg, B. (2006). Five misunderstandings about case-study research. *Qualitative Inquiry*, *12*(2), 219–245. https://doi.org/10.1177/1077800405284363
Forrester, J. (2017). *Thinking in cases*. Polity.
Foucault, M. (1977). *Discipline and punish*. Allen Lane.
Freud, S. (1913). On beginning the treatment (further recommendations on the technique of psycho-analysis 1). In J. Strachey (Ed. & Trans.), *The standard edition of the complete psychological works of Sigmund Freud*, Volume XII (pp. 121–144). Hogarth Press.

14   *Liz Bondi*

Freud, S. (2002a). Analysis of a phobia in a five-year-old boy ('Little Hans') (L. Adey Huish, Trans.). In *Sigmund Freud. The 'Wolfman' and other cases* (pp. 1–122). Penguin Books. (Original work published 1909)

Freud, S. (2002b). From the history of an infantile neurosis (the 'Wolfman') (L. Adey Huish, Trans.). In *Sigmund Freud. The 'Wolfman' and other cases* (pp. 205–320). Penguin Books. (Original work published in 1918)

Freud, S. (2002c). *Sigmund Freud. The Schreber case* (A. Webber, Trans.). Penguin Books. (Original work published 1911)

Freud, S. (2002d). Some remarks on a case of obsessive-compulsive neurosis (the 'Ratman') (L. Adey Huish, Trans.). In *Sigmund Freud. The 'Wolfman' and other cases* (pp. 123–202). Penguin Books. (Original worked published 1909)

Freud, S. (2006). Fragment of an analysis of hysteria (Dora) (S. Whiteside, Trans.). In A. Phillips (Ed.), *The Penguin Freud reader* (pp. 435–540). Penguin Books. (Original work published 1905)

Freud, S., & Breuer, J. (2004). *Studies in hysteria* (N. Luckhurst, Trans.). Penguin Books. (Original work published in 1895)

Geertz, C. (1973). *The interpretation of cultures*. Basic Books.

Gordon, P. (2009). *The hope of therapy*. PCCS Books.

Greene, G. (1971). *The heart of the matter*. Penguin.

Grosz, S. (2014). *The examined life*. Vintage.

Latour, B. (1983). Give me a laboratory and I will raise the world. In K. Knorr-Cetina & M. Mulkay (Eds.), *Science observed* (pp. 141–170). Sage.

Latour, B., & Woolgar, S. (1979). *Laboratory life. The construction of scientific facts*. Sage.

McLeod, J. (2010). *Case study research in counselling and psychotherapy*. Sage.

Merleau-Ponty, M. (2012). *Phenomenology of perception*. Routledge.

Orbach, S. (1999). *The impossibility of sex*. Penguin Books.

Orbach, S. (2016). *In therapy: How conversations with psychotherapists really work*. Wellcome Collection.

Polden, J. (1998). Publish and be damned. *British Journal of Psychotherapy*, *14*(3), 337–347. https://doi.org/10.1111/j.1752-0118.1998.tb00387.x

Richardson, L., & St. Pierre, E. (2005). Writing as a method of inquiry. In N. Denzin & Y. S. Lincoln (Eds.), *Handbook of qualitative research* (3rd ed., pp. 959–978). Sage.

Rustin, M. (1997). The generation of psychoanalytic knowledge: Sociological and clinical perspectives, part one: 'Give me a consulting room …' *British Journal of Psychotherapy*, *13*(4), 527–541.

Rustin, M. (2001). *Reason and unreason*. Continuum.

Ryle, G. (1971). The thinking of thoughts. What is 'le penseur' doing? In *Collected Papers. Volume 2, Collected Essays (1929–1968)*. Hutchinson.

Sperry, L., & Pies, R. (2010). Writing about clients. *Counseling and Values*, *54*(2), 88–102. https://doi.org/10.1002/j.2161-007X.2010.tb00008.x

Winnicott, D. W. (1954). Mind and its relation to the psyche-soma. *British Journal of Medical Psychology*, *27*(4), 201–209. https://doi.org/10.1111/j.2044-8341.1954.tb00864.x

Winnicott, D. W. (1965). *The maturational processes and the facilitating environment. Studies in the theory of emotional development*. Karnac.

2 Hermeneutic phenomenology

Exploring and making meaning of lived experience in psychotherapy research

Kerry Thomas-Anttila and Margot Solomon

Hermeneutic phenomenology and its relevance for psychotherapy research

Hermeneutic phenomenology lends itself particularly to the ontological exploration of experience—that is, the study of being, and particularly of human beingness or *Dasein* (Heidegger, 1927/2008). The literal translation of 'Dasein' is 'being there'; Dreyfus (1991) notes that Dasein is not to be thought of as a conscious object but rather as a human way of being or 'human beingness' (p. 14). For us, hermeneutic phenomenology's focus on valuing the nature of being and revealing meaning within lived experience resonates with the therapeutic endeavour, and concurs with psychotherapy's own concern with the value of human experience. There is an emphasis on being and being-with, including being-with the data (corresponding to being-with the client), an openness to what might arise from being-with the data (as in noticing one's response to the client), and then the written response to being-with the data, which deepens with further engagement, often uncovering the taken-for-granted or a hidden (and elusive) truth (Sheehan, 2015; Smythe, 2011). One's own subjectivity, as well as the intersubjective nature of the engagement between researcher and participant (or text), is acknowledged (here are further resonances with the therapeutic engagement).

However, despite some similarities between hermeneutic phenomenology and psychotherapy, there are crucial differences. Van Manen (2017) cautions against confusing the two and notes that whereas psychology and psychotherapy are interested in examining how people interpret their experience, phenomenology is interested in understanding the 'primal meaning(s) of this experience' (p. 776). Thus, van Manen proposes that a phenomenological question might be 'What is this lived experience like?' or 'How do we understand or become aware of the primal meaning(s) of this experience?' (p. 776). The research then promises 'depthful understanding and meaningful insight' (p. 776), rather than the psychotherapist's 'trying to make sense of the participant trying to make sense of what is happening to her/him' (p. 778). Interpreting the stories told by research participants thus becomes a grappling with the essential and primordial nature of the person's experience, rather than a psychological meaning making of the experience.

DOI: 10.4324/9781003280859-3

Because phenomenology is concerned with the investigation of lived experience, it is ideal for investigating personal learning journeys (van Manen, 2014). Hermeneutics adds an interpretive element, whereby the researcher aims to uncover meanings and intentions that are hidden in the text (Moules et al., 2015; Smythe & Spence, 2020). Subjectivity is valued (meanings of experiences are sought rather than explanations or predictions of behaviour), and findings emerge from the interactions between the researcher and participants (or text) as the research progresses (Moules et al., 2015). This creates the possibility of generating new understandings. An important aspect of this approach is the assumption that our pre-understandings always go before us in interpreting any text and, therefore, that the researcher needs to be able to identify and reflect on their own experiences and assumptions. Gadamer (1975/2013) proposed that neutrality in the context of interpreting data cannot exist; however, if we are sufficiently aware of our own bias (our own fore-meanings and prejudices) then we will also be open to the text's alterity or otherness, and to its being able to show itself in new and different ways.

Although research methodologies and methods are tools for investigating a research problem/issue/question and do not necessarily need to mirror the researcher's own ways of being and understanding the world, we regard hermeneutic phenomenology as being a congruent and satisfying fit for the psychotherapy researcher. It is, however, a demanding and complex endeavour.

What is hermeneutic phenomenology? Its beginnings and philosophical underpinnings

In this section we examine the philosophical underpinnings of hermeneutic phenomenology and provide a brief introduction to its beginnings. Hermeneutic phenomenology is grounded in the philosophy of Martin Heidegger [1889–1976] and Hans-Georg Gadamer [1900–2002], who were interested foremost in the nature of *being*. They in turn were influenced by Edmund Husserl [1859–1938] and his development of transcendental phenomenology. Husserl is widely regarded as the founder of phenomenology (Moran, 2005). He took exception to the Cartesian split between mind and body and proposed to return to the grounding of truths in human experience (Caelli, 2001)—thus his famous appeal 'To the Things!', signifying the importance of beginning not with theory but rather with the *phenomena* themselves, hence restoring to science a philosophy grounded in deeper human concerns (Cohen, 1987).

Briefly, Husserl introduced the term 'lifeworld' (*Lebenswelt*); he believed that the investigation of the lifeworld could form the basis of a new science; this heralded the beginnings of phenomenology as the study of lived experience. He aimed to establish a science of essences and believed that, in order to achieve contact with the essences, the researcher could bracket out the external world as well as one's own individual biases (Husserl, 1913/2014). Heidegger held a different view about the issue of reduction or bracketing; he did not believe that it was possible to bracket or to set aside one's existing judgments or presupposition to arrive at that which is essential. He believed that we bring who we are, including our background, beliefs, and understandings, to any interpretive process, and began to develop hermeneutic phenomenology.

Heidegger: The question of the meaning of 'being'

Following Husserl, Heidegger called into question the notion of humans as principally rational beings, as proposed by, for example, Plato and Descartes (Dreyfus, 1991). Rather than asking *epistemological* questions (concerning the relation of the knower and the known), Heidegger was interested in *ontological* questions—that is, what sort of beings we are, and how we are bound up with the intelligibility of the world. He suggested that as well as being thinking, observing beings we are also 'being beings, coping beings involved in the world' (p. 3). Resonating with Kierkegaard, Heidegger suggested reversing Descartes' famous statement to read 'I am therefore I think' (Dreyfus, 1991, p. 3). Heidegger's most influential work is *Being and Time* (1927/2008) and it is in this work that he began to discuss the question of the meaning of being.

Phenomenology

The word 'phenomenology' has two components—'phenomenon' and 'logos'—and is derived from a verb meaning 'to show itself' (Heidegger, 1927/2008, p. 51). Thus, phenomenology means 'that which shows itself', the manifest. Heidegger also noted that contained within the verb is 'to bring to the light of day, to put in the light' (p. 51). The phenomenological method of investigation, Heidegger stated, does not characterise the 'what' of the objects of researcher, but rather the 'how' of the research. It is rooted in a primordial manner as 'the way we come to terms with the things themselves' (p. 50). Phenomenology, he re-iterated, is the 'science of the Being of entities—ontology' (p. 61). He included in this consideration of 'being' the 'forgotten mystery of Dasein' (p. 132) and proposed that we have taken flight from the mystery and instead have taken solace in what is 'readily available' (p. 133).

Hermeneutic phenomenology

The term 'hermeneutics' is derived from the Greek word 'ἑρμηνεύω' or 'hermeneuō' (Klein, 2000, p. 344), meaning to translate, expound, or interpret. Yet, the etymology of 'hermeneuō' is somewhat unclear. Some link the word with the mythological Greek deity, Hermes, messenger of the gods, whose duty it was to carry and translate messages between the gods, and between gods and men. Kächele et al. (2009), however, maintain that 'hermeneuō' actually derives from a root with a meaning identical to *speaking* (p. 37). They note that the term *hermeneutics* dates from the seventeenth century, that it was formed from *hermeneutike techne*, meaning a procedure to interpret texts, and that it was influenced by the exegesis of the Bible. Hermeneutics is a circular theory,

18 *Kerry Thomas-Anttila and Margot Solomon*

indicating as it does an interplay between an 'understanding' of the whole and an 'understanding' of a part: 'This circle implies a correction based on the feedback between the preliminary "understanding" of the text and the interpretation of its parts' (p. 37). The basic question is: 'What meaning, what significance did and does this text have?' (p. 37).

Heidegger (1927/2008) believed that to be human was to interpret, and that our understandings are inevitably influenced by our own life histories (our fore-structures and historicality). He consciously inserted into phenomenology the hermeneutical, or the 'interpretedness of the world' (Farin, 2015, p. 110.) When he began to embrace the word 'hermeneutics' in his research he translated the original Greek term as '"to communicate" (*mitteilen*), that is, to put into words and share with others' (p. 112). As Farin suggested, Heidegger's hermeneutics do not lead to general theorising about the interpretation of texts but rather to understanding, expression, and communication of meanings and intimations.

Having outlined the nature of phenomenology, and particularly Heidegger's hermeneutic phenomenology, we now move to consider how to proceed with hermeneutic phenomenological research. We will also each give an example from our own research.

Conducting the research

Hermeneutic phenomenological research situates the researcher in their context and in the research; this has implications for the way of going about the research, or the 'method'. Smythe et al. (2008) highlight this when they write that 'Who one is as researcher is fundamental to the thinking of research, for thinking does not happen as a mechanistic process divorced from being in the world. Rather thinking is lived, breathed, and dreamt…' (p. 1390). For a hermeneutic phenomenological study, there is no prescribed method to follow in the traditional sense of 'method' (Gadamer, 1975/2013; van Manen, 1990). Rather than a way of 'doing' the research, it becomes about a way of 'being' with the topic under investigation; the methods that hermeneutic phenomenology offer the neophyte researcher tend to describe a guide for hermeneutic phenomenological direction and leave plenty to the initiative and imagination of the researcher. McCaffrey and Moules (2016, p. 5) offer a set of guidelines 'as an orientation for direction' rather than the ultimate authority. Smythe et al. (2008) suggest eleven 'handholds to offer reassurance to the researcher who seeks something to grasp and hold as they journey into the unknown' (p. 1394).

What we discovered on our research journeys was the need to find an intricate balance between openness and structure and how these both inform each other (Solomon, 2022; Thomas-Anttila et al., 2017). Openness speaks to the researcher's ability to stay open to the journey of thinking and dwelling, writing and reading, dreaming and letting thoughts emerge. Finding my way (Solomon, 2017) with the writing challenged me to stay open to what lay ahead, to not pin down my understanding, to stay with not knowing, and at the same time there was a need for structure in the gathering of the data that spoke to me, my notes in my journal, and the reading I was doing. Anxiety about losing my direction and feeling the pressure to get it done pushed me towards structure, and the method pushed me towards process and staying open. Supervision supported holding the two in a useful and productive way.

Saevi (2013) describes a phenomenon that she terms 'pathic dwelling' (p. 3), remaining attentively open. What is being said? What is the experience that is being conveyed? What are the feelings here and what is being evoked in me? Where do my thoughts take me? The structure of the specific study depends on what is being researched. For example, if the research project includes participants, then it is at the data analysis stage that hermeneutic phenomenology comes into its own, specifically the hermeneutic circling. As dissertation/thesis supervisors, we supervise students who are engaged in hermeneutic phenomenology research projects. One structure is the hermeneutic literature review. Here, the pieces of literature are the data, and the researcher engages with the literature in a hermeneutic way, to more fully understand the topic they have chosen to research. We have found two articles by Boell and Cecez-Kecmanovic (2010, 2014) to be useful resources for those who undertake hermeneutic literature reviews. In a research project at the doctoral level the candidate is expected to engage with the main philosophers (for example, Heidegger, Gadamer) and to craft stories from participant interviews, drawing on philosophical notions as a part of the data analysis process. We provide examples later in this chapter but turn first to one of the most commonly used basic structures for embarking on a hermeneutic research journey, as proposed by van Manen (1990).

Van Manen's stages of the hermeneutic research journey

Van Manen (1990) has proposed six stages:

i   *Turning to the nature of the lived experience.* This involves coming to a point of recognition and realisation of the topic of the research that engages and enlivens the researcher.
ii *Investigating the experience as we live it.* Here we find how to notice and then record what has been experienced. This sets the tone of allowing the subject matter to imbue every part of the researcher's life for a time, as well as a consideration of how to collect data, who to involve, applying for ethics approval, and so on. These first two stages are reflected in McCaffery and Moules' (2016) first guideline, 'the way of hermeneutic practice is determined by the phenomenon not the method' (p. 6). The topic of the study guides us to the underlying meanings surrounding our phenomena of interest.
iii *Reflecting on essential themes* takes the researcher deeper into the process of uncovering the meaning of what has been hidden. The researcher learns how to look at data in a hermeneutical way.

20 *Kerry Thomas-Anttila and Margot Solomon*

iv *The art of writing and rewriting* speaks for itself, an essential and ongoing process in hermeneutic phenomenology. We both would put writing earlier, because writing is an essential ingredient for even achieving the first stage of the research journey. Our tendency as psychotherapists to naturally ponder and reflect facilitates the writing process that takes us on the path of the hermeneutic journey.

v *Maintaining a strong and oriented relation* requires the researcher to be disciplined and to stay with the question they have asked, even though the researcher is likely to find it difficult to see where the research is going. This discipline is paradoxical because, at the same time as staying with the research question, the researcher is required to surrender the need to know, the need to see the outcome of one's endeavour. Hermeneutic phenomenology requires the researcher to enter into 'meditative thinking' (Heidegger, 1959/1966), where the focus is on being present with what is, making possible the discovery of what has been there but hidden from plain sight.

vi *Balancing the research context by considering the parts and the whole.* This challenges the researcher to stay in relationship with the parts and the whole of the question being addressed. It involves reviewing and re-engaging with all the parts and culminates in these coming together. The writing evolves into a document that has coherence of its own and is a statement from the very essence of the phenomenon; yet it also invites the reader on their own journey of understanding. Conclusions are, to some extent, always open to further elaboration.

From our perspective these stages overlap. The consideration of the context, and the parts and the whole of the research, bring us back to the hermeneutic circle. Heidegger (1927/2008) draws on the hermeneutic circle when discussing interpretation. He proposed that 'what is decisive is not to come out of the circle but to come into it in the right way' (p. 195). It is through being open that we enter the circle in the right way. We bring our understanding through our fore-structures. The hermeneutic circle, the back and forth between past and present, between self, other, and context facilitates what Heidegger calls 'the most primordial kind of knowing' (p. 195). Heidegger suggested that to uncover this knowing requires of us to work out these fore-structures in terms of the things themselves. This requires the researcher to engage in a hermeneutic way with the data; to reflect, interpret, write, and reflect and interpret again in intricate detail, considering the parts, the whole, and the context.

The fore-structure of interpretation

Heidegger's notion of fore-structure of understanding fits closely within psychotherapy theory and practice. It recognises that there is already a way that experience is understood and interpreted based on what has gone before. Heidegger's three-fold structure comprises fore-having, foresight, and fore-conception. He described it thus:

In interpreting, we do not, so to speak throw a 'signification' over some naked thing which is present-to-hand, we do not stick a value on it; but when something within-the-world is encountered as such, the thing in question already has an involvement which is disclosed in our under-standing of the world, and this involvement is one which gets laid out by the interpretation.

(Heidegger, 1927/2008, pp. 190–191)

The fore-structures offer the possibility to unpack reflexively our pre-under-standings and to gain more clarity on horizons of understanding (the frame that encloses the way I perceive and understand the world I live in). The following is an illustration of how the three-fold structure was at play in my (Margot's) research:

Fore-having

Fore-having is the existing understanding that we have in advance of whatever is being interpreted. For example, I am the eldest of four siblings; the four of us represented a unit in my mind as all separate but interlocking parts. Thus, as a child, my awareness was constantly drawn towards consideration of the four of us. Thinking in terms of four comes naturally to me so I am attracted to structures that have four categories. I believe that this example suggests what drew me to the fourfold as an underlying structure for the data chapters in my thesis (Solomon, 2017).

Foresight

Inwood (1999) describes foresight as what I set my sights on, or where I choose to focus my interpretation. I already had in my mind the possible relevance of the thinking of Wilfred Bion (1962/2014), a seminal psychoanalyst writing at the same time as Heidegger. I found myself looking for connections between Heidegger and Bion and I looked for ways their ideas might coincide. Being a psychoanalytic psychotherapist and group-analytic psychotherapist was an essential part of my foresight. It is natural to use our pre-knowledge to under-stand new ideas and yet it can mean missing important new ways of under-standing. Over the period of writing my doctoral thesis, I read less in my professional field than usual and chose to focus my reading on the philosophy of Heidegger. I wanted to move outside my habitual ways of understanding and yet they were of course still in play.

Fore-conception

Fore-conception highlights the way in which I only interpret concepts that are within my grasp and that I have already in some way understood. This is evi-dent from my use of psychoanalytic terms to name some of the themes in the data; for example, 'dynamic administration'. This term is used in group analysis, one of my areas of training and practice. It calls the therapist to attend to the close relationship between the practical and the dynamic. In other words, as a teacher of psychotherapy, I hold in mind the students, the setting, and the context, as well as considering possible (and out of awareness) meanings that occur at the boundary of classroom activity (Solomon, 2017). Thus, all my interpretations are enabled by and limited by my fore-structure of understanding. Tacit knowing, a concept coined by Polanyi (1967), resonates here, in the way that fore-structures influence the research journey. We cannot say why or how we know something, but it is there nevertheless, in what Polanyi termed a pre-logical phase of knowing. The hermeneutic phenomenological journey brings into the light this hidden unthought-about-yet-known part of our knowledge.

Crafting stories from interviews and data analysis

We have mentioned the hermeneutic phenomenological method of crafting stories from participant interviews (Crowther et al., 2016). Participants are encouraged to tell stories of their experience of the phenomenon under investigation; the researcher then crafts stories from the interview transcripts and undertakes the data analysis. In this next section we both provide examples from our research. The first example is taken from my (Kerry's) research on psychotherapists' experience of their ongoing learning (Thomas-Anttila, 2017) and is from an interview I conducted with 'Philip', a psychotherapist who spoke about working with people with psychosis. The crafted story is in italics and following this is the initial interpretation of the story (first level analysis), then the discussion of the emerging of possible meanings (second level analysis). Lastly, the third, deeper, level of analysis is achieved through the use of selected philosophical notions.

Learning to be with the unknown: Doing without the handsheet

Psychosis has also taught me about the limitations of psychotherapy. There are people here who have been psychotic since they were 13 years old. I don't mind this work because it's much more about holding and being present and supporting them; however, it takes so much longer and usually needs a much greater wrap-around approach. These people benefit from therapeutic input but it's not enough; you have to think about what else they need.

This is another way of looking at our limits, and of learning. Who do we want to work with, who are we able to work with? I think that in the case of psychosis, even if we can work in a limited capacity it is very valuable.

I saw someone who had been immersed in a profound psychosis for over 20 years, and who had very fixed belief systems. She would come to me and ask me to channel the gods; she told me that I was one of the few who could channel the gods. So, ok, we channel the gods. The curious thing was that after a year of our working together her belief systems didn't shift one iota; I don't think I made the slightest difference in this area. But we met and we would talk. Her parents told me that she became much easier to be with in social situations. That taught me that being with someone like her in a therapeutic way can make a difference in unconscious ways. In her case it meant that she was better able to interact in social situations. However, she remained exceptionally focused on her belief systems.

I really don't know what I was doing with this woman but I do think it is something about the holding, and something about not being overwhelmed and terrified, about being able to sit with the not knowing, the unknown. That is something that I think is best done learning from your own personal therapy. I think it is the ability to be able to sit with terror or the unknown because you have looked into yourself and have not known or not been able to be clear, and you have not fallen apart and you have survived it. This helps us to survive with our clients where you don't know and don't understand, but you can still be with them without feeling that you have to do something absolutely now, you know 'where's my handsheet, my five-part model, my triangular this or that'.

There are several aspects of this story that present themselves. One is the care that Philip was taking in seeing this client, and the nature of that care, and another is the difference between *being-with* and *doing* something. There is also the connection he makes between the learning he received in his own therapy and his ability to be with a client who many therapists might not be happy (or able) to see. He describes a type of being-with that seems to have had, as a consequence, a strengthening of his client's ability to be with others and he adds that it is difficult to pin down the nature of this phenomenon. He seems to be asking: 'How does this happen?' He talks about it as the client 'responding unconsciously to the therapy' and, given that the client's belief systems did not change at all, perhaps Philip is saying that change could not be brought about on a rational/behavioural level. Philip's client was responding to something else, and it is this phenomenon that, although common to therapists, is precisely what becomes difficult to explain and understand. There is often an expectation that therapy practice ought to demonstrate its evidence base; this story shows how this can be less than straightforward.

Heidegger (1927/2008) described the development of being-with as follows: 'Being-with develops in listening to one another (*Aufeinander-hören*), which can be done in several possible ways: following, going along with, and the privative modes of not hearing, resisting, defying, and turning away' (pp. 206–207). This resonates with the experience that Philip is describing. His client was not looking for ways to improve her ability to be with others; she did not sit down with Philip and list ways in which she might address her social difficulties or practise her social skills. In contrast to this, Philip's client seemed more orientated towards *not* changing anything and Philip mentions that her belief systems remained intact. However, over time she became more able to function in social settings. Was this because she had met with Philip often and regularly, and that from those meetings she was able to develop her abilities to be with others? What might happen in this process?

Akhtar (2013) suggested that psychotherapy is not so much a 'talking cure', as it is commonly referred to, as a 'listening cure'. Heidegger (1927/2008) spoke of listening as being Dasein's 'existential way of Being-open as Being-with for Others' (p. 206). Further, that 'hearing constitutes the primary and authentic way in which Dasein is open for its ownmost potentiality-for-Being—as in hearing the voice of a friend whom every Dasein carries with it. Dasein hears, because it understands' (p. 206). In listening to his client, was Philip's readiness to be open and to be with his client a pre-condition for something potentially to happen? Listening is not necessarily a simple and easy process; it was not just about being there and listening to the words. Heidegger suggested that 'Dasein hears because it understands' (p. 206), and Philip's story provides insight into how these elements, that is, Dasein, hearing, and under-standing are able to occur together. He talks about how the experience of terror in his own therapy helps him to be with clients without feeling that he has to 'do something absolutely now'. He infers that being with a psychotic client evokes feelings of terror, and that unless the therapist has developed an ability to sit with terror, they are unlikely to be able to bring listening and understanding together in a way which is helpful for the client. The therapist's experience of being-there with the client is not simply about attending to what the client brings and who the client is; it also includes the therapist's whole experience of who they are and how they have come to understand them-selves. Without that, it is unlikely that there could be a bringing together of hearing and understanding and being-there; a combination which Philip is suggesting enabled important change in his client.

Philip also uses the word 'holding', both at the beginning when he mentions that working with psychotic clients is much more about holding and being present and supporting, and then later when he says 'I really don't know what I was doing with this woman but I do think it is something about the holding'. In writing about listening during the psychotherapy session, Akhtar (2007) spoke about 'a maternal sort of holding' (p. 4) and that for more unwell clients it is important to establish this 'maternal homeostatic attunement' (p. 5). Has Philip learnt from his work with these clients that it is this type of 'holding' that makes change possible, particularly where change is not being sought, but rather that the being-there, the being-open, the hearing, and the understanding, is what is transformative?

I have mentioned Philip saying that with this client he had to sit with the terror of the unknown, that he had survived these feelings in his own therapy, and that now when these feelings are present in the room with a client, he is able to tolerate the state of not knowing. Rather than hurriedly reaching for a piece of theory or a model, he is simply able to be with his client. So, what is Philip's experience of his learning in this situation? What can we say about the helpfulness or otherwise of being with the unknown rather than, for example, taking on the role of 'expert' and offering an interpretation that conveys cer-tainty? Philip speaks about the importance of sitting with the unknown. What is this 'unknown'? How do we describe or obtain a sense of the unknown, given that it is unknown?

Hermeneutic phenomenology 25

In speaking about being with the unknown, Philip describes a particular type of learning that is not about, for example, learning a technique, but rather learning about an aspect of *being*. Philip refers to the '*handsheet, my five-part model, my triangular this or that*' as devices that are created to lessen the fear of being with ourselves and the other, that make us feel more competent, and that we know something more than the other person. What is lost in the doing of this is the ability to let be: 'to let beings be as the beings that they are' (Heidegger, 1930/1998, p. 144). Heidegger described this as engaging oneself with the 'open region', with the disclosedness of beings, and suggests that doing so is not to lose oneself in them: 'rather, such engagement withdraws in the face of beings in order that they might reveal themselves with respect to what and how they are' (p. 144).

This seems an appropriate and respectful description of the psychotherapeutic encounter, wherein the therapist might withdraw, as it were, in the face of the other, in order that the other might reveal themselves. The use of the word 'withdraw' is not meant as a disengagement, but rather an intentionally respectful and engaged openness to the being of the other. Heidegger's term '*Lichtung*', or 'clearing' (1971/2001), supports this interpretation. In *engaged* withdrawal, the being with the other while not losing oneself in the other creates an open clearing, where there is space for whatever might be revealed. We do not fill the clearing up, or cover it over, with a handsheet, model, the feeling that we know something, and the other does not. We wait for, attend to, and become part of, the revealing.

Note on my (Kerry's) writing process

My experience of writing phenomenologically about data is to think of myself less as an active instrument of understanding and more as taking a position of being open to what might emerge. The writing has to proceed at a relatively slow pace; Saevi (2013) recommended dwelling 'comfortably in the space of hesitation' (p. 5). I found it helpful to consider the following points:

i   What matters?
ii   What leaps out?
iii What thoughts am I having?
iv   What interpretive leap am I making?
v   The conversation is always in play—take the reader with me.

Although it sounds strange to say it, I think it is helpful to be able to merge personal boundaries with the boundaries of the text. This means not fighting with the text, not looking at it and demanding that it show something or forcing oneself to apply one's brain to the text in an effort to extract or impose meaning on it, but rather swimming with the text itself, even letting it take over. Saevi (2013) noted that an understanding of the interconnectedness of self and world is needed, and I often reminded myself that I was not writing about

26   *Kerry Thomas-Anttila and Margot Solomon*

the experience of the phenomenon, but rather to illuminate or let show the experience from the perspective of an 'insider'.

Learning from experience

The following story and data analysis arose from an interview that I (Margot) had with a colleague after a block teaching weekend. I was teaching psychotherapy clinical supervision to experienced clinicians. My question was: 'How does the teacher learn as she teaches?' This example includes many of the aspects of 'the thing' (Heidegger, 1971/2001)—i.e., teaching and learning as relating, which is the central finding and title of the thesis. It is in a section of my doctoral thesis (Solomon, 2017) that explores *learning from experience*, a phrase in common usage but coined by Bion (1962/2014). In a similar way to Heidegger, he recommended reading without concern for understanding, rather, putting experience first.

In a new class of ten students A presented herself as experienced and knowledgeable, first to speak whenever I invited input. I soon became irritated by her constant denigration of the psychoanalytic frame and criticism of everything I said. When starting a new class, I usually feel anxiety around meeting the differences between us and finding a way to work together, but also I began to wonder whether my behaviour was inducing A to challenge me in a transference enactment. Was my authority as teacher evoking her need to assert her difference and competence, her independence from the hierarchy of teacher/ learner? Was this my problem, and what exercised me so?

Classes continued on topics such as anxiety and defences against learning in supervisors and supervisees, while A seemed increasingly tense, wondering whether the supervision course was what she needed: all this seemed to reflect something of what I was experiencing with A. I felt pushed beyond my limits and apparently so did A.

Eventually I spoke to the class about the experience of learning new ideas, of the need to open oneself to a new frame of reference while somehow remaining free from the interference of my already-known ideas, not comparing, staying with the unfamiliar. In looking for similarity we can miss something essential in the new perspective we are trying to encounter. I talked about my own foray into hermeneutic phenomenology (hp) and described my first impulse to make sense of hp in relation to psychoanalytic theory rather than immersing myself in this unfamiliar worldview, a maddening exercise that initially stretched me.

A said that as a Buddhist she could not accept systems that seemed hierarchical or dogmatic. A Taiwanese man (B) said for him Buddhism had that quality. He had been happy to leave the oppression he had felt in Taiwan. Tearfully, he told us that for him psychotherapy training had been a helpful challenge. I could see A's excitement as she engaged in this discussion. Later in supervision she presented clinical work and revealed her anxiety in this class where she was new to everything: new to Auckland, to the University, to me and the other students, new to psychoanalytic thinking and new to supervision. I had not thought about that. She had seemed so sure of herself, while I had felt increasingly full of doubt about myself. My irritation disappeared.

Hermeneutic phenomenology 27

When I read this story, the first thing I notice is my psychotherapist's mind at work. I am considering the thoughts and feelings aroused in me as I sit with my students. I ponder them, turn them over, and wait to see what emerges. My own process of reflection is strongly present. The intervention that arises from my reflection does not reveal my thoughts or point to a particular student. It is clear that I am attempting to illuminate the learning process. However, I was not seeing everything and needed to learn from the experience. I missed an obvious part of the mood of what was occurring.

Heidegger used the word 'mood' (*Stimmung*) to describe something that is part of our 'thrownness into the world' (Dahlstrom, 2013, p. 133). 'The mood has already disclosed, in every case, Being-in-the-world as a whole, and makes it possible first of all to direct oneself toward something' (Heidegger, 1962/ 2008, p. 176). Perhaps the mood of anxiety was orienting A and myself to one another. In other words, we were both anxious about something. The mood that prevailed on that occasion brought both of us face-to-face with our existence. Did this then create the possibility for the leap that Heidegger (1962/ 2008) writes about? The leap that takes us into the 'neighbourhood of thinking'. Is the reflection that occurred in me, in Miss A and in Mr. B, part of what begins the process of thinking?

Heidegger (1954/1968) wrote, 'Any kind of polemics fails from the outset to assume the attitude of thinking' (p. 13). He then continued: 'Thinking is thinking only when it pursues whatever speaks for a subject' (p. 13). In other words, this could be referring to the mood of anxiety. Perhaps our shared failure to address the mood that was present in the room created the polemic. Using Heidegger's statement about thinking, one way of making sense of this could be that my reflection process concerning Miss A reveals that I am in a 'polemic'. That may be overstating it, but essentially there is an oppositional undercurrent. Perhaps it is in me, Miss A, and also in the rest of the class; but it is also in the mood. It is as if somewhere there was a truth we should all be following; in this instance, be Buddhist, do not be part of the hierarchy, do not be anxious as we begin this new teaching and learning experience together.

Yet, at the same time, none of us gave up testing the edge of the familiar with what is unknown and yet essential to learning. 'To learn means to make everything we do answer to whatever essentials address themselves to us at the given moment' (Heidegger, 1954/1968, p. 8). This is about being in the moment, being fully present to the experience, listening with, and bearing with. This is what I was attempting to tease out in my thesis, to find what is primordial in the process of learning, which truly means being willing to begin to think. Heidegger wrote, 'applied to the matter before us: we can learn thinking only if we radically unlearn what thinking has been traditionally' (p. 8). This statement resonates with me, yet at the same time feels impossible. It speaks to the struggle experienced by both Miss A and myself, as is revealed in the 'mood' of our exchange. Learning from experience requires the learner, whether teacher or student, to be willing to feel the experience and to allow it to enter into them. Heidegger believed the teacher has to learn more than the

28 *Kerry Thomas-Anttila and Margot Solomon*

student: 'The teacher must be capable of being more teachable than the apprentices' (p. 15). First the teacher has to be willing to question herself and this vignette illustrates that.

This story and analysis form a small section of a much larger analysis. Each theme is present in multiple stories and has been unpacked in a hermeneutic process of writing and rewriting. It is situated in van Manen's last three stages and the writing is ongoing, in what Smythe et al. (2008) named as 'the unutterable circle of writing' (p. 1394). The task is to get beyond one's own fore-structure or horizon. This means writing and rewriting, reading, and dwelling at-depth with the data. The hermeneutic circle invites the writer into a way of being with the data through our familiar way of seeing (the psychotherapist busily reflecting), bringing understanding through our fore-structures. Being open is the key: open to what I know (my fore-structures) and to what I know but is hidden from me (the mood of anxiety), as well as open to what I don't yet know (the experience of Miss A).

Final reflections

As we drew to the end of this writing, we spoke together about the impossibility of conveying in this chapter all that we would wish to say about researching using hermeneutic phenomenology. We have focused on the underlying philosophy and how to go about the research, giving examples from each of our research projects, and we hope that this is useful to future researchers who resonate with researching lived experience and uncovering the often-taken-for-granted. Ogden (2006) wrote that 'writing, after all, is a form of thinking' (p. 1072) and we found this to be particularly true of using hermeneutic phenomenology. It is a reading and writing journey, but we would not want to leave out the talking, questioning, and mulling that took place in supervision meetings, with colleagues, with friends and family, and with ourselves. Reading a text together and thinking about it together always promoted further thinking; the phenomenological writing process can feel at times like breathing rarefied air. It calls for sustained focus, a mixture of surrender, and a willingness to meditate on the phenomenon under investigation, while allowing meanings to emerge. The researcher does not write to say, 'this is the truth'; rather questions of the truth are kept open, and the reader is invited to share a journey of exploration and to arrive at their own understandings and meanings. We hope that, should you engage with this way of researching, it will bring you the joy and satisfaction that we have experienced.

References

Akhtar, S. (Ed.). (2007). *Listening to others: Developmental and clinical aspects of empathy and attunement*. Jason Aronson.

Akhtar, S. (2013). *Psychoanalytic listening: Methods, limits and innovations*. Karnac.

Hermeneutic phenomenology 29

Bion, W. R. (2014). Learning from experience. In C. Mawson (Ed.), *The complete works of W. R. Bion* (Vol. IV; pp. 247–365). Karnac. (Original work published 1962)

Boell, S. K., & Cecez-Kecmanovic, D. (2010). Literature reviews and the hermeneutic circle. *Australian Academic & Research Libraries, 41*(2), 129–144. https://doi.org/10.1080/00048623.2010.10721450

Boell, S. K., & Cecez-Kecmanovic, D. (2014). A hermeneutic approach for conducting literature reviews and literature searches. *Communications of the Association for Information Systems, 34*, 257–286. https://doi.org/10.17705/1CAIS.03412

Caelli, K. (2001). Engaging with phenomenology: Is it more of a challenge than it needs to be? *Qualitative Health Research, 11*(2), 273–281. https://doi.org/10.1177/10497320112911899

Cohen, M. Z. (1987). A historical overview of the phenomenological movement. *Image, 19*(1), 31–34. https://doi.org/10.1111/j.1547-5069.1987.tb00584.x

Crowther, S., Ironside, P., Spence, D., & Smythe, L. (2016). Crafting stories in hermeneutic phenomenology research: A methodological device. *Qualitative Health Research, 27*(6), 826–835. https://doi.org/10.1177/1049732316656161

Dahlstrom, D. (2013). *The Heidegger dictionary*. Bloomsbury.

Dreyfus, H. (1991). *Being-in-the-world: A commentary on Heidegger's Being and Time, Division I*. The MIT Press.

Farin, I. (2015). Heidegger: Transformation of hermeneutics. In J. Malpas & H-H. Gander (Eds.), *The Routledge companion to hermeneutics* (pp. 107–126). Routledge.

Gadamer, H-G. (2013). *Truth and method*. Continuum Publishing. (Original work published 1975)

Heidegger, M. (1966). *Discourse on thinking* (J. Anderson & E. Hans Freund, Trans.). Harper & Row. (Original work published 1959)

Heidegger, M. (1968). *What is called thinking? A translation of Was heisst denken?* (J. G. Gray, Trans., 2nd ed.). Harper Collins. (Original work published 1954)

Heidegger, M. (1998). On the essence of truth (1930) (J. Sallis, Trans.). In W. McNeill (Ed.), *Pathmarks* (pp. 136–154). Cambridge University Press. (Original work published 1930)

Heidegger, M. (2001). *Poetry, language, thought* (A. Hofstadter, Trans.). Harper & Row. (Original work published 1971)

Heidegger, M. (2008). *Being and time*. (J. Macquarrie & E. Robinson, Trans.). Harper & Row. (Original work published 1927)

Husserl, E. (2014). *Ideas for a pure phenomenology and phenomenological philosophy. First book: General introduction to pure phenomenology* (D. O. Dahlstrom, Trans.). Hackett Publishing. (Original work published 1913)

Inwood, M. (1999). *A Heidegger dictionary*. Blackwell Publishers.

Kächele, H., Schachter, J., & Thomä, H. (2009). *From psychoanalytic narrative to empirical single case research: Implications for psychoanalytic practice*. Routledge.

Klein, E. (2000). *A complete etymological dictionary of the English language*. Elsevier.

McCaffrey, G., & Moules, N. (2016). Encountering the great problems in the street: Enacting hermeneutic philosophy as research in practice disciplines. *Journal of Applied Hermeneutics, 1*, 1–7. https://doi.org/10.11575/jah.v0i0.53270

Moran, D. (2005). *Edmund Husserl: Founder of phenomenology*. Polity Press.

Moules, N., McCaffrey, G., Field, J., & Laing, C. (2015). *Conducting hermeneutic research: From philosophy to practice*. Peter Lang.

Ogden, T. H. (2006). On teaching psychoanalysis. *International Journal of Psychoanalysis, 87*(4), 1069–1085. https://doi.org/10.1516/D6D1-TGVX-A4F0-JECB

30   Kerry Thomas-Anttila and Margot Solomon

Polanyi, M. (1967). *The tacit dimension*. Anchor Books.

Saevi, T. (2013). Between being and knowing: Addressing the fundamental hesitation in hermeneutic phenomenological writing. *Indo-Pacific Journal of Phenomenology, 13*(1), 1–11. https://doi.org/10.2989/IPJP.2013.13.1.4.1170

Sheehan, T. (2015). *Making sense of Heidegger: A paradigm shift*. Rowman and Littlefield.

Smythe, E. (2011). From beginning to end: How to do hermeneutic interpretive phenomenology. In G. Thomson, F. Dykes, & S. Downe (Eds.), *Qualitative research in midwifery and childbirth: Phenomenological approaches* (pp. 35–54). Routledge.

Smythe, E. A., Ironside, P. M., Sims, S. L., Swenson, M. M., & Spence, D. G. (2008). Doing Heideggerian hermeneutic research: A discussion paper. *International Journal of Nursing Studies, 45*, 1389–1397. https://doi.org/10.1016/j.ijnurstu.2007.09.005

Smythe, E., & Spence, D. (2020). Reading Heidegger. *Nursing Philosophy, 21*(2), e12271. https://doi.org/10.1111/nup.12271

Solomon, M. (2017). *Teaching and learning as relating: A transformational experience* [Doctoral thesis, Auckland University of Technology]. Tuwhera Open Access Theses & Dissertations. https://openrepository.aut.ac.nz/handle/10292/10990

Solomon, M. (2022). Dwelling in the fourfold. In S. Crowther & G. Thomson (Eds.), *Hermeneutic phenomenology in health and social care research* (pp. 132–147). Routledge.

Thomas-Anttila, K. (2017). *Understanding psychotherapists' experience of ongoing learning: A hermeneutic phenomenology study* [Doctoral thesis, Auckland University of Technology]. Tuwhera Open Access Theses & Dissertations. https://openrepository.aut.ac.nz/handle/10292/11023

Thomas-Anttila, K., Smythe, E., & Spence, D. (2017). Towards an openness of being: The personal nature of learning. *Ata: Journal of Psychotherapy Aotearoa New Zealand, 21*(2), 149–164. https://doi.org/10.9791/ajpanz.2017.14

van Manen, M. (1990). *Researching lived experience*. State University of New York Press.

van Manen, M. (2014). *Phenomenology of practice: Meaning-giving methods in phenomenological research and writing*. Left Coast Press.

van Manen, M. (2017). But is it phenomenology? *Qualitative Health Research, 27*(6), 775–779. https://doi.org/10.1177/1049732317699570

3 Using performative meta-reflexivity in psychotherapy research

Jacqueline Karen Andrea Serra Undurraga

We, psychotherapists, use reflexivity in our research and practice. For example, we might attempt to know how our social positioning impacts our inquiry; explore the assumptions we hold; question why we are feeling and thinking in a particular way; consider how we affect what is happening to our client, our research participant, or ourselves; and so on—but what does 'using reflexivity' and 'being reflexive' entail?

It can be tempting to think that there is *one* reflexivity, *one* way of making sense of our experience. It can seem very straightforward: we just need to become 'aware' of ourselves. For example, Etherington (2017) writes about the importance of reflexivity for research in counselling and psychotherapy. She argues that we need to position ourselves in a transparent manner, acknowledging our involvement in the co-construction of knowledge to make our research more trustworthy and rigorous. Following Etherington's call, it seems that we 'simply' need to become aware of ourselves but, again, is there only one way of doing this? By contrast, Finlay (2002, 2017) and Pillow (2003, 2015) emphasise that there are many ways of conceptualising and using reflexivity. There are *reflexivities*, not one reflexivity. In line with this, I would argue that reflexivity is not a direct and transparent process; instead, there are multiple ways in which we can *relate* to what we are experiencing.

I have conceptualised reflexivities as *affective ways of relating that produce* (Serra Undurraga, 2020). Whenever we are being reflexive we are *relating to* ourselves in a particular way that helps to *produce* that very self, rather than the unveiling process that the notion of awareness implies. For example, it is not simply that I need to become aware of my social position as an author. It is different if, when I am reflexive about my position, I, for example, relate to myself as an identifiable person by declaring my identity categories (woman, Chilean, and bisexual) or if I relate to myself as a situated subject by making visible the contexts in which I am writing (engaged in cultural practices that identify me as having a gender, nationality, and sexuality and grant me different possibilities according to that). These two ways of relating are different reflexivities that would help to produce me as an author and my research in different ways. The first might produce me as a subject who carries social identities and my research as bringing visibility to underprivileged groups. The second might produce me

DOI: 10.4324/9781003280859-4

as a subject-in-the-making and my research as illuminating/troubling how these categories are articulated in the first place.

In this chapter, I develop a conceptualisation and practice of reflexivity that takes seriously how, whenever we are making sense of ourselves, we are helping to produce ourselves and the world. Being accountable for what we help to produce, and to open the possibility of relating and, thus, producing, is ethically important for psychotherapy researchers. In particular, how researchers relate to themselves, participants, academia, theories, readers, and more will help shape their research and what it will do. This is why it is crucial to integrate a meta-reflexive questioning of our productive ways of relating.

I propose that at any moment, depending on the implicit conceptualisation of subjectivity that is operating and the way in which we assume we can access our experience, a particular way of relating to our experience and, thus, a particular reflexivity, will emerge. In line with this, in Figure 3.1 I offer a way of mapping different types of reflexivity using two axes. The horizontal axis relates to different conceptualisations of subjectivity (the list is not exhaustive), while the vertical axis relates to the degree of transparency/opacity we assume when accessing our own experience.

For illustration purposes I will give a hypothetical example; let's say I am doing a phenomenological study on young women's sense of belonging. When analysing the experience of a research participant, I want to use reflexivity to take into account my involvement as the researcher in producing knowledge. For example, in one interview, I notice I feel a wave of anxiety when my interviewee speaks about feeling excluded from her social circle because she does not fit in with the milestones others accomplish. There are multiple ways

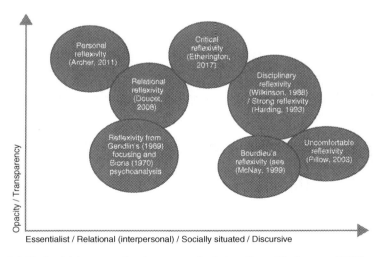

Figure 3.1 Reflexivities as productive ways of relating (Serra Undurraga, 2020).

Using performative meta-reflexivity 33

of reflexively making sense of this anxiety. Also, crucially, how I *make sense of* this anxiety will help to *produce,* in a particular way, not only this anxiety but also both my and the research participant's subjectivities. As the reader might imagine, this also shapes the form and kind of impact my research will have. In Table 3.1, I develop this example using the four possible conceptualisations of subjectivity identified on the horizontal axis of Figure 3.1.

Having focused on the horizontal axis of Figure 3.1, I now move on to make a brief comment on the vertical axis, the transparency–opacity continuum. Here, I can assume a more or less transparent or opaque access to my

Table 3.1 Example of four conceptualisations of subjectivity and their impact on the use of reflexivity and its productions.

Conceptualisa-tions of subjectivity	Broad definition	How I use reflexivity—how I relate to my experience	How the anxiety is produced	How the subjectivities involved are produced
Essentialist subjectivity	Individuals are influenced by others and society but there is a bounded space differ-entiable from these influences.	I might try to uncover how my personal traits, let's say my fear of not being valued, can explain my being triggered with anxiety.	Individual symptom.	I am (pro-duced as) a person with intrinsic traits who is trig-gered by the interviewee as another bounded subject.
Relational subjectivity (interpersonal)	Subjectivity continuously emerges from intimate relationships.	I might be reflexive about how the rela-tionship with the interviewee is enabling this anxiety.	A feeling that emerges inter-personally.	We are (pro-duced as) sub-jects that take shape through our relating to one another.
Socially situated subjectivity	Subjectivity is located in a particular social milieu that gives sub-jectivity its shape.	I might be reflexive about how my and the interviewee's social positioning facilitate this sense of anxiety.	A feeling that reflects the strength of social demands on people in particular positions.	We are, in our intimate feelings, (pro-duced as) sub-jected to our social positioning.
Discursive subjectivity	Subjectivity is constituted (not deter-mined) by discourses that offer frames of intelligibility.	I might consider how my anxiety has to do with the very dis-cursive constitu-tion of alternative ways of life as a pro-blem or a deficit.	A feeling that emerges when not fitting well with a domi-nant discourse.	We are (pro-duced as) sub-jected to, and potentially challengers to/of, dominant discourses.

34 *Jacqueline Karen Andrea Serra Undurraga*

experience, whichever conceptualisation of subjectivity I am holding. If I assume access to experience is transparent, I assume I can directly know how and why I am experiencing something and how I am situated; I just need to become 'aware' of it. If I assume access to experience is opaque, I think there is something in between my experience and my grasping it. This might be, for example, the unconscious, discourses, and/or embodied experience. Assuming a more opaque access to our experience, we think that we can never fully grasp what is going on with ourselves. What are the consequences of these different assumptions in shaping our inquiry and its productions?

The categories I have proposed in these two figures are contestable. How do I draw the lines? What am I leaving out? I offer these figures as tools rather than faithful representations. What I would like to enable with these mappings is twofold: first, I would like to bring to readers' attention some of the many ways in which we can relate to ourselves; second, I would like readers to think about how, when we use any of these reflexivities, we are helping to *produce* ourselves/others/our research/the world in particular ways. This way of conceptualising reflexivity might be thought of within what Pillow (2015) calls *reflexivity as genealogy*, where the assumptions made by each reflexivity are questioned.

My invitation to you in this chapter is not only to use reflexivity in psychotherapy research but to interrogate *how* you are relating when being reflexive and what that relating is *producing*. That is, I encourage you to use what I have called *performative meta-reflexivity* (Serra Undurraga, 2021). In these reconceptualisations of reflexivity, I take seriously into account one of the major challenges to the concept and practice of reflexivity posited by Barad's (2007) post-humanist approach. My reading of their work opens some questions for me: Is there an already formed self to be reflexive about? Is our position something that is there and that we can represent? What does a reflexive research practice produce? These questions lead me to think about reflexivities as *productive ways of relating* and not as simply 'becoming aware' of a self that is already formed. What does it mean/entail to propose that reflexivities are productive? *How* are reflexivities productive? In what follows I address these questions by developing my reconceptualisations of reflexivity using Barad's critique. Later in the chapter, I offer two examples of using performative meta-reflexivity in psychotherapy research.

Barad's post-humanism and reflexivity

Barad (2007) puts forward a critique of the notion of the human as apart from everything and able to reflect: 'Representationalism, metaphysical individualism, and humanism work hand in hand, holding this worldview in place' (p. 134). Reflection and reflexivity inherit this worldview so that when we think about reflexivity, we imagine a fully formed person standing back and making sense of what is going on with them and their situation. Barad's (2007) post-humanism pushes us not to take for granted the distinction between human

Using performative meta-reflexivity 35

and non-human, thus questioning the assumed boundedness of the person engaged in self-reflection.

Barad (2007) brings forth their performative approach by challenging representationalist assumptions. They draw on feminist science studies, post-structuralism, and quantum physics to advance their propositions. Representationalism assumes that there are different ontological units: things to be represented, representations, and someone who does the representing. In contrast, Barad's performative approach posits that we are not *in* the world as if 'we' and 'the world' were already formed and we are merely taking a position *in* it, representing it and ourselves. They stress that we are *of* the world, *part* of the world in its becoming: there is no foundational separation between ourselves and the world; 'we' and 'the world' are continuously being produced and productive. Barad argues that reflection/reflexivity relies on representationalism and that, in research, it only puts the mirror in front of the researcher—i.e., because it tries to represent, it reproduces more of the same. Reflection/reflexivity, for Barad, assumes that subject is bounded and can be defined and positioned, whereas Barad claims, subjectivity is iteratively made: at once produced and productive.

In Barad's post-humanist approach, there is no essential ontological difference between representations and the represented—or between anything. The basic unit is *phenomena,* where all the agencies *intra-act* (see next section) with no intrinsic, *a priori* differentiation, only continuously produced boundaries. The observer and the observed, the representation and the represented, and so on, are not previously defined but come to be iteratively defined in practices. On this basis, Barad suggests using *diffraction/diffractive methodology* instead of *reflection/reflexivity*. Diffraction is a physical phenomenon produced by waves interfering with each other. Waves are not particles but perturbances in a field that cannot be located. Diffraction does not assume previously formed units that can be reflected but attends to what happens when two or more 'things' (scare quotes here because no-thing has foundational boundaries) interfere with each other. What new patterns are produced?

I take up Barad's (2007) criticism of reflection/reflexivity and diffract reflexivity with Barad's post-humanism instead of following their suggestion of moving away from it. Elsewhere (Serra Undurraga, 2020), I have said that I think of different reflexivities as *apparatuses* (Barad, 2007) that generate the agencies at work, whereas 'before' (i.e., without reflexivities-as-apparatus being put to work) there was *phenomena* as an entangled situation with no defined boundaries. For example, if I am having an interpersonal conflict with someone and I use a relational and relatively transparent reflexivity (see Figure 3.1), the conflict might be produced as a stalemate created by a *doer–done to* (Benjamin, 2004) way of relating: myself and the other as relational subjects fitting into roles of this larger relational dynamic. If, instead, I use an essentialist and more transparent reflexivity, the conflict might be produced as the result of a fundamental incompatibility of characters: myself and the other as people with traits. *Reflexivities help to produce the very subjects about which they intend to be reflexive.*

36 Jacqueline Karen Andrea Serra Undurraga

I propose that when we are reflexive on our experience, we are not simply becoming aware of it as if we could stand outside our experience and represent it. Instead, every time we are reflexive we relate to our experience in particular ways that are helping to produce ourselves and the world. This is what I call a *diffracted reflexivity*: reflexivities as affective and productive ways of relating or reflexivities as apparatuses (Serra Undurraga, 2020, 2021). Furthermore, I propose to question our ways of being reflexive using *performative meta-reflexivity* (Serra Undurraga, 2021). Performative meta-reflexivity is a tool that invites you to ask yourself questions such as: How am I relating to myself/others/texts/the world in this situation? What is this way of relating assuming? What is this way of relating helping to produce (including iteratively producing myself and the world)? As part of what 'entanglement' (Barad, 2007)—the fundamental intertwining with/in the world that makes us not bounded 'selves' but relational through-and-through—does this way of relating emerge? This practice is *performative* because it does not assume previously formed identities but understands that identities are always in a process of being constituted.

Whenever we are attempting to reflexively know ourselves, we are helping to produce ourselves; the differentiation between ontology and epistemology collapses—Barad's (2007) neologism, *onto-epistemology*. This is why I do not include my reconceptualisations of reflexivity 'inside' Figure 3.1. My post-humanist notion of reflexivity—*diffracted reflexivity* (Serra Undurraga, 2021)—can help to think about each reflexivity (including all of the reflexivities in Figure 3.1) as a productive way of relating rather than as offering a truth about ourselves. Whenever we articulate reflexive knowledge about ourselves, we do so from an entanglement, and this knowledge helps to further produce ourselves and the world.

The definition of reflexivities as productive ways of relating encompasses implicit and explicit making sense of ourselves as part of the world. Explicit reflexivities are present whenever we offer a question or statement about our involvement in situations. In that sense, performative meta-reflexivity can interrogate more 'traditional' reflexive questions and statements because they are specific, productive ways of relating and not representations of an already formed self. Implicit reflexivities are ways of relating that are part of our constant *implicit* sense-making of ourselves as part of the world. For example, at this moment while I write, I am necessarily relating to myself, the space around me, the imagined reader, etc. These ways of relating sustain an implicit making sense of myself as part of the world. This implicit making sense does not need any explicit reflexive statement about it. These ways of relating can be made explicit with performative meta-reflexivity. I could ask: How am I relating to you as a reader now and what is that helping to produce?

In the next section, I develop how I think that both explicit and implicit reflexivities emerge *as part of assemblages,* including in research. That is, we do not sovereignly decide how we are reflexive. In that sense, I prefer the use of the word reflexivity (rather than reflection): reflexivity has a *reflex* aspect to it; we *find* ourselves relating to ourselves and the world in particular ways.

Using performative meta-reflexivity 37

Performative meta-reflexivity as a tool helps us to critically question these ways of relating and their productions.

Reflexivities emerge from intra-active assemblages

Usually, reflexivity is tied to the notion of a previously formed self that attempts to know itself. This is related to the common notion of agency espoused within humanistic paradigms, assuming a bounded person with intentions (conscious and explicit or not) as the basis of agency. When being reflexive in this case we might be populated by questions about establishing our *personal* motivations, who we are, and who the other is or represents. In contrast, for Barad (2007), agency is not possessed by someone or something but is an enactment. Agency belongs to an *intra-active* (Barad, 2007) configuration of forces: we are never acting alone. The concept of intra-action stresses how there are not previously formed units that then interact, but rather the boundaries that define one thing from the other are iteratively produced. This is consistent with my reading of Deleuze and Guattari's (1987) conceptualisation of *assemblage,* which stresses that subjectivity or any apparent unit is a production of an arrangement of different forces. Each 'aspect' of the assemblage—human and non-human, material and discursive—has its influence on what is being produced. I enclose 'aspect' in scare quotes because these 'aspects' are always in an entanglement and in a constant process of being defined; that is, they are intra-active.

I propose that how we relate to our experience, how we are reflexive, is a product of the *intra-active assemblage* of which we are part and not of ourselves alone. When I am reflexive now, asking myself what I want to achieve in this chapter, a host of agentic forces are at play for this particular reflexive question to emerge: Western individualism and goal-setting, peer-review academic practices, my search for purpose, etc. This does not mean that we are simply 'socially constructed' and have no agency of our own. As Butler (2014) says, this would entail falling into an active/passive dichotomy: discourse constructs the subject, and the subject constructs discourse; both have the same grammar structure. Instead, with Barad (2007), it is true both that each aspect of the assemblage has an influence on what is being produced and that each aspect is iteratively produced. When being reflexive we are at once produced and productive.

Let's consider this hypothetical example. A trainee counsellor articulates the following research question for their dissertation: 'What are the motivations behind counselling students' decisions to become a therapist?' I think of this reflexive research question as emerging from a particular intra-active assemblage: traditionally reflexive assignment and interview questions that ask for the motivations behind the actions a trainee regularly encounters; discourses about people needing to have projects rooted in a personal sense of purpose; the student's curiosity; the student's story; institutional practices that foreground qualitative research using interviews as a method. These and other forces are what intra-actively produce this reflexive question that implies particular ways of relating. When, instead, performative meta-reflexivity asks, as part of what intra-active assemblage does this way of relating emerge, it stresses that we are never reflexive alone; we always—as part of assemblages—*find* ourselves relating in particular ways.

Furthermore, I use Barad's (2007) notion of the *material-discursive* to think about reflexivities not only as a conceptual tool. Each reflexivity as a way of making sense of ourselves emerges in particular material arrangements, which are already discursive. In the same way, reflexivities take shape as particular ways of relating through the force of discourses, which are already material. For example, my use of a relational/opaque reflexivity when thinking about a particular interpersonal conflict (see above) was enabled by a larger material-discursive arrangement: the material, spatial arrangements of my neighbourhood (enabled by economic resources) allow me to go for an undisturbed, thoughtful walk, during which I breathe a discursive ideal of respecting subjectivities as 'having' particular needs and desires—an ideal that is already material in, for example, the distribution of the space that facilitates distance from others.

Following that, when I say that reflexivities are productive ways of relating, I do not mean that we can choose one reflexivity as if it were a thing in itself that produces particular things. I think of reflexivities as part of material-discursive assemblages. This assemblage is what enables this particular way of relating. When thinking about our ways of relating we need to consider the entangled material-discursive aspects that make them possible. At the same time, it is not that specific, predefined reflexivities have certain effects as if they could be separated from their assemblages. An essentialist/transparent reflexivity might produce empowerment as part of an entanglement of, say, people in a disadvantaged situation asserting their identity as valid, and it might produce stigmatisation as part of a therapeutic situation where there is pathologising labelling. Reflexivities are not fully formed things but are constantly being produced and will become different in each entanglement.

I have now described the main aspects of my reconceptualisation of reflexivity as productive ways of relating that emerge as part of intra-active and material-discursive assemblages. Now, why is this important in psychotherapy research? What difference does it make to think about reflexivity in this way? In the next section, I start articulating an answer to that.

Productive reflexivities: Ethico–onto–epistemology

Diffractive reflexivity stresses that the very movement of being reflexive is a way of relating that iteratively produces a self and its world. That is, there is no possibility of being engaged in knowing 'about' ourselves without at the same time *producing* ourselves and our world in particular ways. Knowing is a way of engaging that helps to produce what we know and ourselves as knowers. My conceptualisations of reflexivity have an intra-active and performative onto-epistemology.

Using performative meta-reflexivity   39

I propose a reflexive research practice that is not so much about pinning down who we are being, what is happening to us, or how our subjectivity influences another or our research; all these questions begin with assuming a subjectivity. Instead, performative meta-reflexivity is more about *questioning how particular ways of relating help to produce realities.* For example, in a recent article (Serra Undurraga, 2022), I stress the importance of regularly questioning the ways of relating we unwittingly reproduce in our academic writing (and what they generate) because we cannot assume that we will relate in ways that are consistent with our favourite theories.

Representationalism generates questions about the accuracy of representations as if we could be outside or above what we intend to represent. This can make reflexive practice busy with questions about how well I am capturing my experience. With Barad there is no holding the world at a distance because we are always already entangled. This post-humanist approach to reflexivity then assumes we cannot hold ourselves at a distance in order to know about ourselves. Instead, *we always know ourselves by engaging with ourselves in productive ways.* It is like how you get to know your lover's body by being entangled with it, becoming with it, and helping to make it anew.

Barad (2007) creates the concept *ethico-onto-epistemology* because there is an ethical responsibility for what, in our practices of knowing, we help to produce in the world. This is not a responsibility that falls on us alone as if we had definite and foundational boundaries. However, that does not mean we lack responsibility for considering what we are helping to produce (while being continuously produced). It makes us more responsible because we are not only peeking at the world/others/ourselves but also helping produce them. Furthermore, if we think of ourselves as always entangled, produced, and productive, then what is 'external' is part of us and that makes us more responsible. In the next section, I offer two examples of performative meta-reflexivity in action. Through these examples, I hope to show how this meta-reflexivity is an ethico-onto-epistemological practice.

Examples of performative meta-reflexivity in research

With performative meta-reflexivity we can ask, among others, the following three questions: Which ways of relating am I enacting? What assemblage makes them possible? And what are these ways of relating producing and preventing from happening? These questions help us make visible our ways of relating and recognise how we are entrenched in wider material-discursive practices; they enable us in our becoming *response-able* (Haraway, 2016) for what we help produce and its consequences in the world, and to open possibilities for alternative worlds.

Below, I offer two examples of performative meta-reflexivity in action; the first example is about research that draws on clinical practice and the second is about autoethnographic inquiry. The questioning that performative meta-reflexivity offers helps me to open possibilities for new conceptualisations and

40 *Jacqueline Karen Andrea Serra Undurraga*

practices while remaining close to the affective and productive entanglements of clinical practice and personal experience, respectively, that are crucial to my research.

Research example (1)

As Bondi and Fewell (2016) argue, a crucial type of psychotherapy research is where therapists draw from their own practice to advance new understandings in the field. In my own research, I use performative meta–reflexivity to analyse my reflexive clinical practice—the ways of relating that I enact and their productions—as a means to open up to new ways of thinking about subjectivity and the therapeutic process. In what follows, I offer a brief hypothetical example of what research that draws on questioning my reflexive clinical practice can look like.

Let's say a client struggles to make sense of what they are feeling and I reflexively articulate: *I am feeling unreal now; it is as if we are part of a scripted encounter; I wonder if I am sensing part of my client's experience. Can I stay with this uncomfortable feeling to help them process this?*

First question: What ways of relating am I enacting in this reflexive statement? I relate to my experience assuming it emerges from a relational interpersonal encounter; I relate to my client assuming I might have the capacity to know about them through my own experience; and I relate to the client assuming they need my help to process their experience, which I might be able to, and should, provide. Having thought about the ways of relating that are implicit in my reflexive statement, I would think of it as a relational and relatively opaque reflexivity. I feel a little silly offering this example, thinking how colleagues who work with a relational approach to psychotherapy might find it obvious. But this is precisely why it is important to write about such an example: to open up the possibility of thinking differently about what we take for granted.

Now I move to the second question performative meta–reflexivity invites: As part of which intra-active assemblage did these ways of relating emerge? There are many forces at work I can think of: psychotherapy as a material-discursive practice that privileges human interactions as the main explanatory factor and that places the therapist in a helper role which has some resemblance with the medical model; the clinical setting with me in the psychotherapist role; the affective flow in the session; my client's striving and struggle to make sense of what they are feeling; the physical space of the room; my client's and my stories and experiences and how they are part of ourselves; the brochures about therapy my agency offers; my sense of competence; our racial, social, and economic backgrounds; what I imagine my colleagues would think of this interaction; and so on.

Now the third question that arises with performative meta–reflexivity: What did this reflexivity as part of this assemblage help to produce? It helped to produce me as an agent capable of perceiving and modulating the affective

Using performative meta-reflexivity   41

states of another; the client as a person in need of someone to articulate their affective states; psychotherapy as a space where the therapist can have access and insight into what is going on to the client and in the relationship.

And the second part of the third question: What is this reflexivity preventing from happening? How could it have been different? As part of a different entanglement, I could have related to myself and the client differently; another reflexivity would have emerged. For instance, I could have articulated *I am feeling unreal now, as if we are part of a scripted encounter... I wonder if we are trying to force a 'therapeutic' interaction, assuming I as a therapist need to help the client to make sense of a sensation when actually this sensation might challenge our currently available ways of relating and making sense.* This different reflexivity with my client would have produced me as subject to and questioning the therapeutic material-discursive practices; the client as going through an affective experience that resists symbolisation within our current frames of reference and ways of relating; psychotherapy as a more precarious and critical practice that opens itself to something different.

What we articulate as reflexive knowledge about the client, ourselves, and the relationship is a production of an assemblage of theories, ways of practising, institutional practices, material arrangements, personal relationships with supervisors, peers, and more. To think about our ways of using reflexivity is important because they generate subjectivities, and open and foreclose possibilities. I encourage giving a further reflexive step that performative meta-reflexivity offers to critically consider what we are helping to produce, whether we think this is helpful, or if we might want to move toward alternative ways of using reflexivity to enable different productions. This opens the possibility of new conceptualisations/practices for psychotherapy—the purpose of my research that draws on my reflections on my clinical practice. For instance, in the example my client was produced as a somewhat 'passive' participant in therapy—given their unprocessed feelings, they were helping to produce this sensation of unrealness in me that I was capable and in charge of feeling and understanding. Do I consider this way of relating helpful in this encounter? If not, what alternative ways of relating can I envision? How does this translate into new conceptualisations/practices for psychotherapy?

Research example (2)

In my research, I may use my life experience to consider how the so-called 'personal' is entangled with the conceptual, political, cultural, material, and relational. Being reflexive about my experience using performative meta-reflexivity helps me to make these entanglements visible and be attentive to how my subjectivity is continuously produced/productive. This could be integrated into methodologies like autoethnography. In what follows, I provide an example of what using performative meta-reflexivity in an autoethnographic inquiry can look like. For illustration purposes, I crafted the following scene inspired by my experience as a Chilean immigrant living in Edinburgh, Scotland.

42 *Jacqueline Karen Andrea Serra Undurraga*

I am cycling and there is a flashing light in the distance indicating that pedestrians will meet a red light very soon. Automatically, I start slowing down my pedalling, so I pass just when my light becomes green. A pedestrian is about to reach the sidewalk. When I am a few metres from him he shouts in anger saying I need to stop. My heart starts pounding; I hear myself saying 'I did stop'; he mocks me; I look at him seriously but cannot speak again. I watch him leave and continue cycling.

There is no explicit reflexivity in this example, but there are implicit ways of relating in this scene that can be interrogated with performative meta-reflexivity. First question: How was I relating to him? I find I need to defend my actions from his challenge, but I cannot, in turn, challenge his mocking. Second question: As part of what intra-active assemblage did this way of relating emerge? I can think of my lack of confidence in my English when stressed; my status as a person with limited right to stay in the country; the structure of the streets, the cleanliness and safety of the city, the people around; the anger of this pedestrian; our genders; the movement possibilities that my bike affords me. Third question: What was this way of relating helping to produce? These possibilities: me as a woman cyclist who is accountable to the demands of this man but who is not feeling authorised to challenge his aggression; this man as a pedestrian who feels entitled to hail me; silent witnesses.

Using performative meta-reflexivity here allows me to think about the whole configuration that enabled this way of relating. This is crucial as I could have only thought of it as, say, coming from my shock and lack of confidence. To think about it in that essentialist way would have rendered invisible all other partners and would have dissolved the possibilities of critical engagement in my research: Who gets to feel comfortable enough in the streets to tell others off? I become uncomfortable thinking about what I am helping to produce (including myself). Performative meta-reflexivity opens my critical engagement with this way of relating I found myself enacting, and thus offers the possibility of relating differently. An autoethnographic inquiry, then, can benefit from using performative meta-reflexivity as a tool to make visible how the material, political, discursive, and relational forces are already entangled in our personal experience. Furthermore, it can enable us to become response-able for what we help to produce and to open up alternative ways of relating/producing, thus strengthening the activist, critical, and creative impact autoethnography can have.

Conclusions

I think about the different reflexivities as productive ways of relating and not as unveiling processes. How we relate is not a sovereign decision on our part but emerges as part of intra-active assemblages. This notion of reflexivity as productive ways of relating, which I have called *diffractive reflexivity,* works both when we are making explicit sense of ourselves and when we continuously make implicit sense of ourselves. Reflexivity in that way honours the 'reflex'

Using performative meta-reflexivity 43

part of the word: we cannot avoid making sense of ourselves all the time by relating to ourselves and the world.

With this notion of reflexivity, the practice and tool that I propose is *performative meta-reflexivity*. This tool can ask about the ways of relating in operation; about the assemblages that make them possible; and about what they are both helping to produce and preventing from happening. The purpose of answering the question about the ways of relating is to make our assumptions visible. The purpose of the question about the assemblage is not to offer a complete account of the entangled agencies at work (as if that were possible). Instead, the purpose is, firstly, to think about the human and non-human, material-discursive agencies at work because it allows a richer and more critical understanding of the situation; secondly, to acknowledge our inherent entanglement with the world; and thirdly, to enable us to consider transformations in the whole assemblage and not only in our subjectivity. The purpose of the questions about the productions of ways of relating (what they enable and what they prevent from happening) is: one, to become more response-able for what we are helping to produce; two, to question whether these productions are helpful and generative, for what and for whom; and three, to consider what other possibilities are prevented from being realised by this particular assemblage and way of relating.

Performative meta-reflexivity is in itself another productive way of relating. Asking how we are becoming through productive ways of relating can destabilise the sense of self; it asks us not to hold tightly to the ideas of who we think we/the other/the world are. Sometimes that destabilising might be generative, sometimes it might not. Performative meta-reflexivity as a tool for psychotherapy research can trouble us, make us response-able, and open alternatives. It invites the researcher not only to be reflexive but to question what their ways of relating are helping produce. It opens questions like: What is my way of relating to the academic field helping produce? As part of what entanglements am I as a researcher formulating these questions and not others? What do my ways of relating assume and would it be generative to question that? For whom? My invitation is to interrogate the ways of relating that we, more or less unwittingly, engage in, because they help to produce ourselves, our research and its impact, and the world in which we live.

References

Archer, M. (2011). Routine, reflexivity, and realism. *Dados*, *54*(1), 157–206. https://doi.org/10.1111%2Fj.1467-9558.2010.01375.x

Barad, K. (2007). *Meeting the universe halfway: Quantum physics and the entanglement of matter and meaning*. Duke University Press.

Benjamin, J. (2004). Beyond doer and done to: An intersubjective view of thirdness. *The Psychoanalytic Quarterly*, *73*(1), 5–46. https://doi.org/10.1002/j.2167-4086.2004.tb00151.x

Bion, W. (1970). *Attention and interpretation: A scientific approach to insight in psycho-analysis and groups*. Tavistock Publications.

Bondi, L., & Fewell, J. (Eds.). (2016). *Practitioner research in counselling and psychotherapy: The power of examples*. Macmillan Education/Palgrave.

Butler, J. (2014). *Bodies that matter: On the discursive limits of sex*. Routledge.

Deleuze, G., & Guattari, F. (1987). *A thousand plateaus: Capitalism and schizophrenia* (B. Massumi, Trans.). University of Minnesota Press.

Doucet, A. (2008). 'From her side of the gossamer wall(s)': Reflexivity and relational knowing. *Qualitative Sociology, 31*(1), 73–87. https://doi.org/10.1007/s11133-007-9090-9

Etherington, K. (2017) Personal experience and critical reflexivity in counselling and psychotherapy research. *Counselling and Psychotherapy Research, 17*(2), 85–94. doi:10.1002/capr.12080.

Finlay, L. (2002). Negotiating the swamp: The opportunity and challenge of reflexivity in research practice. *Qualitative Research, 2*(2), 209–230. https://doi.org/10.1177/146879410200200205

Finlay, L. (2017). Championing 'reflexivities'. *Qualitative Psychology, 4*(2), 120–125. https://doi.org/10.1037/qup0000075

Gendlin, E. T. (1969). Focusing. *Psychotherapy: Theory, Research & Practice, 6*(1), 4–15.

Haraway, D. J. (2016). *Staying with the trouble: Making kin in the Chthulucene*. Duke University Press.

Harding, S. (1993). Rethinking standpoint epistemology: What is 'strong objectivity'? In L. Alcoff & E. J. Potter (Eds.), *Feminist epistemologies* (pp. 49–82). Routledge.

McNay, L. (1999). Gender, habitus and the field: Pierre Bourdieu and the limits of reflexivity. *Theory, Culture & Society, 16*(1), 95–117. https://doi.org/10.1177/026327699016001007

Pillow, W. S. (2003). Confession, catharsis, or cure? Rethinking the uses of reflexivity as methodological power in qualitative research. *International Journal of Qualitative Studies in Education, 16*(2), 175–196. https://doi.org/10.1080/0951839032000060635

Pillow, W. S. (2015). Reflexivity as interpretation and genealogy in research. *Cultural Studies ↔ Critical Methodologies, 15*(6), 419–434. https://doi.org/10.1177/1532708615615605

Serra Undurraga, J. K. A. (2020). *Reflexivities as affective ways of relating that produce. Qualitative Inquiry, 26*(7), 920–930. https://doi.org/10.1177/1077800419885408

Serra Undurraga, J. K. A. (2021). What if reflexivity and diffraction intra-act? *International Journal of Qualitative Studies in Education*. https://doi.org/10.1080/09518398.2021.1900622

Serra Undurraga, J. K. A. (2022). *Betraying our best intentions: On the need to interrogate how we relate and what it produces. International Journal of Qualitative Studies in Education*. https://doi.org/10.1080/09518398.2022.2098409

Wilkinson, S. (1988). The role of reflexivity in feminist psychology. *Women's Studies International Forum, 11*(5), 493–502. https://doi.org/10.1016/0277-5395(88)90024-6

4 A psychosocial coming into play
Researching authenticity in therapy, the academy, and friendship

Nini Fang, Anne Pirrie and Peter Redman

This chapter explores psychosocially what it means to practise, research, and live authentically. What role does authenticity play in the creative dimensions of therapeutic practice and academic inquiry? How does it help us to live a good life in the company of others? We attend to these questions by exploiting the indeterminate nature of the psychosocial inquiry as 'a loosely defined, slightly chaotic field of study' (Frosh, 2014, p. 169). The theoretical tussles in trying to define 'psychosocial' (see Layton, 2008) reveal its struggles to be pinned down to a definitional place. The conceptual uncertainty surrounding the term challenges us to resist the temptation to settle too readily on what we know and invites us to *play*. To evoke a felt quality of the psychosocial, we appeal to the creative forces of a triple-act amongst collaborators. This takes the form of sketches that explore issues of personal and professional loyalty, and conformity to notions of occupancy, disciplinarity, and identity in the academy. Indeterminacy and disquiet are the jazz of non-conformists. We let this stream in the background while we explore the elusive contours of the 'psychosocial'. This triple-act is an opening to the processual uncertainty of thinking, researching, and being with others. It foregrounds the generative tension between value and knowledge in academic inquiry (Pirrie, 2019); between truthfulness and rightfulness in therapeutic practice; and between true-self and false-self in relationships. Threaded through these questions are our respective and joint inquiries into 'authenticity'.

An opening act

'So, what is this "psychosocial" that you have been banging on about?', asks Annie, in an apparently playful retaliation to Nini for calling their recent project a 'bloody book' (Pirrie et al., 2021). Nini colours a little as she struggles to come up with a definition of the psychosocial that will provide an opening for her friend. After all, this is an emergent and contested terrain (Redman, 2016). Keen to make the psychosocial sound more tempting, she resorts to quoting a renowned white male professor. 'Psychosocial studies …' she flips through an introduction of a book on the subject and lands her finger on a paragraph. Here she opens the door to Stephen Frosh and lets him do the rest of the

DOI: 10.4324/9781003280859-5

46 *Nini Fang, Anne Pirrie, and Peter Redman*

talking. He explains that this field of inquiry is 'fuelled by an understanding that what is taken to be the realm of the personal, including the "inner world" of psychoanalysis, is produced and sustained by various manifestations of sociality, and vice versa' (Frosh, 2016, p. 3).

'That's quite some nutshell, isn't it?' says Annie, laughing. Her gleeful response is tinged with sympathy towards her colleague, who appears troubled by an odd mixture of pride and embarrassment. She wonders about Nini's version of the psychosocial. 'I shall remain open to it, whatever it is', says Annie, smiling at her friend.

In search of something else, whatever it is

The scope of psychosocial studies as described by Frosh is certainly capacious. This definitional ambiguity is advantageous, for if certainty forecloses the critical dimension of thought, ambiguity keeps it alive (Frosh, 2014). The central task of psychosocial inquiry works around the questions of how the psyche and the social interact. Or more particularly, to quote another grand name, how the psychic and social 'each [permeates] the other in ways that are not fully predictable' (Butler, 2016, p. ix). Multiple approaches and modes of engagement to this question generate what Lapping (2011, p. 2) describes as 'a tussle over meanings and practices' in the collective struggle to put the psychosocial in its definitional place. This is about more than rogue elements of dissent and disquiet aroused by the 'establishment of big names and preferred methods' (Cummins & Williams, 2018, p. xix), both of which are inevitable consequences of the institutionalisation of a particular field of study. Irrespective of one's involvement in those 'tussles', we are impelled to reflect on what lies at the heart of psychosocial studies. What is all the fuss about? What is it struggling *against*? What keeps us at it?

Frosh (2016) contends that one of the major strengths of psychosocial studies is that it does not reside in a single disciplinary constituency. In his view, the richness of this form of inquiry lies precisely in how it resists becoming territorialised and reaches beyond disciplinary singularity. According to Frosh, the institutional boundary-making involved in the demarcation of academic disciplines has proven inadequate in the face of mounting psychosocial problematics that elude stable divisions between the 'psyche' and the 'social'. Consider, for example, the case of political anger stoked by racist violence against the east-Asian communities in the wake of the COVID-19 pandemic (Fang, 2021). In this case, how may we locate the locus of inquiry in either the psyche or the social? To do so would run the risk of reducing a more complex inquiry concerning the co-constitutive interplay between psychoanalytic and sociological processes into unreflexive dichotomisations of either.

Frosh (2016) further argues that psychosocial inquiry can be seen as 'queer' in the sense that it subverts established categories and cuts across disciplinary boundaries:

A psychosocial coming into play 47

What therefore makes psychosocial studies 'trans-' rather than multi- or interdisciplinary is that as a set of practices it is not just a meeting ground for other disciplines, but an attempt to call them into question, to provoke or undermine them through various kinds of sampling of different ideas and procedures (a kind of 'nomadic' practice), all in the name of searching for a systematically critical approach towards the psychosocial subject who belongs everywhere but also, in relation to existing disciplines, can be found nowhere at all. (p. 2)

The prefix 'inter-' denotes 'betweenness or amongness' within temporal and spatial boundaries, with concomitant risks of claustrophobia for insiders and exclusion for outsiders. The prefix 'trans-' points to 'the great outdoors … somehow beyond the reach of disciplinarity' (Baraitser, 2015, p. 212). In the latter, we may find greater freedom to break with received wisdom in search of radically unexpected turns, something we don't already know, something refreshingly new. 'Trans-', therefore, evokes the perpetual motion of going beyond the borders, edges, and limits to create new openings—'to deliberately look for the place where a field meets its breaking points and therefore faces its contingencies, and to reflexively reposition oneself wherever a new liminal space opens up' (p. 209).

Psychosocial, in this sense, struggles against accommodating those who seek the comfort of settling down and belonging. For belonging or settling would risk leaning too readily into 'illusory comforts offered by false compromises' (Redman, 2016, p. 87) or embracing entrenched and sometimes wilfully abstruse forms of discourse that 'narrow the field' and offer the minor consolations of a 'community'. More profoundly, it would mean losing touch with the great outdoors where the psychosocial roams free. Rather, as a transdisciplinary enterprise, it speaks more to those seeking to venture out and transgress academic boundaries. Those engaged in psychosocial studies may on occasion tread into secluded disciplinary sites, but without seeking to '*fully* [emphasis added] belong anywhere' (Baraitser, 2015, p. 209).

'There will always be room for a lot of philosophical disagreement between people who share the same politics' (Rorty, 1999, p. 23). This applies in equal measure to the field of psychosocial studies and provides a timely reminder not to dwell on disagreements and become stifled by institutional legacies. Rather than imagining a better state of affairs from the security of a warm study, we might find ourselves better revitalised by opening the door and sensing the cool breeze of possibility as it crosses the threshold.

This chapter exemplifies the potential of psychosocial inquiry as a form of research practice that sets itself against the normative systems of knowledge and epistemological interventions. We follow up the little stirrings of spontaneous energies that move us between the dialectics of 'how to settle' and 'how *not to* settle'—the very momentum that keeps psychosocial studies going. Settling keeps us down to earth by providing material gravity and meeting our relational need to be part of something. Being unsettled makes us reflect on what

48 *Nini Fang, Anne Pirrie, and Peter Redman*

might be at stake with and through these settlements. As we shall illustrate, oscillating between settling and not-settling is a key dimension of the notion of authenticity and our striving towards it. To bring to light ways in which the psychosocial inquiry affords possibilities for questioning that situates it more authentically within the lived realities of the researchers, we must first let Nini respond to the doorbell of her consulting room that announces the arrival of Susie—a long-term psychotherapy client.

Authenticity in therapeutic encounters

Susie[1] looks unsettled as she enters the room. Planting herself down in the chair, she holds on to the armrests as if preparing for a thunderstorm in the therapeutic terrain. Her subdued smile and offhand comments about the weather do little to disguise her agitation. At the end of the last session, she informed Nini of her desire to 'take a break' from therapy, having been weighed down by the urgency of job-seeking as her Master's studies came to an end and her student visa was expiring. Having considered Nini's suggestion to come in for another session so they could at least discuss this, Susie agreed—adding, as she rose, that the next session might well be the last.

Susie had no idea how much of a blow this was to Nini, who was under the impression that the work had been going well. Susie's ready wit, forthcoming nature, and thoughtful engagement with Nini's psychoanalytic interventions were a breath of fresh air after hours of being confined in a room with all manner of human suffering. Clients come and go, and it would not be the first time that a client wanted out for one reason or another. But Susie's announcement threw Nini. The tremulous tone and the hasty way in which Susie uttered her wish to end had done the job of betraying her real feelings towards their work together. Feeling mortified by Susie's remedial attempt to stress how helpful the work had been for her, Nini felt a bubble had been burst and was left wondering what Susie really wanted to tell her but could not.

The next day Nini rang up her supervisor, hoping to explore what might have been going on with Susie. It was when her supervisor struggled to recall this client that Nini realised how little she has discussed Susie in supervision. Immediately Nini realised how little space Susie had taken in her mind. She suddenly became aware that she had devoted greater attention to other clients who appeared, by comparison, always to be more in need, more distressed, or challenging. 'Sounds like Susie has been taking care of you!' her supervisor quipped. The veracity of that remark stung.

As a Mexican American, Susie had left for the UK as a young adult to pursue a Master's degree in journalism. She had fallen in love with various aspects of life in Scotland and hoped to secure leave to remain. She came to counselling with issues described as 'low self-esteem' and 'difficulties with people', both of which had been compounded by difficulties in finding employment, particularly as a foreigner and a woman of colour. These retrospective glimpses led Nini to wonder what she herself had really wanted to tell Susie but could not.

The similarities in their real-world lived experiences were often beyond the scale of what can be realistically dialogued between a client and a therapist. Through training and experience, Nini had become accustomed to bracketing off parts of her identity so as to remain in touch with what the client brought without getting too caught up in her own distress. However, in what follows, we may come to see how Susie's decision to exit therapy revealed the paradox of bracketing in the therapist's handling of similarities and differences: namely, how (and when) to step up in order to become 'real' for the client; and how (and when) to fall back in order to afford the client scope to bear a close encounter with the other, with all the strangeness that entails in coming into contact with one another.

★★★

This paradox becomes intensified when the encounters take place between members of two different ethnic minority communities. Despite an ever-increasing pressure to diversify the workforce, Merchant (2020) points out how psychoanalysis as a master discourse is replete with nostalgia for whiteness. This unconscious wish, ironically, is often acted upon through an implicit demand on the non-white practitioners or trainees alike to 'blanch' (p. 107) themselves to fit in with the homogenous culture of what a therapist should act, be, and sound like (see also Altman, 2014, and Layton, 2019, on this point). Merchant (2020), an Indian American practitioner who identifies as queer, documents this 'blanching' well:

> Throughout graduate school the violence (and the accompanying rage and shame) of experiencing myself as other was repeated: from being told to seek the services of a writing tutor for my 'grammar' (not only was English my first language but I worked as a tutor at the centre where I was referred), to being asked to delete information about my sexuality in my personal essay for internship (purportedly, in case the information was used against me). (p. 107)

Suppressing individual and cultural differences is the 'psychic deal' we make with the dominant culture in exchange for approval by and access to it (Layton, 2019). The experience of feeling othered can hurt even more at a place of professional community or a training institute that should be a space for solidarity and support. Invoking Winnicott's (1956/2016b) 'impingement', the non-white practitioners here are the ones who must demonstrate 'ordinary devotedness' to the profession's 'preoccupation' with whiteness to allow it to 'go on being' (p. 187).

With regards to Susie, what appeared to be a smooth process and an easy rapport with the therapist was precisely the repetition of her past difficulties where likeability must trump authenticity. Brenman Pick (2018) refers to this type of personality organisation as one of 'precocious development': where the sense of being needed is repetitively engineered and maintained to help ward

50 *Nini Fang, Anne Pirrie, and Peter Redman*

off any real sense of needing others. The latter brings close the early relational trauma where dependence on others often proved futile, subsequently leading to a breach of faith in the relational capacity of others to be genuinely caring. Susie's ready engagement with Nini's comments and the fact that she made few demands on Nini's affective processing were all signs of her adaptation to the particular systems of meanings and manners that, when adopted by the therapist, are seen as *proper* (Dalal, 2009).

And yet, 'speedy flowering … prevents real growth' (Brenman Pick, 2018, p. 100). The relational dynamics described above had reached a critical conjuncture, or a 'breaking point' (Baraitser, 2015, p. 209) when Susie plucked up the courage to seek a way *out*. We might consider this as a pulse of authenticity, breaking through the guise of a good client and cracking open a liminal space where the psychosocial may enter the therapeutic discourse. To Brenman Pick (2018), authenticity has two faces in the therapeutic encounter: one belongs to the patient and the other to the therapist. The authenticity of the therapist finds expression through her alertness to the subtle ways in which the patient's angst manifests itself in relation to the therapist, and her willingness to examine her own contribution to that process. If 'false-self' develops on the basis of compliance to environmental demands (Winnicott, 1965/2016a) then Nini's adaptation to the Eurocentric system of the analytic syntax would also require her to split off core aspects of her lived experience as a woman of colour. Like Susie, she is not from here. To shut out those parts of herself also means to keep politics out of the therapeutic frame (see also Bondi's chapter on this point).

Between them as two women of colour, how could the disparity between Nini's yellow face and her 'white' ways not be experienced as a form of disassociation which normalises the intersectional workings of immigrant status, gender, and race? Furthermore, how might this reproduce in the consulting room what is 'out there' in the social relations in which the racialised subject must adapt to the dominant enterprises and differential syntax to be seen as adequate? With these questions in mind, we now return to the final session with Susie.

★★★

Having declared that it would only be appropriate to acknowledge *all* the help she has received from Nini, Susie has brought a note of 'positive changes' and begins to go through them. She sometimes elaborates upon examples, as if pleading for a good grade for her 'presentation'. And that is exactly what Nini says, when she finally gets a word in edgeways. Susie seems startled by Nini's response, and head down, confides that she had felt nervous coming in today. She was worried that her mind would go blank in the absence of a note. Nini is intrigued by what Susie means when she thinks of 'going blank'. 'Disappearing, as if I had never been here', says Susie hesitantly, her eyes moistening with tears. A palpable air of restlessness settles on the room.

Unexpectedly Susie reaches towards her bag and takes out a portfolio that she lays on the table between them. If this is the last session, she no longer

A psychosocial coming into play   51

wishes to open up about herself. Her hand caressing the cover of the portfolio, she explains to Nini that this is her project on the lives of Mexican immigrants in the US. Susie soon becomes engrossed in telling Nini the story of each photo. Nini listens without interruption, in virtual defiance of all the counselling common sense that what they really should be doing now is addressing the ending. This is Susie's defence against the pain of ending, some Mr Know-how would say. Having silenced Mr Know-how in her head, Nini gently remarks that she is struck by the refrain of the 'border wall' in the accounts of the Mexican immigrants.

Suddenly Susie turns to the page of her own profile and gestures that she would like Nini to read it. Susie's poetic prose, unheard before in therapeutic dialogue, slips the secured moorings of Nini's subjectivity as the therapist, leaving her at sea with the intensity of her own feelings. When Nini raises her head again, Susie eagerly asks her what she thinks. The usual litany of 'it must be really difficult for you' sticks in Nini's throat. This time, thinks Nini, she will turn away from the vague ideal of the 'proper' therapist and make a splash in the mud. 'It *really* is difficult!', she says to Susie, taking the work outside psychoanalysis into the uncertain domains of the psychosocial. Susie replies that she *knew* Nini would understand. It seems that right at the end Nini breaks the illusion that she is one of *them,* someone who should understand but won't.

After seeing Susie off, Nini glances at her watch and hastens to meet Annie, her friend and colleague.

Stepping up and falling back: Authenticity in pedagogical relations

They are striding out along the canal tow-path when Nini becomes aware that Annie is muttering under her breath. 'Stepping up, falling back, labouring, and resting', she repeats, over and over again, striding out to the rhythm of what appears to be some kind of mantra. Annie is setting a brisk pace, gesticulating in a manner they habitually refer to as full Pirrie mode.[2] Nini tucks in behind, enjoying the pocket of wind resistance created by her friend. She is comforted by the knowledge that all she needs to do to ease them both into a more congenial corner is to utter the words 'matcha latte?' Soon their gale-bitten struggle is at an end, and they are sitting opposite each other sipping the pale green beverage.

'It's the teaching. I'm struggling with the teaching', Annie explains. Nini listens expectantly, knowing better than to ask her friend what she is banging on about. For now, it suffices to know that she is probably referring to challenges in teacher education. Annie has previously lamented what she describes as a 'dependency culture' in teacher education. They had begun to discuss how a form of 'precocious development' (Brenman Pick, 2018) was also evident in beginning teachers. Beginning teachers were encouraged to strive for a form of settlement, to ward off any real sense of needing others. This amounted to a systematic denial of their own vulnerability in the context of contingent and

52 Nini Fang, Anne Pirrie, and Peter Redman

unpredictable pedagogical encounters. Annie had speculated that one of the consequences of this was that teachers might be less able to respond ethically and relationally to the needs of their pupils; that they might be less able to embrace authenticity in their practice. The exigencies of day-to-day practice in primary schools meant that many teachers operated with a fairly restricted definition of their responsibilities towards the other, thus seeking to reinforce the authority of the teacher and systematically downplay the constitutive role of the micro-dynamics of face-to-face interaction.

Nini knows from experience that the contours of what Annie wants to say will emerge soon enough. As they have so often remarked on previous occasions, all that is required is conversation, in the sense of a turning towards the other. 'Let me put it in context', says Annie. Nini smiles in relief, toying with the loosely knotted threads of the woollen scarf, relieved that she is no longer relying on it for warmth. 'I'm working with final-year students who are training to be primary school teachers. I am an outsider, if only in the sense that I have never been a primary school teacher. I've been swimming against the tide of habitual practice and have dispensed with conventional "learning outcomes" to persuade the students that education, at all levels, is more about persistent effects than immediate results. I want to counter the prevailing view, in teacher education circles at least, that education is about arming oneself with codified knowledge and implementing "strategies" in the classroom. I want to demonstrate that learning proceeds through inquiry; that it takes unexpected turns through dialogue with others; that it is by definition a psychosocial enterprise.' Nini looks thoughtful.

'I was thinking back to your account of the sessions with Susie', says Annie. 'The paradox of authenticity, if you like, is that you could only bring the therapeutic encounters with Susie to a successful conclusion by choosing *not* to be one of them, someone who *should* understand but won't. I can only fulfil the broader course objectives by *not* doing what I *should* do—i.e., set conventional learning outcomes.'

What does it mean for Nini and Annie to navigate between their authentic and inauthentic selves? Perhaps what they are rejecting are standardised operating procedures, or the tyranny of institutional or disciplinary legacies. These demarcations stifle curiosity by leaving the personal, the cultural, and the social meanings assumed instead of questioned; they regulate thinking and marginalise understanding that is improbable. To engage in psychosocial inquiry, however, requires us to take up a reflexive position on our knowingness and the ways in which we are subjected to knowledge frameworks that govern what and how we think. The purpose of inquiry, as Saville Young and Frosh (2009) point out, is to open out possible, and sometimes self-contestatory, understandings of a reality, instead of settling too readily on a set of interpretations from the standpoint of supposed expertise: to disrupt rather than to conform to what we assume we know. To make way for minoritarian ways of seeing and experiencing, rather than seeking to 'occupy a position that offers a final pronouncement on it' (p. 3).

A psychosocial coming into play   53

Suddenly Nini notices the time, 'Peter is going to call me at 6pm'. 'Peter?' 'Peter from the *Open University*', Nini accentuates. 'Ah, the *Open University*', sighs Annie, wistfully, reflecting on how opportunities for authentic dialogue are often foreclosed in the university sector. 'But do tell me what you were on about with the stepping up, falling back, labouring and resting', says Nini. 'You muttered that continuously on our way here. I'm not even sure you were aware you were doing it'.

'It's a line from a song by Karine Polwart, 'Labouring and Resting', from her album *A Pocket of Wind Resistance* (Polwart & Murphy, 2017), says Annie. She is acutely aware that this opening sentence does not offer much in the way of an explanation. But Nini cocks her head attentively and Annie feels encouraged. 'I set this as the course song for BA4 Theory in Education', says Annie, as if this were an entirely self-evident action. 'Polwart describes how a skein of geese fly in a formation that sustains them. The outstretched wings of the migrating birds create pockets of wind resistance that provide "aerodynamic sanctuaries" for those birds tucked in behind and below. This is both a wonder and a "gale-bitten struggle", for it is not easy to maintain co-operation. Each goose takes a turn in this precious wild goose chase: *stepping up, falling back, labouring and resting*. I wanted to rehabilitate this *being in search of something else, whatever it is*, in relation to educational practice', explains Annie. At the heart of the educational endeavour is an attempt to encourage students to seek 'novel and exciting answers to unexpected questions rather than … answers to questions with which we are already familiar' (Nehamas, 1999, p. xxix). Annie explains that she doesn't want to cram the students with decontextualised knowledge, especially at this late stage in their university careers. She wants them to *understand*; to see connections between things that they didn't already know; to recollect what they already knew; and to ground themselves in their lived experience in order to be able fully to open themselves to the other. 'Socrates was right', she says. 'You cannot carry learning away in a jar.' Nini chuckles. 'But having a harmonious soul (which is how Socrates defined success) or becoming an admirable human being would hardly make the cut in terms of learning outcomes', said Annie, laughing. She explains to Nini that she 'wants the students to fly', and that her friend Julia's response to what she was trying to do had made her smile: 'To be so unequivocally *you* is outstanding. I love it.'

'Julia may be right', says Annie, 'but you have to swim against the tide to maintain this approach when faced with students' expectations that you will tell them what they are going to learn and then teach them it; and institutional pressures to maintain high scores in the annual student satisfaction surveys. I often feel like a lone bird bearing the brunt of an ill wind. If it weren't for the symbiotic dance with you' she says, looking at Nini, 'then I doubt if I could go on. There is a freshness, an openness, to our exchanges that I treasure.' The discourse of conventional academic exchanges is akin to the 'learned insanity' that manifests itself in a 'dialect of sorts that is confined to a very small group of people and has no bearing or meaning outside of that circle' (J. König, personal

54 *Nini Fang, Anne Pirrie, and Peter Redman*

communication, 2018). 'The paradox of authenticity', concludes Annie, 'may be that in order to fly one has to remain grounded in lived experience.'

Closing/opening remarks: What is the psychosocial anyway?

[Phone rings]

PETER: Hullo, Nini!
  [Nini dives in, eager to resume their periodic exchanges on the psychosocial but aware that they would soon have to break off and have dinner.]
NINI: Peter, this psychosocial thing is driving me mad! First, we need to be able to explain how 'this psychosocial' differs from the 'other psychosocial' in health studies. Words like 'psyche' or 'psychic reality' are not always readily understood or appreciated by colleagues outside the field. It can be tricky to find words for the work we are trying to do: to challenge 'subjectivity' which is so often either restricted to external patterns of social meanings and practices or to the internal, psychological processes. Either way, it essentialises the subject and forecloses nuanced explorations of how the inner world may be socially fuelled and how social worlds may be psychically maintained.
PETER: For sure, wouldn't it be nice if it were easy? But perhaps the most compelling definition emerges from our reflections on our own transition into the psychosocial. By paying attention to those moments when we start to seek 'something else', when our disciplinary home no longer accommodates the inquiry. What happens when we don't place these limitations on our thinking, when we become attentive to what is normally excluded, when we push against the limits of the discipline?
NINI: Like how certain strands of psychoanalysis have become outdated for me because they don't allow us to see the 'symptoms' as mutually constituted by psychic process *and* social relations. I knew I had to move on when fossilised psychoanalytic frames were stifling thinking and, worse even, being. Telling you this makes me think of Susie …
PETER: Susie was your 'breaking point'.
NINI: She really was. There had been something else going on in my life that prepared me towards being able to see my 'ending' with Susie as signposting where a way of working ceased to work or apply. Looking back, I realised I was under the same sway of political pressure to secure employment or face being deported as the period of my doctoral studies was coming to an end. I was unable to attend to her psychosocial sufferings as these were exactly what I had been desperate to keep out of my mind. It was necessary for me at the time. But it also meant that I became a version of the false-self with Susie.
PETER: I guess a psychosocial interpretation would be that the environmental conditions for you were not conducive to the emergence of the true self. If Winnicott (1963/2018a) is right, the true self is always hidden and

A psychosocial coming into play 55

cannot be fully known. But one place we experience the true self—if it has been allowed to emerge sufficiently for us to catch a glimpse of it—is in those moments when we rebel against any attempt to reach an accommodation with things that prevent us from entering the intermediate state. What was it Winnicott (1953/2018b) said about intermediate states? Something to the effect that they are neither purely subjective nor objectively perceived, that they exist at the point at which the boundary between reality and fantasy blurs, where we are in touch with what feels vividly alive and with what speaks to us in a profound part of ourselves without us knowing exactly why. Doesn't that describe how and why we feel welcomed into a space, and what is going on when we feel obliged to leave one? In the latter case, perhaps we are in touch with something that prevents us from being fully allowed to *be*.

NINI: That's it, Peter. How can we be unequivocally ourselves when the environment we are in militates against that? It was through these struggles to be unequivocally myself that I strayed from my home, became a stranger, and learned to live with the consequences of my perpetual strangeness. Something in these struggles, I'm not sure what, feels real and worth preserving.

PETER: We risk everything in order to learn something new. We put ourselves in jeopardy.

NINI: We certainly do, so that we can keep thinking alive and our inquiry down to earth. 'Never stay up on the barren heights of cleverness, but come down into the green valleys of silliness.' I love that line from Wittgenstein (1980). To enquire authentically also means noticing when a theory or a concept takes up an epic stance over the intimate questions from our lived world. This is when a theory becomes bigger than life, essentially, demanding that we adapt to it, its language and syntax, in order for it to 'go on being'.

PETER: It appears that we were both drawn to the psychosocial because it seemed to promise something more expansive and open than the 'homes' we were leaving behind. But this openness seems to demand that, to some degree, we remain permanently unsettled—alive to the unknown, escaping, hidden, silent, and not to be defined by what came before us.

NINI: And this 'psychosocial' will always be 'the psychosocial for now' with a sense of timeliness that reflects the context in which we live. A psychosocial without 'guarantees', as you said, 'once more, with feeling'. This also reminds me of Layton's 'ethic of disillusionment'. Perhaps doing psychosocial work requires us to be committed to an ethic of disillusionment. It incites us to reflect on the tensions between innovation and tradition, between the conscious longing to remain true to oneself by resisting conformity and the unconscious longing that seeks to belong. But I guess we both need to head off and make dinner now. It's been great talking to you, Peter. Talk again soon.

56 *Nini Fang, Anne Pirrie, and Peter Redman*

We have engaged in a psychosocial exploration of what it means to practise, research, and live authentically. We hope that our triple-act has offered a brief glimpse of a good life, lived in the company of others. Relating this to research in counselling and psychotherapy, we problematise that, too often, research takes for granted knowledge frameworks that stall and confine thinking. As we have shown, psychosocial inquiry, which contests any preconceived boundaries between the inner and the social world, needs to maintain its porousness and be willing to go to uncertain terrains that may not have been traversed yet in order to keep thinking complex, alive, and close to life. Its privileging of the localised over the global; the particularised over the universal; and the provisional over the certain reflects the processual uncertainty of exploring the crossover between the psyche and social in real time. Our interaction with the world is necessarily partial, which is why it may appear blurred, fragmented, and subject to arbitrary disruption. ('It's cold out, let's go and drink tea.' 'Peter is calling me at 6pm.') Such are the rustlings of the energies that keep us on the go and take us somewhere else. As we run against the buffers of this chapter with the taste of irony in our mouths, we show how not settling (on a disciplinary home; on the known) allows us to settle on a form of inquiry that moves us.

Notes

1 Susie is a pseudonym. This piece of work concluded in 2016—the same year Donald Trump pledged to build a 'big, beautiful wall' on the US–Mexico border. All identifiable information has been carefully removed in this case study.
2 'Pirrie' features as an adjective in *The Concise Scots Dictionary* (Robinson, 1985, p. 497): '1. (of persons) given to sudden bursts of activity, unpredictable, unreliable; 2. quick-tempered, touchy, easily annoyed; 3. hare-brained, scatty.'

References

Altman, N. (2014). *Psychoanalysis in an age of accelerating cultural change: Spiritual globalization*. Routledge.
Baraitser, L. (2015). Temporal drag: Transdisciplinarity and the 'case' of psychosocial studies. *Theory, Culture & Society, 32*(5–6), 207–231. https://doi.org/10.1177/0263276415592039
Brenman Pick, I. (2018). *Authenticity in the psychoanalytic encounter*. Routledge.
Butler, J. (2016). Foreword: Tracking the mechanism of the psychosocial. In S. Frosh (Ed.), *Psychosocial imaginaries: Perspectives on temporality, subjectivities and activism* (pp. vi–xii). Palgrave.
Cummins, A-M., & Williams, N. (Eds.). (2018). *Further researching beneath the surface: Psycho-social research methods in practice* (Vol. 2). Routledge.
Dalal, F. (2009). The paradox of belonging. *Psychoanalysis, Culture and Society, 14*(1), 74–81. https://doi.org/10.1057/pcs.2008.47
Fang, A. (2021). The aggressive potential and the yellow anger. *Psychoanalysis, Culture & Society, 26*, 561–578. https://doi.org/10.1057/s41282-021-00234-4
Frosh, S. (2014). The nature of the psychosocial: Debates from 'studies in the psychosocial'. *Journal of Psychosocial Studies, 8*(1) 159–169. https://eprints.bbk.ac.uk/id/eprint/11514

A psychosocial coming into play 57

Frosh, S. (2016). Introduction. In S. Frosh (Ed.), *Psychosocial imaginaries: Perspectives on temporality, subjectivities and activism* (pp. 1–20). Palgrave.

Lapping, C. (2011). *Psychoanalysis in social research: Shifting theories and reframing concepts.* Routledge.

Layton, L. (Ed.). (2008). Special issue on British psycho(-)social studies. *Psychoanalysis, Culture and Society, 13*(4), 339–427. https://doi.org/10.1057/pcs.2008.34

Layton, L. (2019). Transgenerational hauntings: Toward a social psychoanalysis and an ethic of dis-illusionment. *Psychoanalytic Dialogues, 29*(2), 105–121. https://doi.org/10.1080/10481885.2019.1587992

Merchant, A. (2020). Don't be put off by my name. *Studies in Gender and Sexuality, 21*(2), 104–112. https://doi.org/10.1080/15240657.2020.1760025

Nehamas, A. (1999). *Virtues of authenticity. Essays on Plato and Socrates.* Princeton University Press.

Pirrie, A. (2019). *Virtue and the quiet art of scholarship. Reclaiming the university.* Routledge.

Pirrie, A., Fang, N., & O'Brien, E. (2021). *Dancing in the dark. A survivor's guide to the university.* Tilosophy Press.

Polwart, K., & Murphy, P. (2017). Labouring and resting [Song]. On *A pocket of wind resistance.* Hudson Records.

Redman, P. (2016). Once more with feeling: What is the psychosocial anyway? *Journal of Psychosocial Studies, 9*(1), 73–93. http://www.psychosocial-studies-association.org/volume-9-issue-1-may-2016

Robinson, M. (Ed.). (1985). Pirrie. In *The Concise Scots Dictionary* (p. 497). Aberdeen University Press.

Rorty, R. (1999). *Philosophy and social hope.* Penguin Books.

Saville Young, L., & Frosh, S. (2009). Discourse and psychoanalysis: Translating concepts into 'fragmenting' methodology. *Psychology in Society, 38*, 1–16. https://eprints.bbk.ac.uk/id/eprint/3283

Winnicott, D. W. (2016a). The concept of the false self. In L. Caldwell & H. T. Robinson (Eds.), *The collected works of D. W. Winnicott.* (pp. 28–32). Oxford University Press. (Original work published 1965)

Winnicott, D. W. (2016b). Primary maternal preoccupation. In L. Caldwell & H. T. Robinson (Eds.), *The collected works of D. W. Winnicott* (pp. 185–189). Oxford University Press. (Original work published 1956)

Winnicott, D. W. (2018a). Communicating and not communicating leading to a study of certain opposites. In *Collected papers: The maturational processes and the facilitating environment* (pp. 173–192). Routledge. (Original work published 1963)

Winnicott, D. W. (2018b). Transitional objects and transitional phenomena. In *Collected papers: Through paediatrics to psychoanalysis* (pp. 229–242). Routledge. (Original work published 1953)

Wittgenstein, L. (1980). *Culture and value.* University of Chicago Press.

5 Feminist research in psychotherapy
The strange case of the United Kingdom's 'hostile environment' policy

Emily le Couteur

Utilising a feminist agenda can offer psychotherapists a valuable qualitative framework through which to examine structural issues of oppression and discrimination and provide a coherent counter-narrative to hegemonic ideologies which legitimise such mechanisms of oppression. Using the example of the UK's 'hostile environment' immigration policy, I discuss dialogic and andragogic approaches to fostering a culture of shared values, and a commitment to solidarity, resistance, and action in academic and professional settings, and highlight potential barriers. I draw attention to the role of critical reflexivity, with a view to encouraging research which challenges hegemonic narratives of migration. The chapter addresses androcentric and dehumanising discourses of migration, and explicates the implications for anti-oppressive, feminist research, offering paradigmatic and theoretical frameworks aligned with dismantling systemic oppression, racism, and inequality inherent in hostile environment policy. I draw attention to the role of critical reflexivity, with a view to encouraging research which challenges hegemonic narratives of migration.

★★★

How can psychotherapists resist oppression and discrimination in both their practice and their research? The issues are vast, and the task an enormous one, but so is our potential contribution. Qualitative research, and anti-oppressive, feminist approaches in particular, offer a powerful, legitimate counter position to objective, reductionist, positivist research traditions; an alternate epistemological outlook through which stories of oppression—and resistance—may be prioritised, and multitudinous subjectivities embraced. Key to this is critical consciousness of the power dynamics which govern whose epistemologies are amplified, and whose are stifled. However, research of this ilk first requires fertile soil, based in anti-oppressive pedagogy (Freire, 1967/1970) or andragogy (Knowles, 1970), that is, the teaching of adults as distinct from the teaching of children, in order to nurture the growth of budding adult researchers and practitioners, committed to solidarity with oppressed communities.

Andragogical and dialogical groundwork

Commitment to an ethical agenda of resistance and solidarity is rendered unworkable without reflexive consideration of one's own positionality as 'a

DOI: 10.4324/9781003280859-6

Feminist research in psychotherapy   59

benefactor of oppressor group membership' (Allen & Rossatto, 2009, p. 165). In this work, there is significant potential for acute personal discomfort when examining one's own situatedness in relation to marginalised groups, particularly through the acknowledgement of privilege and complicity in systemic discrimination—something which becomes more pertinent when considering the demographic makeup of my own profession (counselling psychology) and its trainees.

Trainees may tend to distance themselves from individualised complicity (Applebaum, 2012; Whitt, 2016) and the accompanying affective components of guilt and shame (Zembylas, 2019). If unable to acknowledge their complicity in systemic inequalities, they will undoubtedly contribute to their continued reproduction (Applebaum, 2012). Critical, anti-complicity andragogical spaces (Zembylas, 2019) are useful for decreasing trainee resistance and challenging systemic collusion—be it conscious or unconscious—through a reimagining of responsibility as a shared moral imperative to enact change against social injustice (Applebaum, 2012). Zembylas (2019) advocates for a strategic, contextual critique of complicity, situated 'as part of an affective-political contingency' (p. 11), facilitating an engagement with specific and meaningful anti-complicity praxes (Zembylas, 2019).

Further, safe dialogical spaces for trainees can share and shape knowledge and understanding reflexively and reciprocally, allowing for collective awareness and self-development, 'through the confrontation of contradictory voices' (Wortham, 2011, p. 74) and shared responsibility and collective action—*leaning in*, as defined by Reynolds (2013). Learning environments of this ilk can help trainees acclimatise to concepts in anti-discriminatory practice (ADP), and simultaneously critique often (hard) right-wing discourses of ADP as the sole preserve of 'silly… repressive left-wing puritanism' (Hopton, 1997, p. 50). Moreover, supporting crucial critical thinking skills can foster a dialogical dismantling of the dehumanising representations of others—migrants, for example—transmitted by bad actors to infiltrate our shared social and cultural spaces, representations that trainees may have inadvertently found themselves exposed to. Such skills might also bring to light the ways in which the dissemination of these ideas to the populace maintains the political and ideological status quo.

All of the above is geared towards fostering a sense of solidarity within (and directed outside of) the training cohort, thus helping both to 'construct bonds across difference' (Anthias et al., 2013) and to instigate collective action based on shared experience. For example, the concept of politicised identities and solidarity (Lizzio-Wilson et al., 2022) uses social identity theory (Tajfel & Turner, 1979) to demonstrate how politicised, shared values can enhance group cohesion and provide momentum for mobilisation through a shared sense of injustice regarding hierarchical, systemic treatment of oppressed groups (Lizzio-Wilson et al., 2022). At this point, shared values and a commitment to action may blossom into action.

Having made the argument here for an andragogical climate for psychotherapy training that supports students in developing anti-oppressive

60 *Emily le Couteur*

research and practice I now move onto discussing, in some detail, a specific example within the UK context with which psychotherapy researchers might find themselves drawn to engaging. I then turn to the implications of this for anti-oppressive, feminist research.

Why should we be concerned about the 'hostile environment'?

The 'hostile environment' has become shorthand for the 'notoriously harsh' (Griffiths & Yeo, 2021, p. 2), austere, and indifferent machinery of UK governmental immigration policy, and the 'state-led marginalisation of immigrants' (p. 1). Its origins can be traced back to 2012 and a specific set of policy proposals conceived of by the Home Secretary, Theresa May. The majority of these proposals became law under the Immigration Acts of 2014 and 2016. Characterised by the infamous and deeply unpleasant 'Go Home or Face Arrest' vans which were driven around London boroughs home to a high proportion of immigrants, the wider policies and legislation aimed to insidiously introduce immigration checks into every facet of daily life, driving individuals without the proper paperwork out of the country by explicitly inducing a climate of fear.

The hostile environment infiltrates multiple areas of society, including health, housing, policing, banking, driving, employment, schools, and higher education (Liberty, 2019), and denies undocumented or 'irregular' migrants the access to these basic rights and services. It brings border checks to every facet of the quotidian and necessarily makes life as unpleasant and unmanageable as possible. This infiltration is manifest via the 'deputisation' (Griffiths & Yeo, 2021, p. 3) of ordinary citizens—individuals and groups operating within both the public and private sectors, in charities and in healthcare settings, who have been tasked with border enforcement as a form of street-level bureaucracy (Lipsky, 2010) whereby immigration status is checked before employment, healthcare, or housing can be offered (Liberty, 2019).

Racialised policy that positions 'legitimate' against 'illegitimate' citizens engenders deep divisions, and a level of mistrust and suspicion at community level between those offering and those seeking help. These policies have led to discriminatory and racist practices and have had a poisonous effect upon society (Mort et al., 2020), by 'legitimising and even encouraging racism and xenophobia' (Griffiths & Yeo, 2021, p. 13).

Androcentric narratives in immigration discourse

Polarised immigration rhetoric imagines dividing lines between those who are either a help or hindrance to the security, stability, order, and prosperity of the host nation. At the ostensibly more benign end of the spectrum, the social and economic usefulness of migrants may be quantified via ability and willingness to participate in integration and cultural assimilation. While assimilation disregards the enduring connections between migrants' countries of birth and

Feminist research in psychotherapy   61

transnational identities (Anthias et al., 2013), and the need for integration runs the risk of creating hierarchical, racialised boundaries between communities, individuals from rich, developed nations who live in other countries (so-called 'expats'), as Anthias et al. (2013) note, are not subject to interrogation of their linguistic abilities or normative cultural values. Integrational failures are subject to a process of social Othering (Levinas, 1969), and characterised as a threat to social cohesion and national identity. UK readers may recall that during 2016, the then Prime Minister David Cameron singled out Muslim women with a suggestion that they may be deported if not demonstrably showing commitment to learning the English language—part of his rationale being to reduce extremism.

If we momentarily take women as a broad, albeit heterogeneous group, those deemed 'legal', having successfully managed visa application processing and costs, likely face the structural barriers enforced by entrenched inequalities in the economy and labour market. These barriers make them more likely to encounter low-wage, part-time employment (D'Arcy, 2017) and less likely to have access to affordable housing. This is a continuation of neoliberal policy agendas under the umbrella of austerity packages, which have seen the retrenchment of the welfare system, repackaged as a punitive 'regime of conditionality' (Reeve, 2017, p. 65) rendering women's individual security under threat. Additionally, this picture does not even account for the ways migrant women experience gendered divisions of labour. For those women branded 'illegal' or irregular, the offer of even a threadbare safety net is snatched away, as is the case for women with no recourse to public funds (NRPF) status, who may support themselves via informal and precarious employment sectors, be open to exploitation, violence, and abuse, and be forced into submission and dependence upon their husband or partner (Reis, 2019).

Immigration discourse is also inherently and erroneously intertwined with issues of national security, such as terrorism, and is widely weaponised to induce a climate of fear amongst native populations of 'those whose differences are considered to be disturbing and threatening on the basis of ethnicity, faith or national origin' (Anthias et al., 2013, p. 2). The appropriation of the term 'hostile environment' from policy relating to serious crime and counter-terrorism feeds into the criminalisation and delegitimisation of migration (Social Scientists Against the Hostile Environment, 2020). Narratives of migrants as illegitimate or illegal allows them to be constructed as 'a threat to the security and social cohesiveness of the nation within a securitization and criminalization framework' (Griffiths & Yeo, 2021, p. 4), and further inflames anti-immigration rhetoric (Social Scientists Against the Hostile Environment, 2020) and social Othering.

While problematic tropes around terrorism, or the economic migrant, remain largely the domain of young males, where women do represent a threat to national security or financial stability, whether real or artificial, they become emblematic of the deviant status of women who step away from narrowly defined, traditional gender roles. If migrant males may represent an overt

62 Emily le Couteur

physical or economic threat, migrant women, their differentiated versions of femininity, and their bodies represent a clandestine menace to society and 'the fear of having one's nation or culture infected by foreign blood' (Hart, 2005, p. 6). Cultural diversity may also be weaponised as 'potent instruments of polarization' (Randeria & Karagiannis, 2020, p. 228) along gendered and highly racialised lines, whereby immigration is framed as an invasion, *en masse*, of non-Western people into a majority white country, often born out of dehumanising, post-9/11 tropes regarding Islam. As Randeria and Karagiannis (2020) explain, the uncivilised, illiberal Islamic intruder is incompatible with the values of the civilised, liberal host nation—the former synonymous with female subjugation, oppression, and brutality; the latter constituting a beacon of enlightenment, feminine emancipation, and equality.

The hostile environment: Implications for anti-oppressive, feminist research

The imagined migrant woman is at once both weak and dangerous, vulnerable and threatening—a messy, contradictory set of identities which somehow renders her utterly paradoxical and grossly misunderstood, further causing the rhetorical pendulum to swing wildly between detaining and deporting her, or providing caring intervention and a safe place of shelter from harm. The simplistic and polarising foundations of hostile environment policy are once again borne out through notions of deserving and undeserving—who should be welcomed and who should be turned away. Caution may still be required with regards to any narratives which frame women as vulnerable—however benevolent the intention—due to the conflict, brutality, or persecution they may be fleeing which has motivated them to cross oceans and continents, as there is potential to pathologise normal levels of distress and to impose Western, *expert* models of mental health onto non-Western, *non-expert* populations (Summerfield, 1999). Research, and indeed any intervention, should be based not only upon the explicitly stated wishes of the women involved, but also upon 'Indigenous' (Summerfield, 1999, p. 1461) definitions of mental health and wellbeing, and contextually located within their social, cultural, and historical determinants. As Chantler (2012) also notes, the idea of female asylum seekers as strong, capable women as opposed to shattered human beings may inadvertently characterise them as amongst those so-called undeserving claimants—the antithesis of conventional notions of the woman as the victim.

The task then for qualitative, feminist researchers becomes a little clearer, in providing opposing narratives to homogenous, androcentric, dehumanising representations of migrant and asylum-seeking women, through subjective perspectives and nuanced story-telling which seek to humanise women's accounts of migration. Situated within a critical framework, these accounts may provide a non-voyeuristic window into the experiential realities of existence within socioeconomic and cultural structures which reproduce conditions of oppression and discrimination.

Other ways of being and knowing: Critical, disruptive, and anti-oppressive frameworks

Although there is no single methodological formula when approaching disruptive or decolonising research methodologies (Thambinathan & Kinsella, 2021) congruous with dismantling systemic oppression, racism, and inequality, broadly it seems prudent to seek out paradigms imbued with the intention of welcoming oppressed and Othered (Levinas, 1969) groups, whose multiple realities and knowledge claims have been marginalised in favour of orthodox epistemologies. Similarly, there is no one way to *do* feminism, but feminist research perspectives can not only offer a critical, counter-cultural narrative to cold, scientific detachment, but also make room for the relational, emotional, and experiential expressions of meaning-making (Dupuis et al., 2022). They offer a valuable—important, urgent—lens through which to conduct qualitative research on both micro and macro levels of analysis, both in exploring the complex, deeply personal experiences of oppressed migrant women, and in contesting dehumanising, dominating ideological tropes.

Feminist approaches cover an expansive range of epistemological ground, from scientific empiricism through to post-modernism (Stanley & Wise, 1993) and beyond. Addressing some of the research concerns outlined in the previous section may be achieved by an approach which I broadly refer to as *critical* feminism, incorporating what Ponterotto (2005) termed a 'critical-ideological' stance, whereby the research is distinctly value-laden in relation to the researcher's commitment to emancipatory projects and ideals and allowing for the analysis of both the personal and the political. Here, knowledge production is ontologically grounded and located in experiential, human interaction within the social world—'in women's concrete and diverse practical and everyday experiences of oppressions' (Stanley & Wise, 1993, pp. 191–192)—invariably these experiences of oppression then alert us to hierarchies of knowledge claims, and the dynamic systems of power which weaken and strengthen these claims to varying degrees.

Critical feminist, anti-oppressive work cannot make these sorts of claims of itself without recognition of who or what is doing the oppressing, and this invariably requires analysis of power differentials, be they structural, post-structural, or relational (Proctor, 2017). If we consider the narrative of legal–illegal, deserving–underserving migrant women in relation to the axis of knowledge and power, the construction of this widely accepted and legitimised narrative is shaped by relations of power within social and political discourse (Proctor, 2017). Therefore, what is presented as factual is directly shaped by the objectives of those at the apex of the power hierarchy, in order to maintain directives that benefit the powerful (Chung & Bemak, 2012) and the smooth running of the status quo. Traditional feminist researchers tend to theorise power broadly in terms of patriarchal dominance and oppressive, coercive power in the hands of the few (men), subjugating the many (women). However, with the rise of the fourth and fifth waves in counselling and

64 *Emily le Couteur*

psychotherapy (Chung & Bemak, 2012), multiculturalism, and social justice, respectively, have come increasing calls for less dichotomised views of power and oppression, and a greater focus on intersectional (Crenshaw, 1989) understandings—the multidimensional, overlapping experiences of systemic disadvantage faced by women, and a commitment to engage with the experiences of the most marginalised women (Orloff & Shiff, 2016) through anti-oppressive social justice work.

Of course, it is not just systemic power differentials that we need to be awake to. The power that we hold as researchers is sizeable and significant, and needs to be acknowledged, addressed, and mitigated to the best of our abilities. Giving voice (Goodman et al., 2004) to participants is a well-worn phrase in qualitative research circles—seemingly a beneficial technique to ameliorate power imbalances between the voices of both researcher and participant. However, caution is required, as Thambinathan and Kinsella (2021) note: the supposedly 'altruistic' (p. 4) intentions of researchers to give voice to participants can suggest a deficit of ability—they will only be heard when the researcher rides to their rescue. Further, the voices of the marginalised are 'not simply revealed or amplified by qualitative research, but rather are interpreted and transformed in the research process' (Stein & Mankowski, 2004, p. 32). Thus, researchers need to be actively aware of the accuracy of their representations, and the extent to which their own voice becomes 'intrusive' (Lather, 1991, p. 91) in the narrative.

Knowledge construction within research should be a historically and socially situated (Mertens, 2010) collaborative process, but should also be framed within the research relationship as experts (participants) imparting wisdom onto their students (researchers), as a reflexive effort to dismantle ostensibly immutable power imbalances. Fostering this self-determination, through a strength-based approach, and ultimately producing emancipatory work, is grounded in the relationship between researcher and participant; going above and beyond to ensure a level playing field, where there is room for a deep sense of respect, authentic collaboration, and a shared ownership of 'the entire research process' (Thambinathan & Kinsella, 2021, p. 4). For this to be meaningful, participants need to be involved in the research at every stage possible. Financial, academic, and scheduling constraints placed upon researchers may hamper this process—as I have found during my own doctoral research project, which uses both critical feminist and social justice lenses to explore the experiences of marginalised single homeless women—but it is crucial to keep striving for this level of inclusion, and making the case where necessary for authentic collaboration as a key tool in emancipatory work. If our participants do not benefit from the fruits of our research, at least in some way, then who are we doing it for? An embodiment of respect is pivotal to this relational approach, through a commitment to resist treating your research participants as objects of enquiry, to be looked at and studied, thereby reproducing colonial mechanisms of invasion—knowledge as property to be claimed and researchers who lay claim to it (Tuck & Yang, 2014), while simultaneously contorting and erasing its native social

Feminist research in psychotherapy 65

and cultural significance. The relationships we form with our participants ought not to be superficial and unidirectional, if they are anti-oppressive in nature. This is particularly true for women who are marginalised, and therefore may be familiar with objectification by researchers. The time we spend with them, the way we communicate with them, the respect we have for them, the care we show them, and the things we can give back to them, are all elements of relational authenticity that indicate a deeper commitment to anti-oppressive work which seeks to instigate meaningful changes.

Doing critical feminist research intended to disrupt or promote an anti-oppressive agenda may appear daunting, complex, even messy work, but for me, the most exciting qualitative research follows this wayward trajectory. There is no set guidebook. As de Saxe (2012) notes:

> ... it calls on us to reconsider our existing understandings of knowledge, power, and spaces of empowerment ... critical feminist thought, as a discipline, is always evolving and transforming in ways that consistently develop new methodologies of resistance. Through this careful process of constantly reframing and reconsidering, the very nature of our thought processes, and later, our institutions can begin the process of transformation.
>
> (p. 198)

Critical reflexivity as an ethical position

An important step in eschewing the illusion of researcher objectivity is commitment to a reflexive stance, which acknowledges the inevitability of the active role of researcher in the entirety of the research process (Braun et al., 2014), affords a 'more complex and nuanced understanding of issues' (Dupuis, 2022, p. 52) synonymous with qualitative research, and has an important function as a quality appraisal tool in ensuring trustworthiness in the research process (Nowell et al., 2017). Reflexivity may be considered *de rigueur* amongst qualitative researchers, but is noteworthy nonetheless in relation to its ability to provide an additional, critical layer which has important implications, both methodologically speaking, and in terms of interpersonal and systemic power relations.

To be a critical, reflexive researcher is to turn the inquiring searchlight back on oneself; to be critically reflexive is to keenly analyse one's own socio-economic, political, and historical situatedness in relation to Others. Yet it is not just the inclusion of a statement on positionality that defines truly reflexive research: it is a committed, ethical stance to the recognition of multiple power differentials, and a process which needs to be continually, significantly, and explicitly evident (Dodgson, 2019) and enmeshed in the research process, from start to finish. As Shinozaki (2021) suggests, reflexivity does not just occur nominally at the point of data collection, during those synchronous, real-world interactions with participants—it can be embedded within many, if not all, stages, including analysis, dissemination, and the wider process of engaging others in the cause.

66   *Emily le Couteur*

Acknowledgement and critical examination of the inevitable, but not immutable, power differentials in the research process, between researcher and participant, can ameliorate these differentials by opening up co-constructed epistemic spaces. However, this reflexive approach also appreciates the differentially situated identities of researcher and participant, going beyond the insider–outsider dichotomy (Nowicka & Ryan, 2015) common to discourses of migration, which inevitably fall into categorisations of race and nationality.

The reflexive researcher approaches the knowledge co-production process with a keen appreciation for the intersect between multiple identities and positionalities, areas of sameness and difference, and the complex interplay between these.

Ontological and epistemological assumptions too are enmeshed in unequal power differentials; the critical qualitative researcher's task is to understand and articulate the continuum of power which prioritises distinct forms of knowledge and experiences, while constraining and silencing others, embracing multiple realities, and multiple ways of knowing. Crucially, in repudiating the fallacy of researcher objectivity, one's own active role in the knowledge production process can become fundamental in helping to make ethically sound methodological choices, thereby 'actively rebalancing power relations by recognizing community members as knowledge holders' (Thambinathan & Kinsella, 2021, p. 4). Here, the researcher is encouraged to expand their epistemological horizons and look beyond the white, Western, male gaze which has so engulfed scientific understanding and our ways of knowing the world.

As a budding researcher in the embryonic stages of my career, I have been lucky enough to experience doctoral training which has embedded reflexivity as an ethical stance from the very outset of training, allowing me to flourish in the domains of research, practice, and personal development. Reflexive learning and discussion, reflecting as groups upon clinical work, writing reflexively, keeping a reflexive journal (in both research and personal domains), and undertaking personal therapy are just some examples of the holistic, reflexive development I have undertaken. For those without the privilege of this reflexively informed learning environment, the journey to becoming a truly reflexive researcher, and practitioner, is not an easy one. It requires time, dedication, increasing self-awareness, a critical eye, and even soul searching. But the benefits to those whose lives are touched by our work, and to ourselves, are clear and immeasurable.

Emotions in research: Patriarchal disruption as a key research tool

As well as providing important analytical insights pertinent to migration stories, such as the interrelation between movement between places and the emotional attachment of home (Gray, 2008), emotions can help us to better understand some of the gendered implications of migration as the act of crossing geographical and emotional borders, with its associated shifts in identity, role, and

Feminist research in psychotherapy 67

physical and metaphorical place in the world being invariably the root of enormous emotional upheaval. For women who migrate, movement transfers new notions of femininity, sexuality, and womanhood (Espin, 1997) and, for better or worse, a relocation in relation to sexuality and gender roles, position in the labour market, and educational access. These will engender complex emotional responses.

Intensely negative or distressing emotional responses may be the focus of research, or indeed therapeutic intervention, as a presumed inevitability of living under hostile environment conditions, fleeing war zones or religious or political persecution, or making the perilous journey across the English Channel. The emotional toll of these events—what some may conceptualise as post-traumatic stress disorder—bears exploration and significant attention, in better understanding what we can do to support these individuals. However, nuanced and gendered understandings of the issues are vital. As Chantler (2012) notes, both men and women claiming asylum are subject to the same punitive treatment and poor conditions, which are likely to adversely impact upon mental health and wellbeing. However, women's difficulties will be highly differentiated and compounded by numerous factors, including domestic violence, spousal visas, and difficulty in accessing welfare—making dependence on a partner more likely, so heightening the potential for exploitation, coercion, or violence. Where immigration status is precarious, the risk then for these women is that they are rendered invisible—caught between fear of an abuser and fear of the state (Chantler, 2012). However, caution is still required when applying Western models of mental distress to non-Western populations, and an understanding of, and commitment to engage with, the wider sociopolitical forces at play is imperative.

Emotions are at the very core of our work as psychotherapists and psychologists. Clients often cross the threshold into the therapy room because they require some help, encouragement, space, or guidance in managing their emotional lives. Yet emotional responses are not seemingly readily applicable to intellectual endeavours of academic research. However, a willingness to engage with this very personal domain can offer profound insight into socially and culturally quotidian experience, both of oppression and marginalisation, and of resistance. Offered as a refutation of the dualistic mind/body and knowledge/experience ontological claims, which for centuries privileged androcentric claims to rationality above alternate outlooks (Barbour, 2018), emotional and relational aspects of women's experiences, the reconceptualising of emotion as an important analytical tool, and deconstructing notions of an essential feminine frailty, each become a key component of analysis.

If the rational mind is the male domain, then the irrationality of emotions is placed squarely within the realms of the feminine. Feminist approaches do not seek to necessarily (re)claim the rational mind as feminine, nor to contest the essentialist values ascribed to the feminine, but rather to reject dichotomous, rigid categorisation in favour of greater fluidity—the complex, shifting construction of self as emerging from relational and social interactions embedded

68 *Emily le Couteur*

within a social, cultural, and historical basis (Stanley & Wise, 1993). This is particularly true of the reflexively minded, feminist researcher, and of the dynamic and reciprocal research interactions. As Gray (2008), for example, notes, 'emotional reactions are part of human life and are, therefore, never absent from the research situation' (p. 936). Where emotion may be dismissed out of hand as the antithesis of logical thought and reason, therefore having no place in research, when this is considered in the context of dualistic ontological claims it can then be understood as a condition of patriarchal oppression—an ontological power grab that risks closing the door to the notion of welcoming the Other (Levinas, 1969).

When seeking to understand life under the 'hostile environment', for example, and subsequent conditions of oppression, reflection on our own emotional responses as researchers to emotionally difficult terrain feels like an inevitability rather than formality. Where women feel able to share these stories and experiences, and the research boundaries soften—in contrast to scientific detachment—then there is the possibility for pain to be shared, shouldered, and diluted within the research space. Creating an empathic research space is 'guided by an ethic of caring' (Blakeley, 2007, p. 62), which simultaneously allows researchers to reflexively consider what motivates them to such a research project, and to express emotional connection to the project itself, the wider issues it brings to the fore, and the participants at its heart (Blakeley, 2007). The new analytical insights and questions which flourish within emotionally imbued research can seismically shift focus towards exciting, hopeful new outlooks, perhaps inconceivable without a caring, collaborative space.

Such research—and such clinical practice—is mindful of whose narratives we are holding up as legitimate, whose interests we are serving, and who ultimately is benefitting from our endeavours. Such research challenges, rather than is complicit with, the status quo.

References

Allen, R. L., & Rossatto, C. A. (2009). Does critical pedagogy work with privileged students. *Teacher Education Quarterly, 36*, 163–180. https://files.eric.ed.gov/fulltext/EJ851035.pdf

Anthias, F., Kontos, M., & Morokvasic-Müller, M. (2013). Introduction: Paradoxes in integration. In F. Anthias, M. Kontos, & M. Morokvasic-Müller (Eds.), *Paradoxes of integration: Female migration in Europe*. Springer. https://doi.org/10.1007/978-94-007-4842-2

Applebaum, B. (2012). Reframing responsibility in the social justice classroom. *Race Ethnicity and Education, 15*(5), 615–631. https://doi.org/10.1080/13613324.2012.674028

Barbour, K. (2018). Embodied ways of knowing: Revisiting feminist epistemology. In L. Mansfield, J. Caudwell, B. Wheaton, & B. Watson (Eds.), *The Palgrave handbook of feminism and sport, leisure and physical education*. Palgrave Macmillan. https://doi.org/10.1057/978-1-137-53318-0_14

Blakeley, K. (2007). Reflections on the role of emotion in feminist research. *International Journal of Qualitative Methods, 6*(2), 59–68. https://doi.org/10.1177/160940690700600206

Braun, V., Clarke, V., & Rance, N. (2014). How to use thematic analysis with interview data. In A. Vossler & N. Moller (Eds.), *The counselling and psychotherapy research*

Feminist research in psychotherapy 69

handbook (pp. 183–197). Sage. https://uk.sagepub.com/en-gb/eur/the-counselling-a
nd-psychotherapy-research-handbook/book239261

Chantler, K. (2012). Gender, asylum seekers and mental distress: Challenges for mental health social work. *The British Journal of Social Work*, *42*(2), 318–334. http://www.jstor.org/stable/43771637

Chung, R. C., & Bemak, F. P. (2012). *Social justice counseling: The next steps beyond multiculturalism*. Sage. https://dx.doi.org/10.4135/9781452240503.n3

Crenshaw, K. (1989). Demarginalizing the intersection of race and sex: A Black feminist critique of antidiscrimination doctrine, feminist theory and antiracist politics. *University of Chicago Legal Forum*, *1989*(1), 8. http://chicagounbound.uchicago.edu/uclf/vol1989/iss1/8

D'Arcy, C. (2017). *Low pay Britain*. Resolution Foundation. https://www.resolutionfoundation.org/app/uploads/2017/10/Low-Pay-Britain-2017.pdf

de Saxe, J. (2012). Conceptualising critical feminist theory and emancipatory education. *Journal for Critical Education and Policy Studies*, *10*(2), 183–201. https://eric.ed.gov/?id=EJ989410

Dodgson, J. E. (2019). Reflexivity in qualitative research. *Journal of Human Lactation*, *35*(2), 220–222. https://doi.org/10.1177/0890334419830990

Dupuis, C., Harcourt, W., Gaybor, J., & van den Berg, K. (2022). Introduction: Feminism as method—Navigating theory and practice. In W. Harcourt., K. van den Berg., C. Dupuis., & J. Gaybor. (Eds.), *Feminist methodologies: Experiments, collaborations and reflections* (pp. 1–20). Palgrave Macmillan. https://doi.org/10.1007/978-3-030-82654-3_7

Espin, M. O. (1997) *The role of gender and emotion in women's experience of migration, Innovation: The European Journal of Social Science Research*, *10*(4), 445–455. https://doi.org/10.1080/13511610.1997.9968545

Freire, P. (1970). *Pedagogy of the oppressed* (M. B. Ramos, Trans.). Penguin. (Original work published 1967)

Goodman, L. A., Liang, B., Helms, J. E., Latta, R. E., Sparks, E., & Weintraub, S. R. (2004). Training counseling psychologists as social justice agents: Feminist and multicultural principles in action. *The Counseling Psychologist*, *32*(6), 793–836. https://doi.org/10.1177/0011000004268802

Gray, B. (2008). Putting emotion and reflexivity to work in researching migration. *Sociology*, *42*(5), 935–952. https://doi.org/10.1177/0038038508094571

Griffiths, M., & Yeo, C. (2021). The UK's hostile environment: Deputising immigration control. *Critical Social Policy*, *41*(4), 521–544. https://doi.org/10.1177/0261018320980653

Hart, M. (2005). Women, migration, and the body-less spirit of capitalist patriarchy. *Journal of International Women's Studies*, *7*(2), 1–16. https://vc.bridgew.edu/jiws/vol7/iss2/1

Hopton, J. (1997). Anti-discriminatory practice and anti-oppressive practice: A radical humanist psychology perspective. *Critical Social Policy*, *17*(52), 47–61. https://doi.org/10.1177/026101839701705203

Immigration Act 2014, c. 22. https://www.legislation.gov.uk/ukpga/2014/22

Immigration Act 2016, c. 19. https://www.legislation.gov.uk/ukpga/2016/19

Knowles, M. S. (1970). *The modern practice of adult education: Andragogy versus pedagogy*. New York Association Press.

Lather, P. (1991). *Getting smart: Feminist research and pedagogy with/in the postmodern*. Routledge.

Levinas, E. (1969). *Totality and infinity: An essay on exteriority* (A. Lingis, Trans.). Duquesne University Press.

70 *Emily le Couteur*

Liberty. (2019, May 15). *A Guide to the Hostile Environment: The border controls dividing our communities—and how we can bring them down.* https://www.libertyhumanrights.org.uk/issue/report-a-guide-to-the-hostile-environment

Lipsky, M. (2010). *Street-level bureaucracy: Dilemmas of the individual in public services* (30th anniversary expanded ed.). Russell Sage Foundation. http://www.jstor.org/stable/10.7758/9781610446631.3

Lizzio-Wilson, M., Mirnajafi, Z., & Louis, W. R. (2022). Who we are and who we choose to help (or not): An introduction to social identity theory. In M. A. Yerkes. & M. Bal. (Eds.), *Solidarity and social justice in contemporary societies.* (pp.17–28). Palgrave Macmillan. https://doi.org/10.1007/978-3-030-93795-9_2

Mertens, D. (2010). Philosophy in mixed methods teaching: The transformative paradigm as illustration. *International Journal of Multiple Research Approaches, 4*(1), 9–18. https://doi.org/10.5172/mra.2010.4.1.009

Mort, L., Morris, M., & Qureshi, A. (2020). *Access denied: The human impact of the hostile environment.* Institute for Public Policy Research. https://www.ippr.org/files/2020-09/access-denied-hostile-environment-sept20.pdf

Nowell, L. S., Norris, J. M., White, D. E., & Moules, N. J. (2017). Thematic analysis: Striving to meet the trustworthiness criteria. *International Journal of Qualitative Methods. 16*(1). https://doi.org/10.1177/1609406917733847

Nowicka, M., & Ryan, L. (2015). Beyond insiders and outsiders in migration research: Rejecting a priori commonalities. Introduction to the FQS thematic section on 'Researcher, migrant, woman: Methodological implications of multiple positionalities in migration studies'. *Forum: Qualitative Social Research, 16*(2). https://doi.org/10.17169/fqs-16.2.2342

Orloff, A. S., & Shiff, T. (2016). Feminism/s in power: Rethinking gender equality after the second wave. In A. S. Orloff, R. Ray, & E. Savci (Eds.), *Perverse politics? Feminism, anti-imperialism, multiplicity* (pp. 109–134). Emerald Publishing Limited. https://doi.org/10.1108/S0198-8719201630

Ponterotto, J. G. (2005). Qualitative research in counseling psychology: A primer on research paradigms and philosophy of science. *Journal of Counseling Psychology, 52*(2), 126–136. https://doi.org/10.1037/0022-0167.52.2.126

Proctor, G. (2017). *The dynamics of power in counselling and psychotherapy: Ethics, politics and practice.* PCCS Books.

Randeria, S., & Karagiannis, E. (2020). The migrant position: Dynamics of political and cultural exclusion. *Theory, Culture & Society, 37*(7–8), 219–231. https://doi.org/10.1177/0263276420957733

Reeve, K. (2017). Welfare conditionality, benefit sanctions and homelessness in the UK: Ending the 'something for nothing culture' or punishing the poor? *Journal of Poverty and Social Justice, 25*(1), 65–78. https://doi.org/10.1332/175982717X14842281240539

Reis, S. (2019, July 8). *A home of her own: Housing and women.* Women's Budget Group. https://wbg.org.uk/analysis/reports/a-home-of-her-own-housing-and-women

Reynolds, V. (2013). 'Leaning in' as imperfect allies in community work. *Narrative and Conflict: Explorations in Theory and Practice, 1*(1), 53–75. https://doi.org/10.13021/G8ncetp.v1.1.2013.430

Shinozaki, K. (2021). Reflexivity and its enactment potential in gender and migration research. In C. Mora. & N. Piper. (Eds.), *The Palgrave handbook of gender and migration.* Palgrave Macmillan. https://doi.org/10.1007/978-3-030-63347-9

Social Scientists Against the Hostile Environment. (2020). *Migration, racism and the hostile environment: Making the case for the social sciences.* https://acssmigration.wordpress.com/report

Stanley, L., & Wise, S. (1993). *Breaking out again: Feminist ontology and epistemology.* Taylor & Francis Group.

Stein, C., & Mankowski, E. (2004). Asking, witnessing, interpreting, knowing: Conducting qualitative research in community psychology. *American Journal of Community Psychology, 33*(1–2), 21–35. https://doi.org/10.1023/B:AJCP.0000014316.27091.e8

Summerfield, D. (1999). A critique of seven assumptions behind psychological trauma programmes in war-affected areas. *Social Science & Medicine, 48*(10), 1449–1462. https://doi.org/10.1016/s0277-9536(98)00450-x

Tajfel, H., & Turner, J. C. (1979). An integrative theory of intergroup conflict. In W. G. Austin & S. Worchel (Eds.), *The social psychology of intergroup relations* (pp. 33–47). Brooks/Cole.

Thambinathan, V., & Kinsella, E. A. (2021). Decolonizing methodologies in qualitative research: Creating spaces for transformative praxis. *International Journal of Qualitative Methods, 20.* https://doi.org/10.1177/16094069211014766

Tuck, E., & Yang, K. W. (2014). Unbecoming claims: Pedagogies of refusal in qualitative research. *Qualitative Inquiry, 20*(6), 811–818. https://doi.org/10.1177/1077800414530265

Whitt, M. S. (2016). Other people's problems: Student distancing, epistemic responsibility, and injustice. *Studies in Philosophy and Education, 35,* 427–444. https://doi.org/10.1007/s11217-015-9484-1

Wortham, S. (2011). Wondering about dialogic theory and practice. *Journal of Russian & East European Psychology, 49*(2), 71–76, https://doi.org/10.2753/RPO1061-0405490211

Zembylas, M. (2019). Re-conceptualizing complicity in the social justice classroom: Affect, politics and anti-complicity pedagogy. *Pedagogy, Culture & Society, 28*(2), 317–331. https://doi.org/10.1080/14681366.2019.1639792

6 Critical race theory
A methodology for research in psychotherapy

Divine Charura and Sonya Clyburn

This chapter considers critical race theory as a methodology for research in psychotherapy and elaborates on logical steps beginning with racism, and then discusses critical race theory as a methodology for research.

As a Western and Eurocentric endeavour, psychotherapy is riddled with and compromised by racism. In this chapter, we argue that if psychotherapy and other psychological professions are going to be fit for our contemporary diverse world, then it is important that racism within these professions is addressed head on. Psychotherapy—and psychotherapy research—needs to engage critically with ideas about ontology, and, specifically, the reality that people are culturally diverse beings, and not other to a neutral white essence of things. Furthermore, the therapeutic relationship can only be understood in the context of social factors, including systemic racism and oppression of those from ethnically diverse communities (Maharaj et al., 2021). Thus, psychotherapy researchers must face and engage with the social construction of race, illuminating the importance of intersectionality in understanding the experiences of individuals within psychotherapy research and practice (Grzanka et al., 2017; Maharaj et al., 2021). Such research contributes to highlighting the micro-aggressions that perpetuate racism and its operationalisation between individuals in sociopolitical environments in which overt racism is no longer acceptable (Etchebarne, 2021). In line with this, Keating (2020) asserts that it is blatantly wrong to believe the myth that ethnicity is a risk factor for mental health. Rather, he argues, it is discrimination, racialised trauma, oppression, exclusion, and the invisibility of particular groups that are the risk factors for psychological distress. Given that both the practice of psychotherapy and psychotherapeutic research have been shaped by Eurocentric cultures, politics, and bodies of knowledge (epistemologies), we maintain that the very fibre of evidence-based practice and even practice-based evidence in psychotherapy research is informed by particular worldviews, namely, of seeing Eurocentric perspectives as superior to other ontologies and epistemologies. Thus, we assert that the power of research, 'science', and of the impact of 'evidence', even when it results in discrimination and bias, must be critiqued.

This chapter considers critical race theory (CRT) as a methodology for research in psychotherapy. In doing so, we look at and elaborate on logical

DOI: 10.4324/9781003280859-7

Critical race theory   73

steps beginning with racism, and then discuss CRT as a methodology for research.

Racism

The concept of *race* did not come from science or theology, it came *to* science and theology (Wilder, 2013). Systemic and cultural racism have been endemic and pervasive mental and public health issues in many societies for hundreds of years (Maharaj et al., 2021). This is also true for psychology and psychotherapy (Charura & Lago, 2021a; Graham et al., 2011; Lago, 2006; Moodley et al., 2018; Pomare et al., 2021). Racism involves attitudes, dispositions, behaviours, and assumptions of whiteness (Green et al., 2007; Gunew, 2007; Owen, 2007). In the book *Superior: The Return of Race Science*, Saini (2019) argues that race is a social construct, and not a biological trait. The history of race is a reminder that science is not just about theories and data; it is also about which facts and stories regarding human diversity are given pre-eminence and by whom. Saini (2019) highlights the history of how race categorisation of humans came about. She argues that European Enlightenment naturalists and scientists decided that humans could be divided into discrete groups in the same way as some other animal species. This then led to the arbitrary setting of the boundaries for the categories they had decided, based on skin colour, and established sweeping generalisations of cultural stereotypes about temperament, intelligence, behaviour, and innate differences between populations. Ultimately, these pseudoscientific ideas became the bedrock influence of Western medicine for centuries and formed the basis for the Nazi eugenics programme of racial cleansing and the Holocaust (Saini, 2019). Despite these misguided assumptions about race, societal structures remain that perpetuate the myth that race is biologically real.

Similarly, research in psychotherapy and psychological therapies has been conducted with a whiteness Eurocentric lens. Over the decades, prominent influential psychologists and researchers have played a role in advancing the biological perspective on race by highlighting research and championing and interpreting cognitive tests which were racially biased. For example, Hans Eysenck was one of the earliest researchers to perpetuate the notion of heritability of intelligence and race differences in IQ scores. He argued that the observed variability in IQ scores was genetically determined to a high degree (80% heritability) and that the Black–white IQ gap in the US was due predominantly to genetic factors (Eysenck, 1971). A further example is Herrnstein and Murray's (1996) study, which offers assertions that overestimate the influence of genotype on IQ, and on the dynamics of achievement and the role of socioeconomic attainment in US society. One of the flaws in their research was the failure to consider the large environmental influences on IQ, an omission which inadvertently resulted in biased results (Conley & Domingue, 2016).

Although we note examples from psychology research, racism within society and within psychotherapy research is cumulative and complicated and can exist

74 *Divine Charura and Sonya Clyburn*

in many forms. Research in psychotherapy has attempted to maintain white superiority and power. Even today, scientists responsible for medical discoveries have been involved in the maltreatment of people of colour (Saini, 2019). They have minimised and neglected to share the stories, histories, or experiences of those individuals. Consequently, whiteness and white supremacy are in the fibre of our global communities, as well as in psychotherapy literature and research (Andrews, 2016; Gunew, 2007; Newnes, 2021; Saini, 2019). Therefore, we need to pay increasing attention within psychotherapy to how privilege and otherness feature both in research and in the therapy room. We also need to appreciate how having an intersectional understanding of identity offers a complex and more nuanced exploration and understanding of racism and oppression (Newnes, 2021).

We cannot talk about racism without engaging with the critical whiteness literature which has emerged over the last few decades (Andrews, 2016; Garner, 2007; Green et al., 2007; Owen, 2007). The main thesis of the critical whiteness literature is to illuminate the concept of whiteness so that it can be addressed, dismantled, or overcome, with the essential objective of 'the liberation of people of colour around the globe' (Owen, 2007, p. 2003). Andrews (2016) argues that whiteness is rooted in the social structure, and that whiteness underwrites and reproduces systems of racial oppression. If the processes of whiteness can be uncovered, they can be overcome through rational dialogue, and this has implications for anti-racist engagement. Thus, whiteness studies can be identified as a development in the study of racism, as they highlight the responsibility of white people and are meant as a decolonising call to action (Andrews, 2016). We note here Green et al.'s (2007) argument, that 'locating whiteness, rather than racism, at the centre of anti-racism focuses attention on how white people's identities are shaped by a broader racist culture, and brings to the fore the responsibilities that white people have for addressing racism' (p. 390).

Considering these arguments, whiteness is also a system that underwrites and reproduces systemic racism and oppression within the psychotherapy profession. Understanding and challenging whiteness as a structural property of racialised psychotherapy systems (research and practice, etc.) is important for anti-discriminatory practice, as well as for decolonising the psychotherapy profession. Andrews (2016) highlights the challenge of attempting to address, dismantle, and overcome whiteness. We, however, concur that the critical theory of whiteness is necessary, but not sufficient, for the formulation of an adequate explanation of the mechanisms of racial oppression in the modern world (Green et al., 2007). Our position is that engaging with the issues of whiteness and racism in psychotherapy research and practice is important for all. This is the only way we can challenge subjective bias or the privileging of certain groups and theories over others. It is also a way to dismantle the status quo of seeing everyone as culturally neutral, and impartial, whilst on another level ignoring the racism embedded in the structures of our profession and practice.

We are aware of the common criticisms of critical race theory in that it is pessimistic and divisive, but we argue the opposite. We align with perspectives that optimism is inherent to CRT and similar critical frameworks because they are rooted in the belief that white supremacy and structural racism in society and in our profession can be ameliorated (D'Arrigo-Patrick et al., 2017; Su, 2007; Wilcox, 2022). We see CRT as a framework that can bring an episte-mological lens to a social justice agenda in research.

In the following section, we outline some tenets of CRT and illustrate the importance of exposing racism in psychotherapy research. This is a way in which both a critical consciousness and an evidence base can be established in our profession that embed equity in the perspectives of people of colour in research and transformative psychotherapy practices.

Critical race theory

The movement that led to the development of CRT began in the post-civil rights era as schools were being desegrated. CRT is based upon the critical theory of legal scholars and assesses how institutions, such as criminal justice, education, the housing market, healthcare, and labour market institutions, have unequal practices (Delgado & Stefancic, 2001, 2012). The application of CRT practice can be extended to critiquing inequality and racism in psychotherapy and other forms of trauma for people of Indigenous backgrounds. Drawing on the work of some CRT scholars, we summarise some of the themes found in CRT and illustrate them with reference to the psychological and social psy-chology sphere (Delgado & Stefancic, 2001, 2012; McDowell & Jeris, 2004):

1   Challenging the belief that racism is normal or ordinary and the argument that race is socially constructed and not biologically natural.
2   Focusing on what CRT scholars call 'interest convergence' or 'material determinism', the argument is that legal advances (or setbacks) for people of colour tend to serve the interests of dominant white groups. Thus, the racial hierarchy that characterises Western and European societies may be unaffected or even reinforced by ostensible improvements in the legal status of oppressed or exploited people.
3   CRT values the notions of intersectionality and anti-essentialism, which argue that no individual can be adequately identified by membership in a single group. An African American or Black British person, for example, may also identify as a woman, heterosexual, having a faith, and so on.
4   The ultimate goal of CRT is social justice. This can be illustrated by challenging unfair outcomes for ethnic minorities in society and promoting inclusivity in research, and this is seen as an ethical and moral position. This can be exemplified by members from diverse communities being involved in research design, collection and analysis of data, and writing and dissemination.
5   CRT critiques the perspective that racism is primarily an individual or psychological problem. This point can be illustrated, for example, by the

work of Breen (2021), who argues that racial and ethnic minorities (among other socially vulnerable groups) are highly likely to be impacted and have slower recovery rates from disasters. Fussell et al. (2010, p. 24) concur with this and argue that pre-existing inequalities, from socioeconomic status, race, and age due to predisposing factors, exacerbate the limitations in capacity to recover. Thus, systemic racism and discriminatory and racist practices, rather than individual psychological problems, are some of the reasons that people from diverse communities fall behind white people in nearly every aspect of social life (Bonilla-Silva, 2014).

6   CRT argues that white supremacy is ingrained in our institutions and cultural practices and that it is often unrecognisable, creating an 'invisible norm' against which all other races are measured (Delgado & Stefancic, 2001, p. 7). Thus, far from being an exception, racism is experienced by all those who fall outside the identity of whiteness. People from diverse communities have a unique voice in racial matters because of their socially minoritised position and experiences with oppression and microaggressions. For this reason, inclusivity of racially marginalised members of society being authentically (i.e., not tokenistically) represented in research is important. Thus, CRT has an openness and commitment to opportunities for others telling their stories, deconstructing existing narratives, and challenging 'embedded preconceptions that marginalise others or conceal their humanity' (Delgado & Stefancic, 2001, p. 42). In addition, a CRT perspective challenges white-dominated 'truth' and, in the case of psychological research, challenges research methods that are not culturally sensitive or reflective of the impact of the research and approach on participants. In line with this, Delgado and Stefancic (2001) make reference to what they call the 'voice-of-colour thesis':

> The voice-of-colour thesis holds that because of their different histories and experiences with oppression, Black, Indian, Asian, and Latino/a writers and thinkers may be able to communicate to their white counterparts matters that the whites are unlikely to know. Minority status, in other words, brings with it a presumed competence to speak about race and racism.
>
> (p. 9)

7   Another important facet of CRT is counter-storytelling. Oulanova et al. (in press) argue that the act of storytelling can be a powerful tool for creating meaning and disrupting normative myths, narratives, and metaphors about minoritised individuals. CRT emphasises the importance of the telling of counter-narratives through research evidence and of engaging voices of those with the lived experience of being marginalised by the dominant culture. Thus, these counter-narratives resist the 'master narratives', which reinforce systems of oppression (Solórzano & Yosso, 2002, p. 27).

Critical race theory 77

We focus here on the importance of engaging with counter-narratives in the research of those from diverse communities and we draw on examples from the work of scholars from those Black and diverse communities. These include Kenneth Bancroft Clark (1914–2005) and Mamie Phipps Clark (1917–1983), whose famous research and work on the 'Doll Study' presented responses of more than 200 Black children who were presented with a white or brown doll and were asked which doll was beautiful. Their findings showed the children preferred white dolls from as early as three years old. Their research impact and conclusions were that experiences of segregation were psychologically traumatic, became introjected as part of racial identification, and were damaging (Clark & Clark, 1939). Other influential Black psychologists whose bodies of research work counteracted racism and bias in studies towards those of African heritage include research on the psychology of race. This laid the groundwork for challenging many psychologists' and researchers' views of race and misdiagnosis of African American children due to biased psychological testing. For example, see Clark's 30-year review on changing concepts in mental health (Sumner & Shaed, 1945).

In line with this, others continued with research that evidenced that psychological tests which were Eurocentric and did not take into consideration the cultural context of the participants led to bias in the results. For example, Robert Lee Williams, a founding member of the National Association of Black Psychologists, created the *Black Intelligence Test of Cultural Homogeneity* (BITCH-100), which took into consideration the African American vernacular and cultural lived experience. This test showed that intelligence testing was biased and offered a counter-narrative that spoke to African Americans as not intellectually inferior to European Americans, but showed that the differences in speech and lived experience in Eurocentric-based psychometric tests and measures skewed IQ results (Williams, 1975).

These tenets permit examination of whiteness, racism, privilege, intersectionality, and shared stories of oppression and microaggressions. As the term suggests, CRT offers both a critique of theory that is racist or based on racist assumptions, and alternative theory and narratives. We want to highlight that the CRT lens that we used to question and engage with this historical research and brief literature review offered us counter-narratives to resist the 'main' Eurocentric-based psychology narratives on race, ethnicity, identity, and intelligence. This forms the backdrop for the importance of a critical race stance in psychology and in psychometric testing, because to ignore it means to have results that can be negatively biased towards clients from diverse communities whose lived experiences and cultures have not been taken into consideration in the psychometric process.

CRT as a methodology for research

In accordance with the transdisciplinary nature of psychotherapy, and bearing in mind the significant role of ethnic identity in health outcomes, CRT can be utilised as a theoretical framework and analysis tool for psychotherapy research. In this section, we (1) briefly overview the importance of employing CRT as a methodology for psychotherapy research, (2) offer a commentary that emphasises how psychotherapists can engage with qualitative research by firstly clarifying their own ontological and epistemological positions, and (3) propose ways CRT can be used in a range of methods in psychotherapy research.

It has been noted that a methodology is the rationale for the research approach, and the lens through which the analysis occurs (McLeod, 2015). Thus, in this context, methodology describes the general research strategy that outlines the way in which psychotherapy research is to be undertaken. The methodology should impact which method(s) are chosen for research and, hence, these methods are the specific tools and procedures used to collect and analyse data (Howell, 2013; McLeod, 2015).

Examples of methodologies which can be employed to engage with CRT include those that use phenomenology and interpretative phenomenological analysis (J. A. Smith et al., 2022). Such studies focus on describing the *lived experience* of a particular phenomenon, such as, for example, the mental health experiences of international graduate students of colour (Anandavalli et al., 2021).

We have also identified within the literature that participatory approaches to research methods have also been successfully employed in conducting CRT-focused research. This approach focuses on the empowerment of those for whom the research is relevant and ensures that they are fully involved in developing, designing, and undertaking the research, as well as in disseminating the findings (Fine et al., 2021; Hugman et al., 2011). In line with this, it is argued that there remains limited evidence for community-based participatory research in counselling and psychotherapy (Spong & Waters, 2015).

Another consideration is that of grounded theory, which involves the construction of hypotheses and theories through the collection and analysis of data, taking an inductive approach to develop a new theory (Bryant, 2019). Drawing on concerns regarding retention of students of colour in graduate programmes in higher education across disciplines, Hipolito-Delgado et al. (2021) use CRT and grounded theory to propose the importance of increasing ethnic diversity as a way of enriching psychotherapy training programmes, as it enables a wider range of voices and experiences. They also argue that it increases the cultural competence of all students, and they propose a liberatory theory of academic success.

We have also identified a narrative approach in the literature as another preferred method in CRT, as it enables the gathering of multiple-perspective accounts of individuals, communities, and groups. A narrative approach directly addresses dominant and non-dominant discourse in psychotherapy (and other) contexts and acknowledges roles that socially oppressive cultural discourses, such as racial stereotypes, can play (DeVance Taliaferro et al., 2013). Narrative research can take an oral or written form, in which researchers minimally prompt participants on a topic that may highlight a host of issues, including

Critical race theory 79

identifying power differentials within a person-in-environment perspective or socially constructed oppression (DeVance Taliaferro et al., 2013; Semmler & Williams, 2000).

We cannot describe all the methods and approaches that psychotherapists can employ in engaging with CRT in this chapter but, as already noted, we acknowledge the congruence between CRT and a range of other critical methodologies. Additionally, we note that CRT takes an interdisciplinary approach, and can engage a variety of methods, and epistemologies, to illuminate the effects of racism, sexism, classism, and power distribution (Davis, 2022). From our experience, engaging a CRT methodology also enables those from marginalised and diverse communities who have experienced social injustices to speak on their experiences of psychotherapy or on factors contributing to different forms of trauma due to systemic oppression. In line with this, we reiterate in the following section the importance of researchers engaging with their own positioning (ontological and epistemological) to face their own prejudice and bias, and to be ethical.

The importance of clarifying one's ontological and epistemological position with a CRT lens

CRT is far from politically neutral, because it supports the argument that theories (and, indeed, research) are never neutral or objective, but reflect the worldview, social position or perspective, and interests of the theorist or researcher (McDowell & Jeris, 2004). CRT relies on this social-constructionist stance to understand race and racism. It is therefore important for qualitative researchers to make explicit the philosophical and epistemological paradigms and ontological assumptions that underly their research.

Our ontological and epistemological positions that inform our research and our valuing of CRT are rooted in constructionism, which argues that knowledge, reality, or truth can never be truly known (Pring, 2004; Punch, 2005). Rather, reality is highly subjective and, as noted by Blackburn's (2017) perspectivism philosophical stance, is that each subjective position is due to being positioned at different viewpoints. Additionally, we both align with the central theme of a post-modernist philosophical assumption and stance, which embraces and involves complexity, an ethos of 'both/and' rather than 'either/or', and enables us to accept seemingly different or opposing perspectives, paradoxically, side-by-side (Charura & Lago, 2021b; Giovazolias, 2005; Wachtel, 2014). In line with this, Tillman (2002), when writing about culturally sensitive methodologies, postulates that it is important for researchers to challenge their own cultural power. Thus, we note that in engaging with CRT methodology, clarifying one's ontological and epistemological positions is an important process for researchers. It demonstrates continual commitment to challenge, as well as critiquing theoretical dominance and unequal power relations that subjugate, minimise, marginalise, or exclude the multiple lived realities and knowledge bases of their participants (Tillman, 2002).

Importance of reframing ethical principles

All research should be ethical. We start with a quote from Paquin et al. (2019), who remind us about the notion of moving towards a psychotherapy science for all and the importance of conducting ethical and socially just research. They state:

> However, as psychotherapy researchers, we should be grappling with how our own research can address these inequities, including moving beyond studying the impacts of culturally adapting treatments. This involves expanding our scientific objectives to get at the roots of these disparities to directly address society's most pernicious problems (e.g., racism, classism) as well as creating a psychotherapy science for all, not just some.
>
> (Paquin et al., 2019, p. 492)

We align with their argument by reminding the psychotherapy profession about the fundamental principle of 'nonmaleficence—do no harm'. All of us within our profession must adhere to this principle without exception, to protect the rights and welfare of participants, clients, and patients, and to ensure they are not harmed (American Psychological Association, 2017). Paquin et al. (2019) argue that although nonmaleficence is only one of the fundamental ethical principles (along with others such as beneficence, autonomy, justice, and fidelity), 'doing no harm' could be interpreted to mean that psychotherapy researchers should not continue to develop, design, implement, disseminate, or ask participants to engage in research that contributes to systemic oppression or the oppression of others. Given the often-invisible nature of oppressive systems and racism within our professions, we join Paquin et al. (2019) in their call and invite readers to begin engaging with this reinterpretation when developing all facets of their research.

Formulating a research question

As with all research, researchers using CRT as a methodology should select a topic of interest, identify a gap in the literature, and begin formulating question(s) for research (Miller et al., 2018; Paquin et al., 2019; Solórzano & Yosso, 2002). Thus, the research questions and process should be open, exploratory, and directed primarily at how participants make sense of experiences (Delgado & Stefancic, 2012; Miller et al., 2018; Paquin et al., 2019; Solórzano & Yosso, 2002).

A methodology engaging with critical participatory action

The inability to work effectively with diverse cultural groups and failure to consider their sociocultural contexts within psychotherapy can be characterised as cultural malpractice (Nagayama & Gordon, 2001). Whilst inclusion of ethnic minority populations may help determine the external validity of psychotherapy

Critical race theory 81

research and its efficacy, to determine the generalisability of psychotherapy approaches psychotherapy researchers need to do more than simply recruit and include ethnic minorities in psychotherapy research (Nagayama & Gordon, 2001).

The adoption of a CRT perspective on research design, data collection and analysis, dissemination, and implementation of findings has the potential to enable psychotherapy research to build a just society and profession. If new knowledge about ethnic minority populations is to be authentically evidenced, psychotherapy as a profession must come to terms with participative action research and collaborative inquiry approaches (McLeod, 2011; Ponterotto, 2005; K. Smith et al., 2021). We draw here on Winter's (2019) social justice perspective, in which she argues that an illustration of participative action research and collaborative inquiry approaches from a psychotherapy social justice perspective embraces the ideas of 'collaboration as a matter of principle' (p. 180). Thus, in aligning with the aim of CRT's ultimate goal of social justice, a CRT methodology should include approaches in which members from diverse and Black communities are involved in research design, collection and analysis of data, writing, and dissemination. K. Smith et al. (2021) highlight how participatory research is congruent with collaborative emancipatory approaches to research inquiry. This can be found within the methodological traditions associated with critical psychology (Fine et al., 2021). To give voice to the lived experience of people from diverse communities, CRT as a methodology for psychotherapy research can include counter-storytelling, use of poetry, biographies, family histories, parables, chronicles, narratives, stories, fiction, and revisionist histories (Ladson-Billings & Tate, 1995; Solórzano & Yosso, 2002). We concur with Fine et al.'s (2021) argument that participation and inclusion of the voice of those with lived experience of marginalisation and racism is so crucial to social justice research. Put simply, from a CRT methodological design perspective, we therefore note 'no research on us, or about us, or to represent us without us'!

As CRT has an activist dimension, engaging with it enables us to contribute to a paradigm shift. It enables opportunities for taking responsibility for atrocities done by others so that we can build an environment to learn from one another instead of gaining an inheritance of ignorance. In using CRT as a lens in counselling and psychotherapy research to decolonise psychotherapy, we need to strip back some of the structures on which research methodologies and approaches are built. We need an ongoing reflexive process that goes beyond its inclusion as a tick box exercise, and more engagement with immersing ourselves as researchers into a process of critiquing our power in relation to racialised others, and the intentionality and assumptions we hold about them from the very inception of research ideas to the research design, process, and dissemination.

Conclusion

Some see CRT as creating fear and chaos, and many advocate a ban of CRT, stating that it is anti-American or anti-British, villainises white people, and

82 Divine Charura and Sonya Clyburn

propagandises children. However, we argue that having a non-colour ideology in society, and indeed in psychotherapy research, leads to continuous systemic racism and social inequalities. In society, this includes police brutality, voting suppression, access to healthcare, women's rights, gun violence, hunger, and food insecurity. In psychotherapy, this would manifest as perpetuation of the exclusion of people from minority and diverse communities in research and, consequently, a one-size-fits-all intervention approach which lacks cultural humility and disregards diversity and intersectionality. We argue that not allowing CRT to be taught is an attack on free speech and on knowing the truth about the history of our nations and of psychotherapy. As ethical researchers, professionals, and citizens, we should have appropriate respectful conversations which enable us to gain awareness about biases, foster new ideas about each other, and develop new skills for engagement.

For our professions to make a difference in a multi-ethnic, multiracial, multicultural, and diverse society today, we must unveil the truth, so that our present and future generations and professions can be healthy and succeed. We argue, therefore, that what is needed is a paradigm shift in psychotherapy research to authentically include methodologies that are sensitive to and engage with race. It remains important to identify theories from schools of thought which can enable strong critique of the psychotherapy profession, and CRT is one of the theories that can enable research and methodological emancipation from the status quo. Joining our voices with others in our field who have increasingly been speaking about racial injustice, we assert that racialisation and racism, subtle and overt, has impeded the development of our profession to be inclusive of all, within the domains of research and practice. Utilising CRT within research and psychotherapy practice can potentially facilitate greater understanding of our participants and clients through gaining knowledge of their context and lived experience. Thus, as argued by Moodley et al. (2018), 'CRT provides another lens from which to contextualise, organise and analyse information revealed during the practice of mental health care' (p. 86). We acknowledge that many researchers and therapists may have the best of intentions, but without dismantling institutional, structural, and methodological racism in psychotherapy research, a perpetuation of subtle or overt discrimination will continue against racialised groups (Moodley et al., 2018).

To end, we reiterate the benefits of remaining open, of not assuming that as researchers any of us are free of discriminatory bias, or free from the influence of the structural frame which the psychotherapy profession and historical research has benefited from, to the cost and exclusion of other groups, their lived experience, and their epistemologies. Furthermore, decolonising research methodologies informs decolonising research at all levels and stages—from consultation about the research question and participants through to ideas about data sovereignty, and from applying methods such as CRT to data analysis and findings through to dissemination.

References

American Psychological Association. (2017, March). *Ethical principles of psychologists and code of conduct.* https://www.apa.org/ethics/code

Anandavalli, S., Borders, L. D., & Kniffin, L. E. (2021). 'Because here, white is right': Mental health experiences of international graduate students of color from a critical race perspective. *International Journal for the Advancement of Counselling, 43*(3), 283–301. https://10.0.3.239/s10447-021-09437-xhttps://doi.org/10.1007/s10447-021-09437-x

Andrews, K. (2016). The psychosis of whiteness: The celluloid hallucinations of 'Amazing Grace' and 'Belle'. *Journal of Black Studies, 47*(5), 435–453. https://doi.org/10.1177/0021934716638802

Blackburn, S. (2017). *Truth.* Profile Books.

Bonilla-Silva, E. (2014). *Racism without racists: Color-blind racism and the persistence of racial inequality in America* (4th ed.). Rowman & Littlefield Publishers, Inc.

Breen, K. (2021). Disaster racism: Using Black sociology, critical race theory and history to understand racial disparity to disaster in the United States. *Disaster Prevention and Management: An International Journal, 31*(3), 229–242. https://doi.org/10.1108/DPM-02-2021-0059

Bryant, A. (2019). *The varieties of grounded theory.* SAGE Publications Limited. https://dx.doi.org/10.4135/9781529716542

Charura, D., & Lago, C. (Eds.). (2021a). *Black identities + white therapies: Race, respect + diversity.* PCCS Books.

Charura, D., & Lago, C. (2021b). Towards a decolonised psychotherapy research and practice. In D. Charura & C. Lago (Eds.), *Black identities + white therapies: Race, respect + diversity* (pp. 185–198). PCCS Books.

Clark, K. B., & Clark, M. K. (1939). The development of consciousness of self and the emergence of racial identification in Negro preschool children. *The Journal of Social Psychology, 10*(4), 591–599. https://doi.org/10.1080/00224545.1939.9713394

Conley, D., & Domingue, B. (2016). The bell curve revisited: Testing controversial hypotheses with molecular genetic data. *Sociological Science, 3*(23), 520–539. https://doi.org/10.15195/v3.a23

D'Arrigo-Patrick, J., Hoff, C., Knudson-Martin, C., & Tuttle, A. (2017). Navigating critical theory and postmodernism: Social justice and therapist power in family therapy. *Family Process, 56*(3), 574–588. https://doi.org/10.1111/famp.12236

Davis, J. (2022). Disrupting research, theory, and pedagogy with critical race theory in mathematics education for Black populations. *Journal of Urban Mathematics Education, 15*(1), 9–30. https://jume-ojs-tamu.tdl.org/JUME/article/view/423/328

Delgado, R., & Stefancic, J. (2001). *Critical race theory.* New York University Press.

Delgado, R., & Stefancic, J. (2012). *Critical race theory* (2nd ed.). New York University Press.

DeVance Taliaferro, J., Casstevens, W. J., & DeCuir Gunby, J. T. (2013). Working with African American clients using narrative therapy: An operational citizenship and critical race theory framework. *International Journal of Narrative Therapy and Community Work,* (1), 34–45. https://search.informit.org/doi/10.3316/informit.283838607191036

Etchebarne, A. (2021). *Exploring the wellbeing of Black and minority ethnic academics: An interpretative phenomenological analysis* [Doctoral dissertation, University of Manchester]. Research Explorer. https://www.research.manchester.ac.uk/portal/en/theses/exploring-the-wellbeing-of-black-and-minority-ethnic-academics-an-interpretative-phenomenological-analysis(a7704ad8-9f34-4d1c-99e4-d4260928901b).html

84 Divine Charura and Sonya Clyburn

Eysenck, H. J. (1971). *The IQ argument: Race, intelligence, and education.* Library Press.

Fine, M., Torre, M. E., Oswald, A. G., & Avory, S. (2021). Critical participatory action research: Methods and praxis for intersectional knowledge production. *Journal of Counseling Psychology, 68*(3), 344–356. https://doi.org/10.1037/cou0000445

Fussell, E., Sastry, N., & VanLandingham, M. (2010). Race, socioeconomic status, and return migration to New Orleans after Hurricane Katrina. *Population and Environment, 31,* 20–42. https://doi.org/10.1007/s11111-009-0092-2

Garner, S. (2007). *Whiteness: An introduction.* Routledge. https://doi.org/10.4324/9780203945599

Giovazolias, T. (2005). Counselling psychology and the integration of theory, research, and practice: A personal account. *Counselling Psychology Quarterly, 18*(2), 161–168. https://doi.org/10.1080/09515070500143542

Graham, L., Brown-Jeffy, S., Aronson, R., & Stephens, C. (2011). Critical race theory as theoretical framework and analysis tool for population health research. *Critical Public Health, 21*(1), 81–93. https://doi.org/10.1080/09581596.2010.493173

Green, M. J., Matsebula, J., & Sonn, C. C. (2007). Reviewing whiteness: Theory, research, and possibilities. *South African Journal of Psychology, 37*(3), 389–419. https://doi.org/10.1177/008124630703700301

Grzanka, P. R., Santos, C. E., & Moradi, B. (2017). Intersectionality research in counseling psychology. *Journal of Counseling Psychology, 64*(5), 453–457. https://doi.org/10.1037/cou0000237

Gunew, S. (2007). Rethinking whiteness. *Feminist Theory, 8*(2), 141–147. https://doi.org/10.1177/146470010707813

Herrnstein, R. J., & Murray, C. (1996). *The bell curve: Intelligence and class structure in American life.* Free Press.

Hipolito-Delgado, C. P., Estrada, D., & Garcia, M. (2021). Countering deficits: A grounded theory of success from graduate students of color. *Journal of Multicultural Counseling and Development, 49*(1), 4–17. https://doi.org/10.1002/jmcd.12202

Howell, K. E. (2013). *An introduction to the philosophy of methodology.* SAGE Publications Ltd.

Hugman, R., Pittaway, E., & Bartolomei, L. (2011). When 'do no harm' is not enough: The ethics of research with refugees and other vulnerable groups. *The British Journal of Social Work, 41*(7), 1271–1287. https://doi.org/10.1093/bjsw/bcr013

Keating, F. (2020, November 24). *What does it mean to decolonize knowledge and why is it important in mental health research?* [Video]. YouTube. https://www.youtube.com/watch?v=jqUlVpvh5A8

Ladson-Billings, G., & Tate, W. F., IV. (1995). Toward a critical race theory of education. *Teachers College Record, 97*(1), 47–68. https://doi.org/10.1177/016146819509700104

Lago, C. (2006). *Race, culture, and counselling: The ongoing challenge* (2nd ed.). Open University Press.

Maharaj, A. S., Bhatt, N. V., & Gentile, J. P. (2021). Bringing it in the room: Addressing the impact of racism on the therapeutic alliance. *Innovations in Clinical Neuroscience, 18*(7–9), 39–43. https://www.ncbi.nlm.nih.gov/pubmed/34980992

McDowell, T., & Jeris, L. (2004). Talking about race using critical race theory: Recent trends in the Journal of Martial and Family Therapy. *The Journal of Marital and Family Therapy, 30*(1), 81–94. https://doi.org/10.1111/j.1752-0606.2004.tb01224.x

McLeod, J. (2011). *Qualitative research in counselling and psychotherapy* (2nd ed.). SAGE Publications Ltd.

McLeod, J. (2015). *Doing research in counselling and psychotherapy* (3rd ed.). SAGE Publications Ltd.

Miller, R. M., Chan, C. D., & Farmer, L. B. (2018). Interpretative phenomenological analysis: A contemporary qualitative approach. *Counselor Education and Supervision*, *57*(4), 240–254. https://doi.org/10.1002/ceas.12114

Moodley, R., Mujtaba, F., & Kleiman, S. (2018). Critical race theory and mental health. In B. M. Z. Cohen (Ed.), *Routledge international handbook of critical mental health* (pp. 79–88). Routledge. https://doi.org/10.4324/9781315399584

Nagayama, H., & Gordon, C. (2001). Psychotherapy research with ethnic minorities: Empirical, ethical, and conceptual issues. *Journal of Consulting and Clinical Psychology*, *69*(3), 502–510. https://doi.org/10.1037/0022-006X.69.3.502

Newnes, C. (Ed.). (2021). *Racism in psychology: Challenging theory, practice and institutions*. Routledge. https://doi.org/10.4324/9781003119401

Oulanova, O., Hui, J., & Moodley, R. (in press). Engaging with minoritised and racialised communities 'inside the sentence'. In L. A.Winter & D. Charura (Eds.), *Handbook of social justice theory and practice in the psychological therapies: Power, politics and change*. SAGE Publications Ltd.

Owen, D. S. (2007). Towards a critical theory of whiteness. *Philosophy & Social Criticism*, *33*(2), 203–222. https://doi.org/10.1177/0191453707074139

Paquin, J. D., Tao, K. W., & Budge, S. L. (2019). Toward a psychotherapy science for all: Conducting ethical and socially just research. *Psychotherapy*, *56*(4), 491–502. https://doi.org/10.1037/pst0000271

Pomare, P., Ioane, J., & Tudor, K. (2021). Racism in New Zealand psychology, or is Western psychology a good thing? In C. Newnes (Ed.), *Racism in psychology: Challenging theory, practice and institutions* (pp. 110–130). Routledge.

Ponterotto, J. G. (2005). Qualitative research in counseling psychology. *Journal of Counseling Psychology*, *52*(2), 126–136. https://doi.org/10.1037/0022-0167.52.2.126

Pring, R. (2004). *Philosophy of educational research* (2nd ed.). Continuum.

Punch, K. (2005). *Introduction to social research: Quantitative and qualitative approaches* (2nd ed.). SAGE Publications Ltd.

Saini, A. (2019). *Superior: The return of race science*. Beacon Press.

Semmler, P. L., & Williams, C. B. (2000). Narrative therapy: A storied context for multicultural counseling. *Journal of Multicultural Counseling and Development*, *28*(1), 51–62. https://doi.org/10.1002/j.2161-1912.2000.tb00227.x

Smith, J. A., Larkin, M., & Flowers, P. (2022). *Interpretative phenomenological analysis: Theory, method and research* (2nd ed.). SAGE Publications Ltd.

Smith, K., McLeod, J., Blunden, N., Cooper, M., Gabriel, L., Kupfer, C., McLeod, J., Murphie, M., Oddli, H. W., Thurston, M., & Winter, L. A. (2021). A pluralistic perspective on research in psychotherapy: Harnessing passion, difference and dialogue to promote justice and relevance. *Frontiers in Psychology*, *12*, 742676. https://doi.org/10.3389/fpsyg.2021.742676

Solórzano, D. G., & Yosso, T. J. (2002). Critical race methodology: Counter-storytelling as an analytical framework for education research. *Qualitative Inquiry*, *8*(1), 23–44. https://doi.org/10.1177/107780040200800103

Spong, S., & Waters, R. (2015). Community-based participatory research in counselling and psychotherapy. *European Journal of Psychotherapy & Counselling*, *17*(1), 5–20. https://doi.org/10.1080/13642537.2014.996170

Su, C. (2007). Cracking silent codes: Critical race theory and education organizing. *Discourse*, *28*(4), 531–548. https://doi.org/10.1080/01596300701625297

86 *Divine Charura and Sonya Clyburn*

Sumner, F. C., & Shaed, D. L. (1945). Negro-white attitudes towards the administration of justice as affecting Negroes. *Journal of Applied Psychology, 29*(5), 368–377. https://doi.org/10.1037/h0063424

Tillman, L. C. (2002). Culturally sensitive research approaches: An African-American perspective. *Educational Researcher, 31*(9), 3–12. https://doi.org/10.3102/0013189X031009003

Wachtel, P. L. (2014). An integrative relational point of view. *Psychotherapy, 51*(3), 342–349. https://doi.org/10.1037/a0037219

Wilcox, M. M. (2022). *Oppression is not 'culture': The need to center systemic and structural determinants to address anti-Black racism and racial trauma in psychotherapy. Psychotherapy.* Advance online publication. https://doi.org/10.1037/pst0000446

Wilder, C. S. (2013). *Ebony & ivy: Race, slavery, and the troubled history of America's universities.* Bloomsbury Press.

Williams, R. L. (1975). The BITCH-100: A culture-specific test. *Journal of Afro-American Issues, 3*(1), 103–116. http://eric.ed.gov/ERICWebPortal/detail?accno=EJ113500

Winter, L. A. (2019). Social justice and remembering 'the personal is political' in counselling and psychotherapy: So, what can therapists do? *Counselling and Psychotherapy Research 19*(3) 173–181. https://doi.org/10.1002/capr.12215

7 Pasifika research methodologies and psychotherapy

Julia Ioane and Athena Tapu Tu'itahi

Western—and Northern—psychology and psychotherapy are becoming more aware of their cultural heritage, assumptions, and position, and the need both to acknowledge this and to incorporate other worldviews into their clinical and research practices (Ioane, 2017; Waitoki et al., 2018). Whilst this includes Pasifika worldviews, relatively little is known among white European and Northern academic traditions about such methodologies, which are framed within collective cultures and communities. This chapter aims to provide an initial understanding of some current Pasifika research methodologies and methods that have been developed and designed by Pasifika for Pasifika communities. For the purposes of this chapter, we have selected only those research methodologies that we have used in our own research. We think that, appropriately contextualised, these methodologies can also be used among other collective communities and, arguably, in Western cultures and contexts. Thus, this chapter provides information about selected research methodologies and methods that are currently used and how they may be implemented by non-Pasifika researchers in the field. It also discusses the importance of the researcher as being fundamental to the authentic success of a research project, an importance that goes beyond the methodology itself; in other words, the researcher *is* the research. The chapter concludes with some practical implications on how to conduct research with Pasifika communities by both Pasifika and non-Pasifika researchers.

Who we are

Talofa lava, warm Pasifika greetings. My name is Folasāitu Apaula Julia Ioane; I am of Samoan descent, though my ancestors are also from Denmark and Germany, and migrated to Samoa for trade and colonisation of Samoa. I am a New Zealand-born Samoan, having grown up in South Auckland, though fortunate to have spent some of my primary school years in Samoa while my mother took turns with her siblings to care for my grandmother. I am the first university graduate in my 'nuclear' family, though I come from a long line of medical graduates in my extended family: health runs through my blood! I am a clinical psychologist in private practice, working with government agencies

DOI: 10.4324/9781003280859-8

88 Julia Ioane and Athena Tapu Tu'itahi

which work with children, young people, and their families in care and protection and youth justice. I am also an associate professor at Massey University in Auckland, teaching clinical and criminal psychology. I conduct and supervise research with a particular focus on Indigenous research methods and practice alongside Western methodologies and research frameworks.

Ka tangi te titi, Ka tangi te kaka, Ka tangi hoki a hau, Tihei mauri ora
Ko Vaea te Maunga
Ko Polynesian airlines te waka
Ko Ngāti Hāmoa te iwi
Ko Ta'igalaala Ioane tōku Papa
Ko Tautegaatufana Kuresa Ioane tōku Mama
Ko Anthony Joseph tōku tane/hoa rangatira
Tēnā koutou, tēnā koutou, tēnā koutou katoa.

Talofa lava, malo le soifua maua ma le lagi e mamā. O lo'u igoa o Talutoe Athena Tapu Tu'itahi. I come from the villages of Lotofaga, Vaimoso, Pu'apu'a, and Iva in Samoa. I am a descendent of the Sitagata, Siō, Tamasese, and Savelio clans. I was born and raised here in Aotearoa New Zealand and currently reside in South Auckland. My family emigrated from Samoa in the 1960s in search for better opportunities for their 'aiga (family). My family continue to work in their Samoan and Pasifika communities as educators. I am a registered psychotherapist working in private practice and I am also a lecturer in the Department of Psychotherapy & Counselling at Auckland University of Technology. My background is in mental health and Pacific mental health and community. I am passionate about Pasifika Indigenous knowledge and ways of healing and therapies. I am a strong advocate for the advancement of Pasifika and Māori in Aotearoa New Zealand, in particular youth and young women.

Ko mauga o Savaii toku mauga
Ko Moana nui a Kiwa toku Moana
Ko Fuipisia toku Awa
Ko Vaaloa toku vaka
Ko Hamoa toku iwi
Ko Lotofaga, Vaimoso, Pu'apu'a, Iva toku papa kainga
Ko Sitagata Tapu toku hapu
Ko Tauanu'u Perenise toku Papa
Ko Jennifer Tapu toku Mama
Ko Rizvan toku tane
Ko Kalepo mo Luka toku tamariki
Ko Talutoe Athena Maugakiona Tapu Tu'itahi ahau.

Who you are

We assume, respectfully, that you, the reader, are likely to be a non-Pasifika person with a range of knowledge about Pasifika people from nothing or little to a lot. If you are in an environment where there are no Pasifika people, you may interact with Indigenous or other ethnic minority communities in your country or area. Alternatively, you may be an Indigenous member of your community or someone from an ethnic minority, or even Pasifika yourself! Basically, what we are trying to say here is that this chapter can and should be read by anyone who has an interest in working with collective communities and possibly those that may have different worldviews to your own. As you will see in our chapter, we think that we should all be agile in our psychotherapy and psychology practice and research, and make every effort to be as authentic as possible with the communities we aim to serve.

What this chapter does

This chapter will first provide you, the reader, with a brief background about Pasifika people as it is important to contextualise the communities that we are discussing prior to sharing research methodologies. Practically, before you work with Pasifika people, get to know them first. We provide a brief overview of Pasifika people in Aotearoa New Zealand, and an understanding of Pasifika values and vā. Values underpin Pasifika cultures and, whilst the concept of values is universal, the centrality of values to everyday life and to any psychological practice is part of the fabric that is the identity of all Pasifika cultures. This information is crucial as it will need to be integrated in your engagement and relationships with Pasifika people. We then share some Pasifika methodologies and conclude with some recommendations on using such tools in your research.

Pasifika people

There are approximately 25,000 islands in the Pasifika or Oceania (Ministry of Pacific Peoples (MPP), 2021). In Aotearoa New Zealand, tagata Pasifika (Pacific people) make up approximately 8.1% of the New Zealand population, comprising nine major Pacific Island ethnicities: Samoan, Cook Islands, Tongan, Niuean, Fijian, Tokelauan, Tuvaluan, Kiribati, and Rotuman (MPP, 2021).

We are a young and growing population with an average age of 23.4 years, compared to the national average age of 37 years, and we are a population that is steadily growing—at a rate of 29% (MPP, 2021). Many tagata Pasifika who have emigrated to Aotearoa New Zealand have a special link to their mother Pacific Islands and their culture and identity (Thomsen et al., 2018). The term 'Pacific' collectively applies to those who were born in Aotearoa New Zealand and to those who identify themselves as having Pacific Island descent. This is used interchangeably with many variations of the term—e.g., Pasifika, Pasefika, or Pasifiki—each of which is the literal translation for the word Pacific, in different Pacific Island languages.

Pasifika is also a term that describes a behaviour: a way of viewing the world around us and in which we operate. The New Zealand Treasury defines Pacific and its traditions as 'the concepts, perspectives, values, belief systems and knowledge that frame, drive and underpin the way that Pacific people and Pacific New Zealanders behave and respond to issues that matter to them'

90 *Julia Ioane and Athena Tapu Tu'itahi*

(Thomsen et al., 2018, p. 15). We also want to acknowledge that tagata Pasifika is also a heterogeneous group that shares some but not all identities, beliefs, and values.

Whilst this chapter is about Pacific methodologies, we would like to challenge our readers. When non-Pacific people think about Pacific people, they tend to think about us in the context of the Western country in which they lie, such as Aotearoa New Zealand, Australia, the UK, or the USA. Instead, we ask you to think about us in the context of our island of origin in the Pacific. These islands are 'third world' nations which rely significantly on aid and remittances from the Western world whilst, at the same time, trying to build their own economies (Fraenkel, 2006). As we—and especially those of us in the Pacific diaspora—hold a collective identity, which includes our 'aiga in the islands, we ask you to think about research by, with, and for Pasifika people in the Western world *and* to consider how this may also be useful to Pasifika people living in our islands in the South Pacific. How we do well in Western countries is also dependent on and related to how well our families are in our island nations.

Values of Pasifika people

Values are fundamental to the way in which we as Pasifika people live our lives. They underpin our daily conversations, behaviour, actions, and practices. The role of values in Pasifika research is a key element to ensure that processes have integrity and that researchers are safe to work with communities. Respect, reciprocity, and humility or 'fa'aaloalo' are part of the foundation of keeping good relationships. It is the protocols and etiquette that define the respectful and reciprocal behaviour in the 'Vā fealoaloa'i (Lui, 2003; Silipa, 2008, and see below).

Anae (2010) highlights being face-to-face as an integral part of relational respect and reciprocity or fa'aaloalo. Respect and reciprocity are seen through Pasifika values in different cultural protocols, both physical and spiritual, such as funerals and remittances, having sacred guardianship over caring for the land, and feeling spiritually connected to the land. As such, fa'aaloalo is a transferrable concept that is nurtured by cultural custodians at homes, churches, and various education institutions. It can also be defined as reverence, courtesy, and politeness and it is one's respectful actions, words, and appropriate behaviour according to the social or cultural space or vā fealoaloa'i (Silipa, 2008).

Principles of the vā

The vā is a fundamental concept that arguably defines the existence of Pasifika people in Aotearoa New Zealand and in their islands. Vā can simply be referred to as 'space between people or things' (Ka'ili, 2005, p. 89) as is understood among Tongan, Samoan, and Rotuman communities. In Tahiti, it is also referred to as vā, whilst Aotearoa New Zealand and Hawai'i refer to it as wā.

Pasifika research methodologies 91

However, it is more commonly used in Samoan (vā) and Tongan (Tauhi vā) communities. Mahina (2002, as cited in Ka'ili, 2005) expressed the vā in four dimensions of physical, social, intellectual, and symbolic. These are the sacred spaces between people, people and their land, and people and their God.

Tauhi vā is connected to all four dimensions, though it tends to be based more on the social dimension of vā that promotes relationships and spaces between people and other matter (Ka'ili, 2005). Vā within the Samoan context has different types such as vā fealoaloa'i referring to the respectful space between people, and each knowing where they fit within the social structures, roles, and duties within their world (Tuagalu, 2008). Vā tapua'i is one that is grounded in a spiritual foundation consisting of sacred obligations and commitment to family and community (Tuagalu, 2008).

Within research environments, implementing the vā is crucial to genuine engagement and participation by Pacific peoples. This includes having a strong understanding of the role you play as you enter the world of a Pacific participant. This includes being aware of how your identity and role can impact on Pacific people, understanding Pacific protocols of engagement to show your respect of the culture, and prioritising your relationship within them that will supersede interview questions and assessments. Time is needed to build and nurture the vā among Pacific people. However, once this is established, nurturing the vā becomes a reciprocal process between people.

Pacific research methods/methodologies

Talanoa method and methodology

Talanoa is generally known to have been developed as a research method by Tongan researcher Timote Vaioleti (2006). However, it was first introduced by Sitiveni Halapua (2003) as a process of talking openly from the heart (Tecun et al., 2018). Another Tongan researcher, 'Okusitina Mahina, later referred to it as 'talking critically yet harmoniously' (as cited in Tecun et al., 2018, p. 157). Despite this, challenges have also arisen in reference to its application and attempts to distinguish it from other approaches, though it is still regarded as an appropriate research tool similar to individual and focus group interviews (Tunufa'i, 2016).

As a practitioner and researcher, I (Julia) also see it as a method to invoke enquiry with Pasifika people. Whilst some have referred to talanoa as replacing open-ended interviews, this does not take into account the cultural complexities that come with a talanoa. Talanoa is seen as a method to learn and make enquiries about things, though it is also seen as a 'decolonial ethic to research, recognising the power relationships from how one is positioned or relates to the search process' (Nabobo-Baba, 2008, p. 58). Talanoa can also be used to discuss Indigenous research that is not necessarily Pacific. It can be used to invoke conversations, seek wisdom, mediate conflict and tension, and/or share knowledge and wisdom from one generation to the next.

92 *Julia Ioane and Athena Tapu Tu'itahi*

My use of talanoa is an instinctive process that begins at the same time the relationship is being established. Talanoa naturally begins as a conversation to build rapport and create engagement with the other person(s). Conversations range from current daily activities to one's identity and family. Such conversations are unstructured, with no conscious attempt to direct or guide the nature or content of talanoa. As the talanoa warms both parties to the relationships, there is a natural point where it begins to steer towards the purpose of the visit. However, this only happens when both parties feel a mutual sense of comfort and trust with one another. On many occasions, the purpose is already enacted as the talanoa continues—without any direct effort from either party. It is an open, unstructured process yet it is filled with cultural protocols, connotations, and practices that are often unseen by Western and individualised researchers. It is a process of 'feeling' the talanoa rather than 'practicing' or 'speaking' the talanoa.

Teu le vā

The origin of the Teu le vā methodology was birthed from a symposium held in 2007 in a partnership between the Pasifika Caucus of the New Zealand Association for Research in Education and the Ministry of Education's Pasifika and Research and Evaluation teams (Anae et al., 2010). Anae and her colleagues further developed the outcomes of the discussions and recommendations of the symposium into 'Teu le vā: Relationships across research and policy in Pasifika education: A collective approach to knowledge generation and policy development for action towards Pasifika education success'. This shortly became known as the Teu le vā approach. This approach was developed to uphold safe cultural practice and relationships within the Pacific communities and researchers in Aotearoa New Zealand. There are three Teu le vā principles and six guiding principles:

1 The importance of nurturing the relationships between researchers and policy makers.
2 Sharing collective knowledge to develop optimal relationships.
3 Having a clear focus for research and policy efforts (Anae et al., 2010).

The six practices of Teu le vā are as follows:

1 Engage with stakeholders in Pasifika education research.
2 Collaborate in setting the research framework.
3 Create a coordinated and collaborative approach to Pasifika education.
4 Grow knowledge through a cumulative approach to research.
5 Understand the kinds of knowledge used in Pasifika education research and policy making.
6 Engage with other knowledge brokers.

Pasifika research methodologies 93

This methodology is useful as it is founded on the pan-Pacific concept of vā and 'Teu le vā' (Tuagalu, 2008) or nurturing and maintaining of the vā or relationship. This is a foundation of care, mutual respect, and reciprocity from which any research can be entered into.

This methodology adds to the growing platform of Pacific methodologies and gives Pasifika researchers an opportunity to ground their research in a methodology that aligns with their values and worldview. It also safeguards Pasifika communities and individuals who are research subjects by inviting them into the research planning process from initiation. It uses a core Pasifika value of vā to anchor the research in values of respect, humility, and reciprocity.

My (Athena) research positions my Samoan worldview and identity as linked with my family, culture, community, ancestors, cosmos, and the relational space that links us (Tapu Tu'itahi, 2018). It is with this understanding that I chose Teu le vā methodology (Anae, 2010) in my dissertation as it incorporates the Samoan worldview that I hold. Teu le vā dictates how I related and engaged with all others in my research: community elders, other Pasifika academic staff, Pasifika and non-Pasifika peers. I attended to the relational space by being aware of the sacred space between us, using respectful or formal language, acknowledging one's title or cultural/community status, supplying or paying for food and refreshments, and noticing how I conduct myself in people's homes by taking my shoes off or asking if they would like to start with prayer. I am acutely aware of my position as a Pasifika researcher and how I conduct conversations and communications. I recognise the significance of respectful protocols that uphold and nurture relationships particularly when interacting with elders, community leaders, supervisors, and colleagues.

The strength of Teu le vā is that the notion of vā is widely known around the Pacific and in Māori as the Wā (Salmond, 2003). Therefore, it has global connotations that connect Indigenous peoples within the Pacific. In addition to this, Teu le vā can be adapted to any research area as it emphasises core values of relationship and respect. Therefore, it can be utilised in a wide variety of fields and sectors such as health, social work, business, education, and justice to name a few. This makes the Teu le vā adaptable and versatile, and as aforementioned, I have used this methodology within the field of psychotherapy. This has never been done before, and thus creates a new avenue for future psychotherapy researchers to ground their research in.

It would also be useful to have clinical and cultural academic supervision to formulate one's research. Having a Pacific academic and practitioner as a supervisor helped the research process come together. It helped to integrate the two worlds of academic research and have it grounded in a Pacific methodology. This enables a worldview and research perspective that can be thought about in a Western education framework.

In this context, it is not insignificant that we are both women. Within Pasifika communities, gender roles are assumed to be known, though this does not stand alone as it is also affected by other intersectionalities such as age, social status, and role in the village.

94 *Julia Ioane and Athena Tapu Tu'itahi*

Kakala framework

The Kakala framework was originally developed by Tongan Professor Konai Helu-Thaman drawing on the kakala (garland) as a metaphorical framework for research practice among Pacific communities (Thaman, 1992). It was a framework originally designed with three stages of Toli, Tui, and Luva. Further adaptation was made with Teu (Taufe'ulungaki et al., 2007) at the beginning of the process and two final stages of Mālie and Māfana to conclude the process (Fua, 2021). In brief, the stages include Teu (preparation), Toli (data collection), Tui (data analysis), Luva (report and dissemination), Mālie (evaluation), and Māfana (final evaluation). It is a process that requires one to be mindful in their approach to participants and to be collaborative in their analyses, dissemination, and evaluation. Teu involves a process of consultation and review with appropriate parties to ensure the research will be of benefit and value to its target audience. Furthermore, the evaluation and final evaluation refers to having further talanoa with its target audience (community) to review and interpret findings and identify its implications for the community. It is a co-partnered approach working together with the community it intends to serve.

The Kakala framework provides the opportunity for a step-by-step approach to conducting research with Pasifika communities. I (Julia) have also used it as a process to review whether a therapeutic process can be adapted within a Pasifika context (Ioane, 2022). Given that the Pasifika worldview is collective and communal, it is our view that any research about Pasifika communities needs to be applied. This means that it needs to have relevance, it needs to have a purpose, and it needs to have an outcome in order to authentically serve Pasifika peoples. Pasifika people in Aotearoa New Zealand and arguably across the globe have experienced many social and economic disparities and any research needs to include an element to improve equity among this vulnerable yet resilient population. How do we do this? We do this via the first stage of Teu. Teu requires one to start the preparation for the study. This involves researching the community of interest though making sure that the research is not limited to reading materials such as peer-reviewed journals and grey literature. We believe that this also involves having a talanoa and meeting with the Pasifika community. It is well documented that Pasifika communities are not necessarily reflected in academic literature and therefore thinking outside of the box is required to hear the voices of these communities (Kidman & Chu, 2019). Furthermore, Pasifika worldviews are not often reflected in the world of research and academia (e.g., Pacific methodologies) and therefore consultation at the grassroots level is a necessity. Consultation can look like calling a community meeting to see what is going on in our Pasifika communities. That is, what is working well? What is not working well? A researcher can then look at how things can either be strengthened or improved so that it is going to be of value to Pasifika peoples. Another option is to target particular key members of the Pasifika community with expertise in the area to seek their knowledge, guidance, and advice. This all contributes to the preparation and responds

Pasifika research methodologies   95

appropriately to the collective identity of Pasifika—by asking Pasifika people for their views. The process of data collection begins, and it is here by which Pasifika methodologies are to be undertaken. Data are only as good as the way in which they are gathered, so method and methodology are just as important as the data itself.

As noted previously, Pasifika people are relational beings and are more likely to engage depending on their relationship with the research and researchers. Part of the methodology and method involves the way in which you relate, and it is this process alone that determines the authenticity by which participants engage. Two widely held values of Pasifika people are respect and humility; so, whilst we may not always fully understand the purpose of the research, as the researcher is in a position of authority, we are still likely to engage. Thus, the challenge researchers face is whether the engagement of participants is authentic and genuine or simply a matter of respect towards the researcher and their work.

Following Toli is Tui (data analysis). We are aware that whilst there are Pasifika methodologies available, data analysis within a Pasifika framework/worldview is currently limited. We challenge Pasifika researchers to consider the development of a data analysis tool to assist in the translation of data to applied knowledge in the relevant field of interest. Luva (report and disseminate) is a process which highlights the reciprocity of the relationship between the researcher and participants. The participant has provided the researcher with the knowledge and wisdom in the area of interest. The researcher will now reciprocate by providing the findings of their research. In some cases, it is not uncommon for Pasifika research to go back to the community to discuss the results and then both groups work towards the interpretation of such findings. This highlights the collective identity for Pasifika people. Finally, we conclude with Mālie and Māfana—both are the evaluation of such a project. It is seen as a 'so what?' of the cycle. It determines whether the research has done what it said it was going to do. In addition, it also responds to a 'where to from here?' for the research. What will it influence? What will encourage Pasifika communities to flourish and thrive? It is at this point that we can truly understand whether the fragrance of the Kakala is exactly what it was intended to be. In other words, it is at this point that we can truly understand whether the research has impact on the Pasifika community it proposed to serve.

Fa'afaletui

Fa'afaletui is a Samoan concept that was initially discussed in focus groups of Samoan elders as part of a talanoa study by Tamasese et al. (1997). It was here that fa'afaletui originated as a Samoan research method in which elders 'viewed themselves to be a part' (p. 23). This method fundamentally describes the way that information is gathered among different groups or 'fale'. Groups were defined depending on cultural appropriateness according to age, gender, and

96 *Julia Ioane and Athena Tapu Tu'itahi*

relative status. In forming culturally appropriate groupings, discussion of subjects that may be considered tapu or taboo could be introduced with ease. The fale then proceed to weave or 'tui' together the different discussions, topics, and perspectives, and in this process critically reflect on what was discussed. The fa'afaletui method entails discussion, consultation, and validation of important knowledge with all the different community groups and members (Tamasese et al., 2005). Fa'afaletui is translated as fa'a = to make, fale = groups or houses, and tui = the critical process of weaving together different expressions of knowledge from within groups (p. 302).

Fa'afaletui emphasises the value of gathering different perspectives, naming three important perspectives in Samoan culture: the person on top of a mountain, the person sitting on the top of a tree, and the person sitting in a canoe near a school of fish. All the voices that are included in the fa'afaletui enrich the conversation as no one person is left out.

In my research (Tapu Tu'itahi, 2018), I (Athena) have engaged in fa'afaletui as a way to understand different points of view. I found that it deepened my understanding of the research as it gave me many threads to weave together. It must be noted that it can be challenging for a researcher to incorporate many different thoughts and opinions into recordings. However, noting your own thoughts and biases that may arise adds to the richness of the data. In my experience, this method of gathering information, consultation, and discussion leading to consensus came naturally to me as I had seen this process in my family, church, and community groups. Yet it also mimicked some formal research methods taught in academic tertiaries of posing research questions, collating data, looking at the scope of my research, checking my own biases, and being transparent with my work.

The process can be time consuming and there is a lot of transcribing as there are many discussions and focus groups. Going back and forth critically reflecting and consulting has layers of themes and insights that are all valuable. Therefore, a robust research team is needed to help process and translate the data. Fa'afaletui is effective for community scale projects and further development is appropriate so it can be applied to smaller scale research projects.

Pacific research guidelines

When researching Pasifika communities, regardless of whether you are Pacific or non-Pacific researcher, guidelines have been created and provided to support those engaged in such research (Health Research Council of New Zealand, 2014; Massey University, n.d.; University of Otago, 2011). We encourage you to review these prior to any research with Pacific peoples. These guidelines highlight the worldview of Pacific peoples in relation to their values, principles, and protocols. They address concepts of authentic engagement, partnership, and ensuring the safety of Pasifika peoples are protected. The *Pacific Research Guidelines* from the Health Research Council provide information on guiding themes that frame Pacific research. They highlight engagement, respect, and the significance of Indigenous Pacific knowledge. A key feature is the principle of non-maleficence that prioritises a commitment to protect and guard from any harm during a research project. An ongoing concern among Pasifika communities is the lack of consultation and feedback that is provided when researchers undertake studies within and for their community. Even if you are not engaged in Pacific research, these guidelines offer useful frameworks for promoting research that is culturally sensitive, respectful, appropriate, and safe, and, thus, are helpful to other researchers in positions of power and/or privilege.

These guidelines are also helpful in providing *practical steps* in the development, design, and implementation of research with Pacific people. Massey University's Pacific guidelines draw on Pacific principles to be implemented in the research. This includes the respect for relationships and those who hold the knowledge. This draws attention to the message rather than the messenger. It is the notion of 'action speaks louder than words' where one's behaviour and presentation will be the decisive factor as to whether one participates with the research. Given that Pasifika people are generally respectful and humble, they are most likely to participate in research. However, the challenge for researchers is the authenticity of their participation. This is mediated by prioritising the relationship, such as taking time to spend with participants, sharing food, and making sure that names are pronounced appropriately. Respecting knowledge holders is shown by researchers having the humility to genuinely acknowledge that participants are the experts and therefore the time they spend with you as the researcher is to be honoured and acknowledged appropriately.

Using Pasifika research methodologies

Before this can be answered, we recap on some of the values and principles of Pasifika worldviews that we have mentioned. The universal values of respect, reciprocity, and humility are foundational to the existence of Pasifika people. These values are paramount to relationships and how Pasifika people live and interact with one another including the environment and the spiritual world (Ioane & Tudor, 2022). As the values of Pasifika people are universal, these values would not be new to non-Pasifika communities. However, it is the interpretation of how these values would be implemented in a Pasifika context before that *is* the point of difference. For example, respect towards Pasifika people means that the approach is to be people-focussed right from the outset of research. An example of this is to engage with Pasifika people and seek their views on what warrants research in their community. This responds to a 'by Pasifika, for Pasifika' approach where research is led by the Pasifika community.

The past three decades have seen the catalogue of Pasifika methodologies and research steadily grow and develop. Since Smith's (1999) call to decolonise Indigenous research, Pasifika researchers were strengthened and challenged to carve out their identity and bring forward their Pasifika epistemologies.

Today there continues to be a resurgence to claim our Indigenous ways of knowing and learning as well as question the hegemony that has been accepted in the past. Historically, Pasifika communities were researched in clinical trials within Western methods that ultimately excluded the Pasifika community. This put us on the periphery of the research process with little to no recognition of the ethical boundaries of ownership of information and consent. This has shifted significantly towards collaboration with Pasifika, Indigenous knowledge being central, and research standards that promote working together in a reciprocal relationship.

This was not only a move to decolonise research but also an ethical shift towards claiming, demanding, and owning space for Indigenous knowledge and worldviews. The ethical foundation guides and navigates how to invite, include, listen to, plan, and talanoa together in your research. Tagata Pasifika value and recognise this way of relating as the vā that connects us. It is the values of respect and reciprocity, alofa and fa'aaloalo, in following protocol that you as a researcher may be welcomed in.

I believe that Pasifika and non-Pasifika researchers can use these methodologies. However, it is the actions and interactions of standing side-by-side, the preparing and planning, sharing together, working and breaking bread together—that is the measina or taonga of understanding Pacific methodologies and research. The sacred Indigenous knowledge that is shared for the village, community, or group can be offered to both Pasifika and non-Pasifika researchers on the conditions that there are Pasifika researchers co-leading the research team and a Pasifika cultural research advisory/navigation group.

Recommendations for using Pasifika research methodologies

Given the ongoing demand for Pasifika research that is tailored towards authentic engagement with Pacific communities, we are of the view that Pacific research does not necessarily have to be 'led by Pacific, for Pacific'. Whilst this would be the gold standard, we are very aware of the lack of resourcing for Pacific researchers. However, this should not hinder progress with Pasifika research in Aotearoa New Zealand. We propose two solutions for this question.

Solution 1: We believe that any research with Pacific people must be led or at the very least co-led by Pasifika researchers. This is to ensure safety of all researchers as well as protecting Pasifika communities in Aotearoa New Zealand. Furthermore, as a means to improve equity within the academic community, prioritising Pacific leaders to lead and guide research contributes to the development of an authentic partnered approach with Indigenous people and members of the academic community. It is well known that recently there have been more and more calls for academia to reflect Western and Indigenous worldviews. Parsons et al. (2016) conclude that Western ways of understanding need to acknowledge and make room for Indigenous worldviews in order to promote transformational change across systems. Kilian et al. (2019) found in their research of non-Indigenous researchers conducting Indigenous research that institutional barriers and policies often prevented the implementation of recommendations. Whilst this is not a focus of this chapter, we do acknowledge the systemic issues that become barriers to the authenticity of Indigenous research and encourage all researchers to incorporate this as they develop recommendations for their research.

Solution 2: There have been countless times where we are asked to be advisory group members for research that involves Pacific. This is often seen as acceptable practice. However, our concern is that an advisory group is consulted depending on the requirements of the researchers or what the researchers deem appropriate to consult. We believe that this is a fundamental flaw among researchers. You will not know what you do not know, and often many errors and mistakes have been made when researching Pasifika communities and have been attributed to ignorance. On the other hand, or at the very least, we do see value in having an advisory group. However, the terms of reference or the relevance and appropriateness of the advisory group must be discussed with the group first. The extent to which researchers are accountable to the advisory group must also be discussed. The success of this will rely on the quality of the relationship and the ability of both parties to honour and acknowledge Pasifika values and principles of practice.

Conclusion

Pacific research methodologies are available for Pacific and non-Pacific researchers to use when working with Pacific communities. However, there are also instances whereby research with Pacific communities does not necessarily require the use of Pacific methodologies at all times. We ask researchers to always consider the appropriateness of Pacific methodologies and to engage with having Pasifika people lead or (at least) be part of the research team or consult appropriately with a Pasifika advisory group.

It is important to recognise the true meaning and value of relationships within a Pasifika worldview. The identity of Pasifika people is relational (Tamasese et al., 2005) and therefore your role and identity as a researcher will be pivotal to how such communities engage. Therefore, any research with Pasifika people must partner with Pasifika communities right from the outset. To engage and consult with Pasifika communities partway or towards the end of research highlights a lack of integrity and respect to truly serve Pasifika people. We encourage the use of Pasifika methodologies with Pasifika communities, though this needs to be implemented alongside having Pasifika people as part of the research journey, and not just as participants.

References

Anae, M. S. (2010). Research for better Pacific schooling in New Zealand: Teu le va—A Samoan perspective. *MAI Review, 1*, 1–24. http://www.review.mai.ac.nz/mrindex/MR/article/view/298.html

Anae, M. S., Mila-Schaaf, K., & Coxon, E. (2010). *Teu le va—Relationships across research and policy in Pasifika education.* Ministry of Education, New Zealand. https://www.education counts.govt.nz/__data/assets/pdf_file/0009/75897/944_TeuLeVa-30062010.pdf

Fraenkel, J. (2006). Beyond MIRAB: Do aid and remittances crowd out export growth in Pacific microeconomies? *Asia Pacific Viewpoint*, *47*(1), 15–30. https://doi.org/10.1111/j.1467-8373.2006.00300.x

Fua, S. J. (2021). Kakala research framework: A garland in celebration of a decade of rethinking education. In M. 'Otunuku, U. Nabobo-Baba, & S. J. Fua (Eds.), *Of waves, winds and wonderful things. A decade of rethinking Pacific education. Selected papers from the 2011 Vaka Pasifiki Education Conference* (pp. 65–79). https://www.usp.ac.fj/institute-of-education/wp-content/uploads/sites/132/2021/11/Of-Waves-Winds-Wonderful-Things_FINAL51.pdf

Halapua, S. (2003). Walking the knife-edged pathways to peace. Inaugural public lecture of the Ratu Mara Friendship Foundation.

Health Research Council of New Zealand. (2014). *Pacific health research guidelines.* https://gateway.hrc.govt.nz/funding/downloads/Pacific_health_research_guidelines.pdf

Ioane, J. (2017). Talanoa with Pasifika youth and their families. *New Zealand Journal of Psychology*, *46*(3), 38–45. https://www.psychology.org.nz/journal-archive/Talanoa-with-Pasifika-youth-and-their-families-private.pdf

Ioane, J. (2022). Faifai mālie–Balancing ourselves in our journey with Pasifika communities in person-centered and experiential psychotherapy and counselling. *Person-Centered & Experiential Psychotherapies*, *21*(2), 129–143. https://doi.org/10.1080/14779757.2022.2067586

Ioane, J., & Tudor, K. (2022). Family-centered therapy: Implications of Pacific spirituality for person-centered theory and practice. *Person-Centered & Experiential Psychotherapies*, 1–19. https://doi.org/10.1080/14779757.2022.2100812

Ka'ili, T. O. (2005). *Tauhi vā: Nurturing Tongan sociospatial ties in Maui and beyond. The Contemporary Pacific*, *17*(1), 83–114. https://www.jstor.org/stable/23721933

Kidman, J., & Chu, C. (2019). 'We're not the hottest ethnicity': Pacific scholars and the cultural politics of New Zealand universities. *Globalisation, Societies and Education*, *17*(4), 489–499. https://doi.org/10.1080/14767724.2018.1561247

Kilian, A., Fellows, T. K., Giroux, R., Pennington, J., Kuper, A., Whitehead, C. R., & Richardson, L. (2019). Exploring the approaches of non-Indigenous researchers to Indigenous research: a qualitative study. *Canadian Medical Association Open Access Journal*, *7*(3), E504–E509. https://doi.org/10.9778/cmajo.20180204

Lui, D. (2003). *Family: A Samoan perspective.* Mental Health Commission.

Massey University. (n.d.). *Pacific research guidelines and protocols.* https://tinyurl.com/3bmy5hhe

Ministry for Pacific Peoples. (2021). *Pacific Aotearoa status report: A snapshot 2020.* https://www.mpp.govt.nz/assets/Reports/Pacific-Peoples-in-Aotearoa-Report.pdf

Nabobo-Baba, U. (2008). Decolonising framings in Pacific research: Indigenous Fijian Vanua research framework as an organic response. *AlterNative: An International Journal of Indigenous Peoples*, *4*(2), 140–154.

Parsons, M., Fisher, K., & Nalau, J. (2016). Alternative approaches to co-design: Insights from Indigenous/academic research collaborations. *Current Opinion in Environmental Sustainability*, *20*, 99–105. https://doi.org/10.1016/j.cosust.2016.07.001

Salmond, A. (2003). Maori epistemologies. In J. Overing (Ed.), *Reason and Morality* (pp. 237–260). Routledge.

Silipa, S. R. (2008). *Punavai o le malamalama: Spring of illumination: Framework of significant learning concepts and domains in the web of Samoan epistemologies: Cultural context, artefact and traditional oratory.* Working Paper Series, 16. McMillan Brown Centre, University of

Pasifika research methodologies   101

Canterbury. https://ndhadeliver.natlib.govt.nz/delivery/Delivery ManagerServlet?dps_pid=IE786828

Smith, L. T. (1999). *Decolonizing methodologies: Research and Indigenous peoples.* Zed Books.

Tamasese, K., Peteru, C., & Waldegrave, C. (1997). *O le taeao afua the new morning: A qualitative investigation into Samoan perspectives on mental health and culturally appropriate services.* New Zealand Health Research Council.

Tamasese, K., Peteru, C., Waldegrave, C., & Bush, A. (2005). Ole taeao afua, the new morning: A qualitative investigation into Samoan perspectives on mental health and culturally appropriate services. *Australian and New Zealand Journal of Psychiatry, 39*(4), 300–309. https://doi.org/10.1080/j.1440-1614.2005.01572.x

Tapu Tu'itahi, A. (2018). *Navigating the boundaries of two cultural worlds while re-negotiating a space for myself: My journey as a Samoan woman in the AUT psychotherapy course* [Dissertation, Auckland University of Technology]. Tuwhera Open Access Theses & Dissertations. https://openrepository.aut.ac.nz/bitstream/handle/10292/11996/TapuTuitahiA.pdf

Taufe'ulungaki, A., Johansson Fua, S., Manu, S., & Takapautolo, T. (2007). *Sustainable livelihood and education in the Pacific project—Tonga pilot report.* Institute of Education, University of the South Pacific, Suva. http://repository.usp.ac.fj/5383/1/SLEP_TO_Jan_07.pdf

Tecun, A., Hafoka, I., 'Ulu 'ave, L., & 'Ulu 'ave-Hafoka, M. (2018). Talanoa: Tongan epistemology and Indigenous research method. *AlterNative: An International Journal of Indigenous Peoples, 14*(2), 156–163.

Thaman, K. H. (1992, June). Looking towards the source: A consideration of (cultural) context in teacher education. In *Pacific teacher education forward planning meeting: proceedings.* Institute of Education, USP, Suva. http://www.directions.usp.ac.fj/collect/direct/index/assoc/D770044.dir/doc.pdf

Thomsen, S., Tavita, J., & Zsontell, L-T. (2018). *A Pacific perspective on the living standards framework and wellbeing* (DP 18/09). https://www.treasury.govt.nz/publications/dp/dp-18-09

Tuagalu, I. (2008). Heuristics of the Vā. *AlterNative: An International Journal of Indigenous Scholarship, 4*(1), 107–126. https://doi.org/10.1177/117718010800400110

Tunufa'i, L. (2016). Pacific research: Rethinking the talanoa 'methodology'. *New Zealand Sociology, 31*(7), 227–239.

University of Otago. (2011). *Pacific research protocols.* University of Otago. https://www.otago.ac.nz/%20research/otago085503.pdf

Vaioleti, T. M. (2006). Talanoa research methodology: A developing position on Pacific research. *Waikato Journal of Education, 12*, 21–34. https://doi.org/10.15663/wje.v12i1.296

Waitoki, W., Dudgeon, P., & Nikora, L. W. (2018). Indigenous psychology in Aotearoa/New Zealand and Australia. In S. Fernando & R. Moodley (Eds.), *Global psychologies* (pp. 163–184). Palgrave Macmillan.

8 Queering psychotherapy research
Collaborative autoethnography and fossicking

Trish Thompson and Daniel X. Harris

This chapter explores the ways in which collaborative autoethnography can offer a creative-relational means of queering traditional methods and relationships in psychotherapeutic, as well as research, contexts. Drawing on the work of American psychotherapist, psychiatrist, and author Irvin Yalom, we explore the ways in which sharing vulnerabilities and experiences of 'outsiderness' to/with one another can allow not only a trusting therapeutic relationship to be established through creative collaboration. Finally, we consider the process of our inquiry: how our research approach—our 'queer methods'—as collaborators, and former therapist/client, can extend and enrich traditional approaches to both research and psychotherapy.

> A queer methodology, in a way, is a scavenger methodology that uses different methods to collect and produce information on subjects who have been deliberately or accidentally excluded from traditional studies of human behavior. The queer methodology attempts to combine methods that are often cast as being at odds with each other, and it refuses the academic compulsion toward disciplinary coherence.
>
> (Halberstam, 1998, p. 13)

Scavenger methodology

The notion of queering methods—whether in research contexts or therapeutic ones—is not new—see Kong et al. (2003), Browne and Nash (2010), Ferguson (2013), Jackman (2016), and Fish and Russell (2018), amongst others. Autoethnography, as one contemporary methodology that aims to disrupt traditional approaches to research, psychotherapy, and storytelling, 'is situated within a larger set of shifts and changes in qualitative (and post-qualitative) inquiry that followed the "crisis of representation" in anthropology and other disciplines' (Holman Jones & Harris, 2018, p. 2), shifting from the truth-claims of traditional research to the subjective acknowledgements of qualitative knowledge-production and research activities and relationships. Autoethnography is now well-established in fields as diverse as psychology, sociology, social work,

DOI: 10.4324/9781003280859-9

education, anthropology, cultural studies, and more. Here we explore the ways in which critical autoethnography, especially used in a collaborative psychotherapeutic methodology, draws productively on the process of 'scavenging' across multiple disciplines, practices, and lived experiences in order to make collective sense of the power of queering in these overlapping worlds. We distinguish, in metaphoric terms, between scavenging, fossicking, prospecting, and noodling—all Anglo-Australian terms that carry meaning and histories around gathering, informality, and relationality. In this chapter, we use a critical autoethnographic approach in a dialogic format (Holman Jones & Harris, 2018) in order to call attention to mutuality of trust in psychotherapeutic relationships, as well as the reciprocal relationship between personal and cultural narratives in critical autoethnography, a mutuality that seeks to effect change not only in individuals but in socioculture more broadly.

Much has been written, too, about the changes to research and therapeutic practice during the COVID-19 pandemic and multiple lockdowns. The relative success of the 'pivot' to online therapeutic methods for many has led to widespread speculation about what other previous 'necessities' of therapeutic engagement and research practices might be challenged, changed, or abandoned altogether. In 2020, we (Trish and Dan) began 'queering' our therapeutic methods as we too moved to conducting our sessions online, not unlike many other academics and psychotherapists (Békés & Aafjes-van Doorn, 2020; Shklarski et al., 2021). The shift drew our attention to the ways in which it altered our engagement as well as our own expressions of 'self' in our respective roles, from the previously 'known' and 'expected' into an expanded 'other', beyond the constancy of the therapy room (Harris & Thompson, 2020, 2021a, 2021b). In the course of writing these articles and this chapter, we have had rich discussions about time, space, money, confidentiality, and power, amongst other areas of enquiry.

The co-writing of our first article about long-term therapy in late 2020 felt like another extension of this already enhanced therapeutic engagement. Like Gale and Wyatt (2009), we have come to know ourselves differently while getting to know each other through collaborative writing, inviting us to attend more intentionally to our respective narratives woven together from dynamic spaces of both different and shared perspectives, identities, and histories (Yalom, 1991). Like Gale and Wyatt (2009), we too 'have come to see who [we are] as being always in process' and 'in our writing we have come to place more emphasis on the *how* than either the who or the what' of our individual stories (p. 13). The 'we' of us who write this chapter are as much in flux as an event that is unfolding, as are the practices of empathic therapy or ethical research.

Whether as therapist/client, researcher/co-participant, or co-authors, hybrid engagement now offers exciting possibilities not just for a pandemic period to be tolerated, or for a novel change of perspective, but potentially for lasting changes to methods as well. Cultural theorist Sarah Ahmed encourages readers to queer everyday practices as an intervention that 'disturbs the order of things' (Ahmed, 2006, p. 161), allowing possibility to emerge from the breach. In this

104   *Trish Thompson and Daniel X. Harris*

chapter, we encourage readers to consider the ways in which both research and therapeutic practices are relational—including creative-relational (Harris, 2020; Wyatt, 2018)—and not only can manage but maybe even rely on disturbing the order of things in order to facilitate real change and wellbeing.

Pioneering psychotherapist Shaun McNiff (1992, 2009) has led the discourse of what he calls 'expressive arts therapy' for over four decades in detailing the ways in which the range of creative arts modalities can play a powerful role in psychotherapy, can help to heal the mind, soul, and relationships, and enhance the accepted processes of psychotherapy. While art therapy as a field has been growing in acceptance and diversity of approaches since his first work on the matter in 1981, *The Arts and Psychotherapy*, McNiff has consistently explored the ways in which the imaginative and even mystical quality of creativity and arts can combine with the more 'scientific' aspects of psychology and psychotherapy to assist clients and therapists in their shared healing journey. As a foundational arts therapy scholar, we include the 'core questions' he returns to again and again, over 40 years of practice:

> How do you start a session? How does art heal? Why do you drum while people are painting? How much structure do I need to provide? Should I make art together with my clients? How do I deal with the pain and turmoil that this work generates in me? How do I take care of myself when I am working with toxic psychic materials? How effective am I in helping others? How can I improve?
>
> (McNiff, 2009, p. 7)

These, we assert, are questions that do or should concern all therapists, and the arts offer ways of responding that assist both client and practitioner. One beautiful aspect of McNiff's (2009) sustained practice is his acknowledgement that 'uncertainty, toxins, and negative emotions are essential to the work that we do. It is natural for people to feel threatened when invited to express themselves in unfamiliar and vulnerable ways' (p. 8). We too have found that our collaborative writing method/s raises discomfort in ourselves as well as others. While we are clear that the work we are doing is not (trained) in the discipline of art therapy, nor do we claim it as such, there are important overlaps for those who imagine that what we are proposing is new or radical; it is neither.

Anthropologist and philosopher Tim Ingold (2022) asserts that any (research) process that extracts data from a world we then turn away from, in order to construct our version of knowledge about it, is deeply unethical; yet so much of contemporary mental health provision, as well as research 'knowledge creation', does just that. Ingold works to distinguish between harmful binaries such as wisdom/knowledge and self/soul, but he also writes against binaries in general. As we put forward here, binaries are at best reductive and sometimes downright harmful. For instance, while the imbalance of the power relationship between client and therapist has understandable professional implications,

Queering psychotherapy research 105

the binary of 'one who holds knowledge' and 'one who has a deficit' creates a distance that may not be therapeutic, despite the best of intentions. For those who are gender diverse, or who experience mental ill health, or for researchers, co-participants, therapists, and clients (to name just a few), binaries define by contrast, and in doing so reinforce an 'us/them' mentality. The methods that we (Trish and Dan) use as co-authors, and advocate here, look at the fluid nature of how it is to be 'in relation' with another; moving from experiences of feeling different from and similar to one another from one moment to the next (Harris & Thompson, 2021a).

Ingold's (2022) notion of *wisdom* being different from *knowledge* can help understand more deeply the agency brought by both therapy clients, as well as non-researcher participants.

Ingold compares increments of knowledge accruing to adding stones to an isolating wall, 'with which it shores itself up' (p. 3) and alienates the subject from the world; for Ingold, 'knowledge breeds inattention' (p. 3), a kind of turning away from new experience. In this respect, we draw on his premise that 'Knowledge treats the world as its object' (p. 3) but wisdom seeks to be at one with the world through attention and attunement. Too often, in therapeutic and research relationships, the knowledge accumulated by the researcher/therapist is activated as a dualism in which the measure of the efficacy of the relationship is that the therapist/researcher is agentic, and the client/co-participant is receptive. Ingold defines contemporary knowledge-making as a process of capture, a desire to take possession of. By contrast, our queering of methods in/as collaborative autoethnography holds difference but invites messiness, crossover, and interpolation. We seek, in Ingold's words, to enter each other's milieu, to choose radical openness to the world, and to each other. In our collaborative writing as client and therapist, Dan often took the lead and Trish was willing to express uncertainty and vulnerability, inversing the familiar positions we occupied in our therapeutic relationship. The result was a shared voice that strengthened us both.

We use our autoethnographic lens to better understand culture (psychotherapeutic and research practice) through personal experience. By taking a 'queering' approach to both autoethnography and therapy, it becomes possible to

> draw on the practices and politics of queer and queering to offer narrative and theoretical disruptions of taken-for-granted knowledges that continue to marginalize, oppress and/or take advantage of those of us who do not participate or find ourselves reflected in mainstream cultures and social structures—which includes research methodologies.
>
> (Holman Jones & Harris, 2018, p. 4)

We reflect on our 'scavenger methodology' of using what we find at hand in order to deepen our practice: reading, writing, shared memes, TikTok videos, whatever works. As mental and emotional wellbeing is a sociocultural practice, we informally gather (or 'fossick', 'prospect', or 'noodle') shiny discarded (or overlooked) shards of shared sense-making in our improvisational collaborative practice.

By joining the personal and the cultural, we remind ourselves and others of the interconnectedness of belonging and wellbeing. We began joining the personal and cultural, the dialogic and reflective, in our sessions, and then during the COVID-19 pandemic, in a shared Google document. Dan had been invited to contribute an article to a psychotherapeutic journal in Melbourne, Australia, and in turn invited Trish to co-write it with them. The resultant process was a dialogic experiment that used online conferencing platforms, an online shared document, and email exchanges. Our first output was 'A dialogue on hope: Long term therapy and borderline personality disorder' (Harris & Thompson, 2020). This then went on to be rescoped and extended for Victor Yalom's American online site *Psychotherapy.net online*, as a two-part article series: 'Long-term psychotherapy and BPD, Park 1: A dialogue on hope', and then 'Long-term psychotherapy and BPD, Part 2: A dialogue on trust' (Harris & Thompson, 2021a, 2021b). Now, nearly two years on, we have discontinued our therapeutic relationship but our co-authoring one continues to grow. Trish asks questions now about how to take this productive collaborative writing experience back into her sessions with other clients:

Trish: *How does a therapist help a client without acknowledging when the social hegemony excludes their subjectivity? I remember working with a client a couple of years ago. She worked for a community organisation, she held strong views around social justice, and looked for opportunities to speak out about issues that were important to her. She was in a relationship with a man at the time, and identified as queer. Although she was happy with her partner, there was a deep sadness about part of her that felt hidden, not validated, not seen by others. Her relationship fitted into the heteronormative narrative, but it did not tell the whole story. It did not represent all that she was. As therapists, sometimes we can make the mistake of encouraging clients to think that all they need to do is believe in themselves, to not worry about what other people think, to do what is best for them. But sometimes the choice to be yourself might mean you lose a relationship, or you are 'othered' at work, or in your family, or that you feel profoundly alone.*

Another client comes to mind who often felt despair about others making normative judgements about her for which she did not give permission, and there was nothing she could do about this. There is power in the collective, and when the collective thinks a certain way, steeped deeply in heterosexual privilege, to stand up to it can feel exhaustingly hard. Diversity is something people say they value in schools and workplaces while in the same breath they are having 'boy meets girl' conversations with friends as if that is how the story goes.

As I write this, I bring to mind the deep sadness these clients express. They believe in themselves; they don't lack conviction in their identities or a desire to live authentic lives. What they recognise is the human yearning to belong, and to be acknowledged by the tribe as an integral part of the whole. To have their internal sense of self seen and reflected back by those around them. A dissonance in this area is hard to bear.

Dan, by contrast, thinks and writes about how their collaborative writing relationship with Trish not only continues to 'queer' their notion of the

Queering psychotherapy research 107

therapy relationship, but queers their understanding of their own mental health and gender transitioning:

Dan: *I'm thinking about time in relation to my 'transmasculine journey', which is different from my transness of yesterday, or 10 months ago when I started testosterone, or 10 years ago, when I first packed, or 50 years ago, when I first tried to pee standing up. I've been having conversations—some of them with Trish—about how quickly and yet invisibly maybe the queerness of this non-binary time is passing. What will I feel/look/ think like in five years' time? How different might my facial hair be? My chest? My redistribution of body mass? My bottom growth? But even more importantly, perhaps, how different might be my perception of the world, and the world of me? I described recently to a friend what I called my 'slide' into masculinity. What does that mean? At the time I meant that at the beginning of all of this, I never identified with men, although certainly I've always identified with masculinity. But as the testosterone builds up in my body, as I see myself reflected in my mirror and in those around me, I can feel the masculinity growing, and affirming and affinity growing, and I wonder if in five years I will 'be' in my mind a guy and in the world a guy and it will be, maybe, unremarkable to all of us. I want to hold or at least remember this liminal and trembling interim space of non-binary. I am not confident I can—or want to—hold it for long. I struggle with the binariness of my mind. I'm of a certain age, a certain sociality, maybe just a certain biology, I don't know. It's hard for me to hold non-binary orientations, even though I feel them inside in certain ways. Ambivalence. Androgyny. I feel both male and female, not kind of sometimes male and sometimes female, or not either. However, the more I'm 'allowed' to express my maleness, the happier I feel, and this is what makes me think that I will continue sliding along that road maybe into maleness. But what relevance does this hold for queer methods of a not-yet therapeutic model?*

Like queer and even transgender orientations, it is not so much about what certain bodies do with other bodies (Halberstam, 1998), but rather ways of seeing the world, and resisting a static kind of intelligibility. If we apply this to therapeutic relationships, where the relationality and efficacy of what is being 'done' between bodies is not limited to our static identities, roles, or even recognitions in those roles (as 'counsellor', 'client'), then how free might we be to problematise those categories as an extension of attending to the 'behaviours' or 'emotions' under consideration, rather than being limited to roles. This is not about levels of sharing, or content, but rather about thinking of the work of therapy as more fluid than both working on one person's 'problems'.

Queering methods

Queer and transgender scholar Jack Halberstam (2005) draws on Michel Foucault (e.g., 1996) to articulate the shift from queerness as sexuality-related to queer as a way of living, moving, befriending, and taking up space. In laying out their logic of 'queer time' and 'queer space', Halberstam reminds us that queer friendships, networks, and relations are threatening to hegemonic society not related to a way of having sex, but rather as a way of life. While not all LGBTIQA+ persons, says Halberstam (2005), live their lives in radically different ways from their heterosexual counter-parts, … part of what has made queerness compelling as a form of self-description in the past decade or so has to do with the way it has the potential to open up new life narratives and alternative relations to time and space.

(p. 2)

This is the kind of queering that we are concerned with in this chapter, and in taking collaborative writing into therapeutic spaces and relationships. Much as things have changed for queer folks since Halberstam wrote these words over 15 years ago, the power of queer as method, as relationality, as worlding, has only begun to expand into research and therapeutic methods. More recently, Halberstam (2018) asked readers to consider the ways

we might privilege friendship networks over extended families when assessing the structures of intimacy that sustain queer lives, and we might also think about transgenderism in particular as not simply a contrapuntal relationship between bodily form and content but as an altered relation to seeing and being seen.

(p. 87)

As Trish suggests above, working therapeutically with queer-identified clients involves more than simply validating their experience and building their self-esteem. How can therapists assist in the work of re-worlding heteronormative social structures, kinship systems, and altered relations in 'seeing and being seen' within psychotherapeutic and diagnostic contexts?

Transness, Halberstam (2018) suggests, can help us think differently about 'different life narratives, alternative ways of being in relation to others, and new practices of occupying space' (p. 87). This is the promise of bringing 'queer methods' into therapeutic spaces and relationships, and applying them to tra-ditional hierarchical therapist/client power structures. What might be possible, while still therapeutically effective and ethical, if outdated structures of us/them, therapist/client, diagnostician/diagnosed, well/unwell were to be, colla-boratively, dismantled as the shared work of therapy?

Dan: *Becoming a transmasculine person in middle age over the past few years has led me to think in new ways about my mental health and wellbeing too as something that has no end. I have repeated for years one therapist's statement that therapy (or the psyche) is like an onion—just more layers, always more layers to peel away. You don't go to therapy to 'fix' something, you go for deeper understanding, an unfolding of the self. And there's always more to understand. A lifetime of fluidity in different ways. I'm grateful for the liberatory links between my diagnosis with borderline personality disorder and my having the self-acceptance to transition into greater (outward) masculinity.*

In co-writing with Trish, I reflect on how powerful the simple act of permission-giving can be, and was for me. I think about how a lover in Toronto called me handsome and invited me to engage in ways with her sexually that I had desired but never dared experiment with. I'm still befuddled at why/how someone else can/should/did unlock that/something for me that I was not able to unlock for myself, even after coming out gay as a teenager, and doing so much 'work' on myself. Kinship. Being seen. She allowed me to flex a kind of masculine muscle, a queer masculinity that was more than butch but might have been butch then/or at another time in history/or at another place now/or if I were a different person.

The interaction invited me into being someone new.

Then my feelings expanded and showed me there was something more there. The experience didn't want to be bounded, limited.

Then I became a little braver, did a little more. It was iterative.

And therapy is so much the same. It's a process of being seen, validated, invited. Trish has taught me a lot about being a therapist who co-creates with her clients, not 'solves' them or heals them. Is therapy like that itself a creative method?

Trish: *I will never forget Gary (not his real name), the first client I ever had when I worked at a counselling service in Melbourne, which served both the HIV+ and LGBTQI+ community. This client had many stories to share, and happened to be a natural storyteller—animated, humorous, dramatic—and I found myself drawn to him immediately. The story that stood out in the early sessions was the one about the doctor who shared his HIV diagnosis with his mother without him knowing or giving permission, thereby taking away his ability to author this story for himself. He and his family came to Australia to escape a difficult life in his country of origin, and to have a better life in Australia. But the narrative that followed this family was one of fear and disconnection, and of not quite belonging in their new home, which was meant to promise so much. People come to therapy to tell stories and to find meaning. Very often they want to change the story but believe that the problem lies within their identity and how it disconnects them in their relationships with others (White, 2007). Gary told me many stories over the years, like the one about the day he made muffins because it was something he could do instead of killing himself. He heard the idea on the radio, and he had the ingredients. It saved his life. And so, his story goes on and it changes, as all things must.*

Queering methods in psychotherapy

Psychiatrist, author, and psychotherapist Irvin Yalom (2002) tells us, 'The great majority of individuals seeking therapy have fundamental problems in their relationships; by and large people fall into despair because of their inability to form and maintain enduring and gratifying interpersonal relationships' (p. 47). In 2022, the medical model of mental health still dominates much of the curriculum for degrees in psychology and related fields. While the biosocial model encourages broader thinking around what factors contribute to people's experiences of mental health challenges, the common pathway to access help in Australia is to be diagnosed with a mental health disorder by a GP (general practitioner), with cognitive behavioural therapy (CBT) considered the gold standard treatment.

Was Yalom 'queering' traditional psychiatry by relocating the problem from inside the patient (client) as some disorder or disturbance, to between the client and other people? An interpersonal rather than personal problem, and likely one that had roots in earlier interpersonal relationships. Yalom is particularly known for his devotion to group psychotherapy, and its ability to create a social microcosm. In the space of the group, participants are able to pay attention to their interactions with others in the group and see in real time, or as Yalom (2002) calls it, 'the here and now' (p. 46), the ways in which interpersonal relationships evoke the very concerns that brought them to therapy in the first place. Yalom used this idea of the social microcosm in his individual work with clients too, as his belief was that the remedy to the suffering of his patients was to examine the relationship between client and himself as therapist, as a way of revealing the 'problem' and to explore other possibilities in relating to him and thereby others. This puts the therapist clearly in the frame of the work, as an active participant and as one who influences and is open to influence.

More broadly, then, what can therapists understand about a client's relationship to society, not simply those with whom they are in direct relationship? What if the 'problem' is more about the attitude, beliefs, and behaviours of society and the oppressive impact of this on the client? For straight-identifying therapists such as Trish, as members of the mainstream or dominant culture, there is an opportunity when working with queer clients to bring this representational relationship into awareness and disrupt it. This is very much about understanding how the heteronormative narrative of the straight therapist holds systemic power and may suppress the narrative of the queer client. It is about resisting the endowed position of 'knowing' in order to find ways of 'being with' so that differences in experience and identity stay in awareness but give way to a mutual responsiveness that is attuned to the macro and micro, the outside of the therapy room and the inside, and that maybe cultures and communities can become irrelevant while humans are finding a way forward together.

Gabor Maté (2021) explores the notion of therapist 'enoughness', particularly when faced with 'unfixable aspects' of our clients' lives. The temptation to 'know' and 'fix' in the face of this can be seductive, and it might also be a protective mechanism that therapists can use to stay separate from their clients, and to understandably prevent becoming overwhelmed by the trauma that may be present in the room. In resisting the binary of helper/helped, Maté offers the idea of five levels of compassion (ordinary human compassion, compassion of curiosity and understanding, compassion of recognition, compassion of truth, and compassion of possibility) as a way of queering the idea of therapist being the most 'enough' in the room and ministering to the other. In order to 'see the essential reality of the human being before you' (p. 7), Maté says that therapists need 'clear eyes' and to be willing to see what is possible for growth in their own lives, in order to be with and for growth of clients with authenticity.

Trish: *Sara came to see me with some ideas about what she would like to get out of attending sessions, particularly related to her growth as a woman of trans experience. She spent the early sessions testing the waters, and as she told me later, she wanted to give me*

Queering psychotherapy research 111

a clear message that she felt strong in her trans journey. When I think back on that now, and consider the tender and vulnerable terrain we have traversed, I wonder how she saw me then—maybe as someone who had the power to make her feel 'less than', given the heteronormative group I represented. Was she saying to me, 'I've come so far to embrace who I am, please don't tear this down'? If I were to unconsciously sink into my therapist chair and draw on my 'knowledge' of working with gender diverse clients, immediately I enact the binary of distance/closeness, so far are we from one another that neither of us can be seen. How do we be close, these two women of such different beginnings?

There was a session a few months into the work that was pivotal, I think. She was relating a story about trying on her sister's clothes, and this being an experience of joy, but it also had secrecy around it. A memory of my own was immediately evoked and as I sat with Hannah I was filled with fondness for a teenage Trish, who would try on all manner of combinations of clothing in front of a full length mirror. With the bedroom door firmly shut, the mirror gave me some idea of how I wanted to take some version of what I saw as being a woman, into the world. I remember the delight in the experience but also how careful I was to protect it. As this recollection evoked such self-compassion, I told Hannah about it, and in the telling I reflected on our shared journey into womanhood. Although Hannah cried in that moment, she was able to let me know what the moment offered her. 'You see me', she said. And it felt to me that the moment offered even more—a shared experience of being seen, of moving towards, a getting of wisdom rather than a use of knowledge. As Ingold (2022) puts it: 'Where knowledge makes us safe, wisdom makes us vulnerable.' (p. 3).

Hannah loves to write and often brings something she has written to sessions. She is part of a women's storytelling group, and she strongly believes in the healing power of shared stories. She might begin a session reading to me; her words might speak of pain but mostly they convey images of how she is finding strength in her voice, or what she calls 'her dragon is roaring'. We have incorporated the written word into our work almost organically, including agreeing to brief email exchanges with reflections about the sessions. We make suggestions to one another about useful books and articles to read, movies or series to view, and we find examples in art and life to help us see where we are going. And we notice that we are part of what we observe.

As with Hannah, the collaborative writing with Dan has brought forth a profound awareness to a part in me that is like a deep pool of water. It feels calm and still and yet it is in flux, a flow that is multidirectional. I don't know where it starts and ends or whether it is for me or for others, though I think it must be both. And as time has gone on, it feels stronger and more embodied and is changing me and how I work. It resists capturing in order to define it. I lean into it and trust.

Bringing to presence

Ingold (2022) argues the need to 'bring things to presence: not to discover the truth *about* them, but to discover the truth that comes *from* them, in the experience … for wisdom lies *beyond* the facts' (p. 4). Neither good researchers, nor good therapists, limit themselves to the empirical facts. Being effective at either requires intuition, care, and improvisation. Why then does training for

112 *Trish Thompson and Daniel X. Harris*

both largely remain focused on learning, and then following, established protocols bounded by rules and antecedents, at a time of rapid cultural, technological, and social change? There are those within both our fields who do advocate for emergent methods and unorthodox approaches, but they are not the majority. Ingold moves into new materialist territory when he describes the potential of two-way relationships as queering of methods:

> For to observe, it is not enough merely to look at things. We have to join with them, and to follow. And it is precisely as observation goes beyond objectivity that truth goes beyond the facts. This is the moment, in our observations, when the things we study begin to tell us how to observe. In allowing ourselves into their presence rather than holding them at arm's length—in attending to them—we find that they are also guiding our attention. Attending to these ways, we also respond to them, as they respond to us. Study, then, becomes a practice of correspondence, and of care.
>
> (Ingold, 2022, p. 4)

Things—or clients/co-participants—can tell us how they want to be joined (or not joined) with, and collaborative writing offers another tool for a different kind of dialogue. We offer collaborative autoethnographic writing as a 'queer method' in research and therapeutic relationships because it asks readers to join with their co-participants, not just as fellow travellers, but as collaborators. Collaborative autoethnography, or collaborative writing in general, allows the client, the co-participant, the encounter, to guide the attention of the practitioner, and this attunement helps level the hierarchies of power. Yet while some art therapists and others, like Yalom, might find collaborative writing pretty standard fare, most in the psychotherapeutic community still advocate for a 'single' role for therapists working with clients, a clinical role that demands distance, neutrality, and a sole focus on the client.

Fossicking for queer methods

By abandoning outmoded binaries like certainty/uncertainty, us/them, (client/therapist?), queering methods can invite new possibilities in contexts as diverse as psychotherapeutic practice, and research relationships. This kind of re-seeing, or sifting through discarded or overlooked gems in the client/therapist relationship extends not only psychotherapeutic practices, but research practices as well. Ingold (2022) reminds us that we cling to the idea of scientific knowledge based on data out of a deep anxiety about the chaos of life. The only answer, he suggests, is to move from a position of seeking understanding to succumbing to a process of undergoing, 'that at once strips away the veneer of certainty with which we find comfort and security, and opens to pure possibility' (p. 8). Ingold leaves us with a taste for that aspiration, or what he defines as 'the temporal overshoot of a life that always wants to run ahead of itself' (p. 10). We, too, want to run ahead of ourselves in trying new ways of writing, researching, counselling, and being counselled. The risk is greater, but so are the rewards. For us, as for Ingold, the potential lies in the difference he makes between ignorance and not-knowing. Not-knowing, we claim, is the ever-vulnerable and open position of possibility, and of healing, care, and attending.

In this chapter we have tried to suggest the ways in which 'queering' methods by dismantling binaries in both therapeutic and research encounters can be productively disruptive and offer new ways of understanding human (and more than human) experience. In conclusion, we offer the following invitations as a place to start, for those interested in trying out these approaches for themselves. Queer methods might include:

- Discarding identity-based labels in favour of relational ones (or no labels at all).
- Encouraging therapists, clients, researchers, and participants to move toward more relational identification of needs (i.e., 'I'm looking for a therapist who can affirm my transmasculinity') rather than 'I'm looking for a lesbian therapist'.
- Embracing more creative-relational, collaborative ways of working in therapeutic or research relationships, without seeing them as 'additional' roles but rather enhancement of the core client–therapist exchange.
- Considering the purpose of researching methods on psychotherapy as moving away from the idea of capturing knowledge in order to define and apply, to observing and illustrating phenomenological processes as they unfold and offer expansion to all participants.
- Being willing to respond to the evolving experiences of diversity in all its forms, and to advocate that peak bodies for health professionals review and update materials on a regular basis in order to support their members' professional growth.

Through our practice of collaborative writing about ourselves-in-culture (autoethnography), we invite others to queer the boundaries that separate, to disrupt traditional practices that may limit healing and experiencing withness, and in doing so to queer our own notions of selfhood and otherness.

References

Ahmed, S. (2006). *Queer phenomenology: Orientations, objects, others.* Duke University Press.

Békés, V., & Aafjes-van Doorn, K. (2020). Psychotherapists' attitudes toward online therapy during the COVID-19 pandemic. *Journal of Psychotherapy Integration, 30*(2), 238–247. https://doi.org/10.1037/int0000214

Browne, K., & Nash, C. J. (Eds.). (2010). *Queer methods and methodologies: Intersecting queer theories and social science research.* Taylor & Francis.

Ferguson, J. M. (2013). Queering methodologies: Challenging scientific constraint in the appreciation of queer and trans subjects. *Qualitative Report, 18*(13), 1–13. https://doi.org/10.46743/2160-3715/2013.1539

Fish, J. N., & Russell, S. T. (2018). Queering methodologies to understand queer families. *Family Relations, 67*(1), 12–25. https://doi.org/10.1111/fare.12297

Foucault, M. (1996). Friendship as a way of life. In S. Lotringer (Ed.), *Foucault live: Collected interviews 1961–1984* (pp. 204–212). Semiotext(e).

Gale, K., & Wyatt, J. (2009). *Between the two: A nomadic inquiry into collaborative writing and subjectivity.* Cambridge Scholars Publishing.

Halberstam, J. (1998). *Female masculinity.* Duke University Press.

Halberstam, J. J. (2005). *In a queer time and place: Transgender bodies, subcultural lives.* New York University Press.

Halberstam, J. (2018). *Trans★: A quick and quirky account of gender variability.* University of California Press.

Harris, A. M. (2020). Creative-relational inquiry: The power of the small. *Departures in Critical Qualitative Research, 9*(2), 25–29. https://doi.org/10.1525/dcqr.2020.9.2.16

Harris, A., & Thompson, T. (2020). A dialogue on hope: Long-term therapy and borderline personality disorder. *Psychotherapy & Counselling Today, 2*, https://www.pacfa.org.au/portal/Portal/Publications-and-Research/Publications/Magazine.aspx

Harris, A., & Thompson, T. (2021a). *Long-term psychotherapy and BPD, Part 1: A dialogue on hope. Psychotherapy.net Online Journal.* https://www.psychotherapy.net/article/long-term-psychotherapy-and-bpd-part-one

Harris, A., & Thompson, T. (2021b). *Long term psychotherapy and BPD, Part 2: A dialogue on trust. Psychotherapy.net Online Journal.* https://www.psychotherapy.net/article/long-term-psychotherapy-and-bpd-part-two

Holman Jones, S., & Harris, A. (2018). *Queering autoethnography.* Routledge.

Ingold, T. (2022). On not knowing and paying attention: How to walk in a possible world. *Irish Journal of Sociology*, 1–17. https://doi.org/10.1177/07916035221088546

Jackman, M. C. (2016). The trouble with fieldwork: Queering methodologies. In C. J. Nash & K. Browne (Eds.), *Queer Methods and Methodologies* (pp. 113–128). Routledge. https://doi.org/10.4324/9781315603223

Kong, T. S., Mahoney, D., & Plummer, K. (2003). Queering the interview. In J. Holstein & J. F. Gubrium (Eds.), *Inside Interviewing: New lenses, new concerns* (pp. 91–110). Sage.

Maté, G. (2021). *Helper syndrome: When are we enough? Psychotherapy Networker.* https://www.psychotherapynetworker.org/magazine/article/2577/helper-syndrome

McNiff, S. (1992). *Art as medicine: Creating a therapy of the imagination.* Shambhala Publications.

McNiff, S. (2009). *Integrating the arts in therapy: History, theory and practice.* Charles C. Thomas Publishers.

Shklarski, L., Abrams, A., & Bakst, E. (2021). Will we ever again conduct in-person psychotherapy sessions? Factors associated with the decision to provide in-person therapy in the age of COVID-19. *Journal of Contemporary Psychotherapy, 51*(3), 265–272. https://doi.org/10.1007/s10879-021-09492-w

White, M. (2007). *Maps of narrative practice.* Norton.

Wyatt, J. (2018). *Therapy, stand-up, and the gesture of writing: Towards creative-relational inquiry.* Routledge.

Yalom, I. (1991). *Every day gets a little closer: A twice told therapy.* Basic Books.

Yalom, I. (2002). *The gift of therapy.* Piatkus Books.

9 Critical heuristics in psychotherapy research

From 'I-who-feels' to 'We-who-care—and act'

Keith Tudor

Informed by the author's reading of the literature, their own heuristic enquiry, and subsequent publications about heuristic research, as well as their experience of supervising a number of students' own heuristic research—on cultural identity, shame, grief, exercise, psychological infanticide, ambivalence, humour, abrupt endings, and racial microaggressions—this chapter offers a critical reflection on heuristics as a research method and methodology in psychotherapy.

Drawing on both existential philosophy and perceptual psychology, as well as humanistic psychology, to the development of which it also contributed, the heuristic method of research of Clark Moustakas (1967, 1990, 2000/2015; Douglass & Moustakas, 1985) offers a reflective and disciplined approach to research enquiry. While heuristic research is predominantly used to foster and further *self*-enquiry, it is also used to offer depictions of the researcher's enquiry about and, importantly, *with* others. In this sense, psychotherapy itself, as well as the education/training and supervision of its practitioners, may be usefully conceptualised as heuristic practice, for discussion of which see Beck (1979), Moustakas (1990), O'Hara (1986), Merry (2004), and Stevens (2006).

Notwithstanding this connection, heuristics appears as something of a poor relation in the practice of research and an absent one in the literature. It doesn't warrant an entry in Schwandt's (1997) *Qualitative Inquiry: A Dictionary of Terms*; and, despite the fact that, in four editions of the book *Qualitative Inquiry and Research Design* (from Creswell, 1997, to Creswell & Poth, 2018), phenomenological research has been presented as one of five approaches to such inquiry, heuristics has only been mentioned once in passing in the fourth edition. Even in Finlay's (2011) in-depth review of phenomenology, in which she identifies six approaches in and to phenomenology research—descriptive/empirical, hermeneutic/interpretive, lifeworld, interpretive phenomenological analysis, first-person, and reflexive–relational—she refers to Moustakas' (1990) heuristic approach as a reflexive–relational one. This is also true of books about research in psychotherapy and counselling: an early book on the subject edited by Dryden (1996) offers nothing on heuristics, and in McLeod's (2001, 2003) books on research in this field, it gets one brief mention in each. One exception to this is the book *What is Psychotherapeutic Research?* (Loewenthal & Winter, 2006) in which, due to the good offices of Del Loewenthal who promotes heuristic research, there are three chapters reporting research based on the heuristic method (Birchard,

DOI: 10.4324/9781003280859-10

116 *Keith Tudor*

2006; Rose & Loewenthal, 2006; Stevens, 2006). There are also a number of articles on heuristic research in the *Journal of Humanistic Psychology*. More recently, Sultan (2019) has written a whole book on *Heuristic Inquiry*; and I have published two chapters which focus, respectively, on heuristic method and methodology (Tudor, 2017), and on methodology and practice, with specific discussions about a heuristic approach to the literature view and re-view, and to the use of participants (Tudor, 2022).

Informed by my reading of the literature, my own heuristic enquiry (Tudor, 2010), and subsequent publications about heuristic research (Tudor, 2017, 2022), as well as my experience of supervising a number of students' own heuristic research—on cultural identity, shame, grief, exercise, psychological infanticide, ambivalence, humour, abrupt endings, and racial microaggressions—this chapter offers a critical reflection on heuristics as a research method and methodology in psychotherapy.

In terms of identifying with the focus of this particular enquiry, the first of seven concepts Moustakas (1990) identifies as constituting heuristic research, here—and with Jonathan's encouragement—I say something about and give some references to this.

Research

I have a long association with research (for details of which, see Tudor, 2017), in which I have focused on different forms of conceptual research (Leuzinger-Bohleber & Fischmann, 2006). Over the years I have been keen to promote methods and methodologies that are consistent and compatible with the practice of psychotherapy and have resisted—and encouraged others to resist—the pressure to adapt to or conform to what practitioners, researchers, policy-makers, and funders outside psychotherapy often privilege, i.e., empiricism, randomised controlled trials, and quantitative data. It's not that I think these are irrelevant to researching the human condition, it's simply that they are not the most relevant—and, indeed, this perspective is part of my motivation for editing this book (see also Chapter 15).

Criticality

I have also had a long interest in critical thinking—personally, professionally, and politically (for further details of which, see Tudor, 2018). A strong element of this has been to practice in, with, and with regard to, and to think and write about: groups more than individuals; the cultural and political context of psychotherapy; homonomy more than autonomy; we-ness and we psychology more than individual(istic) psychology; and the social and political applications of psychotherapeutic concepts. In this context, while I appreciate the contributions made to the inner life, including unconscious, non-conscious, and intrapsychic processes, reflexivity, etc., I am critical of the widespread and wholescale privileging in psychotherapy of reflection over action and whence and hence the title of this chapter.

Heurism

One of the criticisms of heuristic—and autoethnographic—research, and, more broadly, of psychotherapy itself, is that it is self-focused, self-referential, and,

Critical heuristics in research   117

ultimately, self-centred. As someone who was initially drawn to transactional analysis through radical psychiatry, and who appreciates the emancipatory origins and effects of person-centred psychology; who has contributed to the interplay between politics and psychotherapy (Totton, 2000) for some years (from Embleton Tudor & Tudor, 1994, onwards, and especially through my editorship of *Psychotherapy and Politics International*, 2012–2022), and who is argumentative (Tudor, 2016), and critical (Tudor, 2018), I have a lot of sympathy with such criticism. Ever since I came across heurism and, specifically, heuristic research some 15 years ago, and as much as I value, use, and promote it, I have had a nagging sense of disquiet, especially given its focus on the self, with regard to its cultural and political relevance. I have reflected on this disquiet and unease and, to some extent, addressed it in my own work (Tudor, 2017, 2022), as well as encouraging others to do so (see, especially, Grennell, 2014; Hammond, 2016; Hill, 2022; and McCann, 2022). I realise that this concern, issue, experience, and knowledge of the phenomena (of disquiet and unease) have become, in Moustakas' (1990) term, a 'lingering presence' (p. 11), and so I am particularly delighted to be transforming this nagging or lingering into these lines and pages. Thus, in this chapter, in order to promote the philosophical congruence between methodology and method, and consistent with the critical perspective of the book, I address two areas of heuristic enquiry—language, and self *and* society—discussion of which I suggest and hope will help transform heuristic research in psychotherapy.

Language

From the Greek εὑρίακειυ, and cousin to εὕρηκα (heúrēka) meaning 'I have found it', the word heuristic means to find, to find out, to discover, to devise, to invent, and to procure. Most, if not all writers about heuristic research emphasise this sense of discovery: Douglass and Moustakas (1985) state that 'Perhaps more than any other component, passion in the process of discovery distinguishes heuristic search from other models of human science' (p. 41), while Moustakas (1990) suggests that 'The process of discovery leads investigators to new images and meanings regarding human phenomena, but also to realizations relevant to their own experiences and lives' (p. 9). In his (one) reference to heuristics, McLeod (2003) describes it as 'a powerful discovery-oriented approach to research.' (p. 97). What follows from this, then, is that the language used in and about heuristic research reflects—or should reflect—the language of discovery, which, as Souba (2011) puts it, 'entail[s] "languaging" the unknown' (p. 53). In this sense, I suggest that the language of heuristics is engaged, descriptive, experiential, open, reflective, creative, improvised, emergent, shared, unique, and uncertain. This is different from that of the dominant empirical paradigm in research in general, in health and psychology, and in much of psychotherapy. Thus, in the face of theoretical bias that privileges certain forms of knowledge and science over others, and vested interests in

118 *Keith Tudor*

research funding, it requires some courage to maintain the philosophical congruence of a particular approach and to follow its logic through the research.

One example of this in psychotherapy research is with regard to the literature review. The 'gold standard' of such a review is predominantly viewed as being a systematic one. This, however, is only one kind of literature review amongst others (for a discussion of which, see Munn et al., 2018), and, moreover, is based on a specific methodology of empiricism (see Xiao & Watson, 2017). Also, systematic literature reviews tend to restrict the source material to what is regarded as scholarly work—i.e., certain forms of writing in certain forms of publication (peer-reviewed journals). If we are adopting and embodying a heuristic approach and wanting to maintain a consistency between methodology (the philosophy underpinning the method) and method (the practice), then we need to conceptualise and undertake a heuristic *way* of viewing and re-viewing the literature about our chosen area for research (for further discussion of which, see Tudor, 2022). This approach also extends to *what* we are viewing and re-viewing: Moustakas (1990) himself writes about returning to 'lyric poetry, autobiography and biography' (p. 10), while Sultan (2019) notes a wide range of 'sources of information' (p. 108) which include, in addition to literature and transcripts, 'artifacts such as memos, photos, audio recordings, and works of art' (p. 108).

There are debates within and beyond heuristic research about its philosophical—and, therefore, methodological—basis. Patton (2002) views it as a form of phenomenological inquiry; and, as I note above, Finlay (2011) categorises it as a reflexive–relational approach to phenomenology research. Within heuristics, it is a little more complex—a complexity in which I discern three strands.

1 Heuristic research does not prescribe a methodology

This is the position put forward by Douglass and Moustakas (1985): 'As a conceptual framework of human science, heuristics offers an attitude with which to approach research, *but does not prescribe a methodology* [emphasis added]' (p. 42). This perspective is quite radical (as in getting to the roots) in that it demands that the researcher articulate their own methodology. In this sense or strand, I suggest that heuristic research is more amenable than many other Western approaches to engagement with cross-cultural research (see Djuraskovic & Arthur, 2010; Grennell-Hawke & Tudor, 2018; Hill, 2022; McCann, 2022; Williams, 2020).

2 Heuristic research is based on specific methodology—and underlying philosophy

Following on from their point about discovery, Douglass and Moustakas (1985) state that the object of such discovery is 'the nature of the problem or phenomenon as it exists in human experience … [and thus that] this orientation makes palpable a theoretical marriage of existential philosophy and perceptual

Critical heuristics in research 119

psychology' (p. 42). Given Moustakas' emphasis on experience, and the theoretical influences on his own work (including those of Buber, Kierkegaard, Bridgman, Gendlin, Polanyi, Jourard, and Rogers), I suggest that Moustakas and his heuristic research is better described as experiential and existential, and, therefore, drawing on an underlying philosophy of experientialism (which goes back to the work of Immanuel Kant), and existentialism (which is reflected in Moustakas' work by Kierkegaard). This is also consistent with Douglass and Moustakas' (1985) distinction between heuristics and phenomenology:

> Whereas phenomenology encourages a kind of detachment from the phenomenon being investigated, heuristics emphasizes connectedness and relationship ... phenomenology loses the persons in the process of descriptive analysis, in heuristics the research participants remain visible .... Phenomenology ends with the essence of experience; heuristics retains the essence of the person in experience.
>
> (p. 43)

Sultan (2019) notes another distinction between the two which is that while, in phenomenological research, it is not necessary to have any personal experience of the subject under investigation, in heuristic research, it is—though this has also been questioned by researchers who either ignore or modify this requirement or expectation (see Kumar & Casey, 2017; Shantall, 1999).

In her work, Sela-Smith (2002) criticises Moustakas (1990) for confusing the issue of methodology by laying out (in the first three chapters of his book on *Heuristic Research*) its experiential base and then (in the last two chapters of the same book) promoting a more phenomenological focus and, therefore, basis to heuristic inquiry. In discussing Moustakas' shift of emphasis from subjective experience to external observation, especially with regard to validation, Sela-Smith (2002) speculates that he did so 'in attempting to make his method more acceptable to positivist science' (p. 79).

Clearly heuristic research is closely aligned to humanistic psychology (see Douglass & Moustakas, 1985). In addition to phenomenology, experientialism, existentialism, and humanism, a number of researchers have drawn on other methodologies to inform their heuristic inquiry: narrative (Sela-Smith, 2002); hermeneutic (Ferendo, 2004; Haertl, 2014); transpersonal psychology (Ferendo, 2004; Meents, 2006); holism (Ozertugrul (2015, 2017b); constructionism (Schulz, 2015); empiricism and social constructionism (Sultan, 2019); and imaginative, creative approaches (Williams, 2020).

3 Heuristics is both a methodology and a method

In many ways, this is consistent with models that define and emphasise *approaches* to research such as humanistic (American Psychology Association, 2005; Polkinghorne, 1982) and person-centred (Barrineau & Bozarth, 1989), in that they describe both a method (practice) and a methodology (theory of practice).

120   *Keith Tudor*

In all of this, language is crucial in defining and clarifying the terms of the research as well as the position of the researcher. In her discussion of the language of research and, specifically, in Moustakas' (1990) method, Sela–Smith (2002) identifies three languages:

1 'I feel'-oriented language

This is the language of the experiencing 'I' and of surrender to the research process, implicit in the first three chapters of Moustakas' (1990) work; it is for Sela–Smith (2002), 'the language of internal focus, the "I", feeling in the present and alive in the moment, even when the present "I" is remembering a painful past, for it is the feeling that connects the past to the present' (p. 79).

2 First-person 'reporting'-oriented language

This is 'a third-person abstraction of the experiencing "I". It is an external language, even though it may be the individual doing a self-report .... The stance is past-focused.' (pp. 79–80)

3 Third person 'reporting'-oriented language

This is this the same perspective on language as the second kind (above), the only difference being that is reported by a third person.

Having made these distinctions, Sela–Smith goes on to make an important point:

> Whenever the second language stance (reporting) is substituted for the first stance (feeling), there can be confusion of the first with the third stance (observing). I think I know what an experience is in general, but I do not connect to the specific, present, alive, feeling, where what is felt can be truly known, which can lead me to the tacit levels where my feelings are connected to meanings.
>
> (p. 80)

On this basis, I suggest some revision of the language used in heuristic research in order to encourage greater precision and congruence between methodology (or underpinning philosophy) and method.

From inquiry to enquiry

I have always been surprised that the one or, by now, two generations of heuristic researchers have uncritically adopted Moustakas' (US English) spelling of the word 'inquiry'. Traditionally, in UK, New Zealand, and other forms of English, 'inquire' is used for formal (and legal) investigations, while 'enquire' means 'to ask'. Given this, and the association of phenomenological therapy (e. g., Spinelli, 2006) and heuristic research with discovery, asking, and facilitating

Critical heuristics in research 121

self-search, i.e., *asking with*, as distinct from the certainty of investigation and finding, i.e., *investigating into*, 'enquiry' seems more congruent with the spirit and practice of heuristics.

From illumination as a stage or phase to a process or series of moments

Along with discovery, illumination is at the heart of heuristic enquiry. As Moustakas (1990) himself puts it: 'Heuristic inquiry is a process that begins with a question or problem which the researcher seeks to illuminate or answer' (p. 15). Taking inspiration from the Greek origins of heuristics and its association with discovery, it is clear that illumination is a process. Indeed, in his original description of this 'phase', Moustakas (1990) writes about it as 'a process ... that occurs naturally ... a breakthrough ... an awakening ... [happening] at once ... [a] process' (pp. 29–30). Such illuminations do not occur conveniently between the heuristic stages or phases of incubation and explication and so should not be viewed as forming a certain and invariant part of a stage theory but, rather, as illuminative, 'eureka' moments through the research.

From literature review to literature view—and re-view

As I have suggested elsewhere (Tudor, 2022) and above, in research, the term 'literature review' usually refers to a specific method, with its underlying methodology, of reviewing literature. As heuristic research proposes a different view of this process, I suggest the terms 'literature view' and, later in the process and write-up of the research, 'literature re-view' as more consistent with heuristics and less confusing with other approaches.

From data collection to gathering information from immersion and dialogue

Similarly, data collection carries a sense both of objectivity and of ownership, each of which are problematic from a heuristic perspective—see also Kukatai and Taylor (2016) for Indigenous perspectives about data sovereignty. As Sultan (2019) puts it: 'Data collection for heuristic research transcends the mere idea of gathering information. In heuristic inquiry data collection is about immersing yourself within your topic through self-dialogue, as well as dialogue with individuals who share your interest' (pp. 122–123).

From interviews to open and co-creative dialogue

Even when heuristic researchers do engage participants—who are usually referred to as 'co-researchers'—the 'interviews' are semi-structured. While the word 'inter-view' suggests some interaction and dialogue, generally speaking, it represents more of a one-person psychology (Stark, 1999) in which the researcher is inter*viewing* the subject who, thereby, becomes more of an object. Kvale (1994) examines this in his work on *InterViews* as conversation informed by hermeneutics and phenomenology. The term 'open and co-creative dialogue' reflects an approach to research which represents a two-person psychology.

122 *Keith Tudor*

From analysing the data to dialoguing with the data

Similarly, the language of 'analysis' and 'analysing' doesn't sit so well with a heuristic approach founded in humanistic psychology and, ultimately, relational therapy. Although Moustakas (1990) uses the phrase, like Sela-Smith, I speculate that he did so in order to accommodate a more positivist approach to research and writing. Given Buber's (1937) influence on the concept of dialogue in humanistic psychology, I suggest that this word represents a heuristic relationship to data. This is well presented in Ozertugrul's (2017b) heuristic self-search inquiry into one experience of obsessive-compulsive disorder in which he uses a dialogic/dialectic approach to data. Nevertheless, and notwithstanding the specific and even partial focus of any research, Sultan (2019) argues that the purpose of self-dialogue 'is to attain a holistic understanding of the phenomenon being explored through self-exploration and self-disclosure' (p. 85).

Self *and* society

According to Sela-Smith (2002), Moustakas' (1990) work represents a shift of focus in research 'from the self's experience of the experience to focusing on the idea of the experience' (p. 53), a shift that she attributes to Moustakas' own resistance to experiencing unbearable pain. As a result, Sela-Smith argues, there are some significant differences between what Moustakas introduced as his theory of heuristics, especially in the first three chapters of his book *Heuristic Research* (Moustakas, 1990), and his application of the heuristic method, as presented in the last two chapters of the same book. Based on her re-reading of Moustakas and the experience of her own heuristic *self-inquiry*, Sela-Smith (2001) identifies six components in heuristic research—i.e., self-experience, inward reach (for tacit awareness and knowledge), surrender, self-dialogue, self-search, and transformation. Using these components as factors, she then conducted a review of 28 research documents whose authors claimed to have followed Moustakas' research method, of which she considered only three to have fulfilled the method successfully. In advancing her critique, she draws on Wilber's (1997) analysis of knowledge, based on two axes that form four quadrants, all of which, according to Wilber, need to be represented in any knowledge system (see Figure 9.1).

Sela-Smith's (2001, 2002) critique of Moustakas' methodological and epistemological inconsistency is useful in a number of ways:

Individuality

Interior view	Interior—'I' Intentional Subjective	Exterior—you (it) Behavioural Objective	Exterior view
	Interior—'we' Intersubjective Cultural	Exterior—them (it) Interobjective Social	

Collectivity

Figure 9.1 The four quadrants of knowledge systems (Wilber, 1997).

Critical heuristics in research   123

- In re-aligning heuristic methodology and method (theory and application, as she puts it), especially with regard to refocusing on experience, as distinct from the idea and phenomena of experience.
- In reclaiming the value of the interior 'I', and, therefore, reasserting the importance of the researcher's lived experience of the focus of their particular enquiry—which she encapsulates in the phrase '*I-who-feels*' as summarising the experience of living in the upper-left quadrant of Wilber's model.
- In acknowledging the process of resistance to feeling in the (re)connection to the 'I-who-feels' (a phrase she uses to represent the upper-left quadrant of Wilber's conceptualisation of knowledge systems). From this perspective, resistance is futile.
- In promoting the importance of surrender; indeed, she views surrender (to the feelings of the experiencing 'I') as the vehicle for self-transformation as it 'carries the researcher to unknown aspects of self and the internal organizational systems not normally known in waking state consciousness' (Sela-Smith, 2002, p. 59).

Sela-Smith's work is also important in challenging researchers to consider the purpose of co-participants and the nature of validity in heuristic research: 'Validity of the self-experience is established by *similar* [emphasis added] experiences of others; yet validity in subjective discovery-research is not possible by *comparing* [emphasis added] to others' experience' (p. 76). She goes on to argue that, if co-participants are used in heuristic self-search enquiry, they are valuable

> as reflectors of possible areas of resistance that may be out of conscious awareness in the form of denial, projection, or incomplete search. This sends the researcher back into the self to continue the self-search into deeper or more distant tacit dimensions, thus allowing the transformation to be more expansive.
>
> (p. 78)

However, in emphasising the self-search nature of heuristic self-search inquiry (HSSI), and deeper engagement with and exploration of the interior 'I', intentional and subjective knowledge, Sela-Smith appears to surrender to individualism. While there are numerous references in her article to the concept 'I-who-feels', there is only one reference to consciousness of the 'we' (the lower-left quadrant in Wilber's conceptualisation); and most of her references to 'transformation' are to 'self-transformation'. For those of us who are concerned about the extrapsychic as well as the intrapsychic, and who draw on the tradition of 'we' psychology (Künkel, 1984) more than individual(istic) psychology, or, indeed, who draw on other, non-Western wisdom traditions, this poses a problem. In this part of the chapter, I suggest three (re)solutions of this problem which help us shift from 'I-who-feels' to a 'we-who-care' perspective.

124   Keith Tudor

Expanding experience

In heuristic research, it is widely accepted that the researcher needs to have experience of the subject they are researching. This is not to say, however, that they cannot or should not draw on the experience of others, even if the focus of the research is themselves (following Sela-Smith's point on the reflective role of co-participants as noted above; see also top-left quadrant of Figure 9.2). Moreover, the researcher may want to research the experience of others with the same or similar experiences, a process that may include the creation or co-creation of depictions that capture something of a collective experience (which represents research conceptualised in the bottom-left quadrant of Figure 9.2). Indeed, for Moustakas (1990), an important element of the explication phase of the heuristic method is when 'The researcher brings together discoveries of meaning and organizes them into a comprehensive depiction of the essences of the experience' (p. 31). This emphasises the individual or subject-*in-context*, an 'I' whose experience encompasses and is informed by that of others. Sultan (2019) highlights the difference between these approaches more sharply when she suggests that for the researcher engaged in HSSI to ignore the experience of others is 'leaning towards the arrogant, as it assumes that only the experience of the researcher is valid, which is dismissive of others' experiences of a potentially universal phenomenon' (p. 27).

I suggest that Wilber's (1997) quadrant model is a useful framework for thinking about expanding the range of experience(s) that interest heuristic researchers in ways that maintain the philosophical congruence and theoretical integrity of the research. It doesn't mean that all heuristic research has to encompass all quadrants, though it may. Figure 9.2 summarises Wilber's four quadrants with regard to heuristic research.

Taking this further, if we are truly living a 'we' psychology, we might consider starting our consideration of the subject of research enquiry by consulting others—for instance, those in marginalised communities who may have useful insights into what we or I might research. I remember being touched by a

Interior—'I' Intentional Subjective Researched through heuristic self-search inquiry (Sela-Smith, 2002)	Exterior—you (it) Behavioural Objective Researched through a range of literature reviews
Interior—'we' Intersubjective Cultural Researched through heuristic enquiry involving co-participants (Moustakas, 1990)	Exterior—them (it) Intersubjective Social Researched through heuristic literature reviews (views and re-views), for example, through 'heuristic engagement' or 'heuristic comparison' (Hiles, 2001)

Figure 9.2 The four quadrants of Wilber's (1997) knowledge systems applied to heuristic research enquiry.

Critical heuristics in research   125

conversation with a colleague some years ago about undertaking a doctorate in which she said that she didn't particularly mind what she researched and that if I knew of something that might be useful, she'd be open to suggestions about possible topics to research. While this could be interpreted as representing a certain disengagement and passivity on my colleague's behalf, I experienced and read it as not only generous but genuinely other-centred, embodying what Schmid (2006) views as constituting 'a Thou–I relationship and an "epistemology of transcendence"' (p. 240).

Consensual validation

Qualitative research has its own perspectives about validation and verification— see Lincoln and Guba (1985), Eisner (1991), and Creswell and Poth (2018)— which challenge traditional and hegemonic (quantitative) perspectives on this aspect of research. (My particular favourite in this regard is Lather's (1993) concept of 'voluptuous validation' in which the researcher sets out to under- stand more than can be known and to write towards that which they do not understand.) This is no less true in heuristic research, about which Moustakas (1990) is very clear: 'Since heuristic inquiry utilizes qualitative methodology in arriving at themes and essences of experience, validity in heuristics is not a quantitative measurement that can be determined by correlations or statistics. The question of validity is one of meaning' (p. 32). Drawing on Bridgman's (1950) emphasis on the subjective basis of validation and Polanyi's (1969) emphasis on the responsibility of the researcher, Moustakas (1990) continues by asking—and answering—a crucial question of the heuristic researcher:

> Does the ultimate depiction of the experience derived from one's own rigorous, exhaustive self-searching and from the explications of others present comprehensively, vividly, and accurately the meanings and essences of the experience? This judgment is made by the primary researcher, who is the only person in the investigation who has undergone the heuristic inquiry from the beginning formulation of the question through phases of incubation, illumination, explication, and creative synthesis not only with himself or herself, but with each and every co-researcher. The primary investigator has collected and analyzed all of the material—reflecting, sifting, exploring, judging its relevance or meaning, and ultimately elu- cidating the themes and essences that comprehensively, distinctively, and accurately depict the experience.
>
> (p. 32)

Although Moustakas places great emphasis—and responsibility—on the researcher, he does suggest that verification is enhanced by returning to parti- cipants involved in the research, while Sultan (2019) asserts that embodied reflexivity includes and integrates self–self, self–other, and self–world reflexiv- ities. Moustakas' (1990) view of verification is that it is a process whereby the

126   *Keith Tudor*

researcher ensures 'that the explication of the phenomenon and the creative synthesis of essences and meanings actually portray the phenomenon investigated' (p. **x**). Thus, and drawing on Eisner's (1991) standard of 'consensual validity', I suggest that other colleagues, including peers, supervisors, examiners (for an example of which, see Tudor, 2018), and peer-reviewers, add to the credibility of heuristic research.

Writing about what he had learned from his experience of working with people, Rogers (1961) states that 'What is most personal is most general' (p. 26). He continues: 'what is most personal and unique in each one of us is probably the very element which would, if it were shared or expressed, speak most deeply to others' (p. 26). Similarly, Moustakas (1990) writes: 'The heuristic process is autobiographic, yet with virtually every question that matters personally there is also a social—and perhaps universal—significance' (p. 15). From the point of view of the person receiving what is personal and shared, whether that is a finding from psychotherapy or research, both these statements suggest that generalisability—a common element, requirement, or standard of validity in research—is also personal, i.e., in the eye of the beholder. Thus, I would add to the researcher, co-researchers, and colleagues as assessors of the relevance and significance of research, the public, including funders, policymakers, and lay readers.

In the context of research in the bicultural nation that is Aotearoa New Zealand, such consensual validation begins (ideally) at the planning stage of any research in order to assess its relevance and potential benefit to Māori as tangata whenua (people of the land). Useful in this is *Te Ara Tika Guidelines for Māori Research Ethics* (Hudson et al., 2010), which provide a framework that triangulates various levels of tika (in this context, research design)—mainstream, Māori-centred, and kaupapa Māori (i.e., that based on Māori customary practice)—with manaakitanga (cultural and social responsibility), whakapapa (relationships), and mana (justice and equity). Honouring this process shifts the focus from an individual(ist) paradigm (or quadrant), represented by the statement 'I-who-feels', to a more collectivist one, represented by the statement 'we-who-care'.

Contextual realism

Given the nature of the heuristic method, and perhaps especially in the phases of initial engagement, immersion, and incubation, there is some antipathy in heuristic circles to external constraints on these processes. Two such constraints, which are commonly experienced by heuristic researchers, and (in my experience) especially students, are: time and evaluation.

Regarding time, Moustakas (1990) is very clear:

> The heuristic research process is not one that can be hurried or timed by the clock or calendar. It demands the total presence, honesty, maturity, and integrity of the researcher who not only strongly desires to know and

Critical heuristics in research   127

understand but is willing to commit endless hours of sustained immersion and focused concentration on one central question, to risk the opening of wounds and passionate concerns, and to undergo the personal transformation that exists as a possibility in every heuristic journey.

(p. 14)

While I agree with Moustakas' view of the demand—and intensity—of heuristic enquiry, and with Sela-Smith's (2002) critique of research conducted and driven by a time clock, I also appreciate what Taft (1933/1973) and others say about the inevitability of time limits, and that these also need to be acknowledged and addressed. As Taft (1933/1973) observes: 'time represents more vividly than any other category the necessity of accepting limitation as well as the inability to do so, and symbolizes therefore the whole problem of living' (p. 12). In the case of the Master's students I currently supervise, this 'limitation' is an allocation of 450 hours in which to write a research dissertation, heuristic or otherwise. Just as Sela-Smith (2002) writes about resistance—in relation to 'unbearable pain' (p. 53), by means of 'denial, projection, or incomplete search' (p. 79), and to Wilber's upper-left quadrant or any self-search—I wonder about the heuristic researcher's resistance to the reality of clock time, by which most researchers have neither 'endless hours' nor the material resources to afford such hours. After all, as Woolf (1929) acknowledges, a woman must have money as well as a room of her own to write fiction. In her work, Sela-Smith (2002) is clearly prioritising and advocating for the personal, individual, subjective interior, for, as she puts it (with reference to Wilber's model): 'Without the Upper Left [quadrant] adequately represented, all others will suffer' (p. 83). I suggest that a holistic view of life, including research, has to represent and, therefore, balance the content and processes of all quadrants—and that authentic engagement with this includes surrender to and enquiry about the resistance to the context and limitations of the research.

For many, evaluation is synonymous with assessment and, as such, has a negative connotation; and, in an academic context, like Sela-Smith, I am concerned about research that is conducted and driven by assessment criteria. As she puts it: 'The spontaneous creative synthesis, the story with embedded transformation, seems to disappear as a research manuscript is formed to fit the requirements of objective positive science' (p. 76). At the same time, I would apply a similar analysis as applied above to the limitation—or reality—of time and resources to that of evaluation.

All research is evaluated and needs to be valuable. If the research lies only within the upper-left quadrant of Wilber's model, and especially if it is embargoed and unpublished, then it runs the risk of being self-referential. In the case of the Master's students (referred to above), one of the learning outcomes by which their dissertations are assessed is to 'Reflect on and evaluate the significance of the research in the discipline area' (Auckland University of Technology, 2022, p. 127). This requires the student and especially those using heuristic and autoethnographic methodologies to reflect out of the box—or

128   *Keith Tudor*

quadrant—to include the interior we, i.e., other known colleagues with whom the student identifies or associates (bottom-left quadrant in Figure 9.2) as well as the exterior them, i.e., the discipline area more broadly (bottom-right quadrant). Personally, I don't think enough is made of this particular learning outcome, for an evaluation of which, see Tudor and Francis (2022).

Conclusion: Personal, theoretical, and social transformation

Heuristic research is clearly transformative on a personal level, a point that Moustakas (1990) makes and Sela-Smith (2002) emphasises, and to which numerous research dissertations, theses, and articles attest. Indeed, it is one of six components Sela-Smith identifies as intrinsic to heuristic enquiry—i.e., that 'There is evidence that transformation has taken place by way of a "story" that contains the transformation and may transform those who "read" it' (p. 69). Heuristic research is also viewed as more general and universal. Perhaps echoing Rogers' (1961) maxim, 'What is most personal is most general' (p. 26), Moustakas (1990) writes: 'The heuristic process is autobiographic, yet with virtually every question that matters personally there is also a social—and perhaps universal—significance' (p. 15). However, both Moustakas' and Sela-Smith's visions of the transformative potential of heuristic research rely heavily on the impact of the story of the researcher's self-transformation (and, for Sela-Smith, of the impact of their acceptance of surrender), as it were, the 'I-who-feels-and-communicates-effectively'. A key to addressing this is the researcher's own positionality, which may—and, arguably, should—draw on social as well as individual consciousness.

On a theoretical level, as part of the large family of Western qualitative research theories (including methodologies and methods), heuristic research has helped make a paradigm shift to claiming and re-claiming the value and validity of subjective experience and knowing. Heuristic researchers are also making exciting connections between heuristics and developmental action inquiry (see Ozertugrul, 2017a); heuristics and social constructivism (Sultan, 2019); and, here in Aotearoa New Zealand, between heuristics and kaupapa Māori research theory (see Grennell, 2014; Hill, 2022). Such initiatives help shift heuristic research itself into areas of 'we psychology', represented more by the 'we-who-care-and-act'.

However, as far as the wider, social, transformative impact of heuristics is concerned, Sela-Smith (2002) is quite hesitant: 'When researchers fully immerse themselves in the Upper Left quadrant of experiencing the feelings by moving through resistance and remaining focused until self-transformation occurs, I suspect that there will there be a potential for social transformation' (p. 83).

Given the state of the world, and the need for social and environmental action, suspecting potential appears (to least to me) a little slow. Writing about tacit knowing, Polanyi (1966) suggests that:

> Having made a discovery, I shall never see the world again as before. My eyes have become different; I have made myself into a person seeing and

Critical heuristics in research   129

thinking differently. I have crossed a gap, the heuristic gap, which lies between problem and discovery.

(p. 143)

The question now is whether heuristics can help researchers cross the research–practice gap, which lies between discovery and action and, in this context, most particularly, psychosocial action. I hope that, by suggesting a certain de-centring of the researcher and a heuristic re-centring of the research, this chapter has answered—or begun to answer—this question.

References

American Psychology Association Division 32 (Humanistic Psychology) Task Force. (2005). Development of practice recommendations for the provision of humanistic psychosocial services. Copy in possession of Keith Tudor.

Auckland University of Technology. (2022). *Postgraduate handbook 2022*. https://student.aut. ac.nz/__data/assets/pdf_file/0018/510048/AUT-Postgraduate-Handbook-2022-V1. 3-September-2022-Final.pdf

Barrineau, P., & Bozarth, J. (1989). A person-centered research model. *Person-Centered Review*, 4(4), 465–474.

Beck, G. (1979). Heuristic psychotherapy [Unpublished paper]. Merrill-Palmer Institute.

Birchard, T. (2006). Researching sensitive and distressing topics. In D. Loewenthal & D. Winter (Eds.), *What is psychotherapeutic research?* (pp. 153–168). Karnac.

Bridgman, P. (1950). *Reflections of a physicist*. Philosophical Library.

Buber, M. (1937). *I and thou* (R. G. Smith, Trans.). T. & T. Clark.

Creswell, J. W. (1997). *Qualitative inquiry and research design*. Sage.

Creswell, J. W., & Poth, C. N. (2018). *Qualitative inquiry and research design* (4th ed.). Sage.

Djuraskovic, I., & Arthur, N. (2010). Heuristic inquiry: A personal journey of acculturation and identity reconstruction. *The Qualitative Report*, 15(6), 1569–1593. https://doi.org/ 10.46743/2160-3715/2010.1361

Douglass, B., & Moustakas, C. (1985). Heuristic inquiry: The internal search to know. *Journal of Humanistic Psychology*, 25(3), 39–55. https://doi.org/10.1177/0022167885253004

Dryden, W. (Ed.). (1996). *Research in counselling and psychotherapy: Practical applications*. Sage.

Eisner, E. W. (1991). *The enlightened eye*. Macmillan.

Embleton Tudor, L., & Tudor, K. (1994). The personal and the political: Power, influence and authority in psychotherapy. In P. Clarkson & M. Pokorney (Eds.), *The handbook of psychotherapy* (pp. 384–402). Routledge.

Ferendo, F. J. (2004). A heuristic and hermeneutic inquiry: Ken Wilber and personal transformation [Unpublished doctoral thesis]. Union Institute and University.

Finlay, L. (2011). *Phenomenology for therapists: Researching the lived world*. Wiley.

Grennell, N. (2014). *What is the experience of being both Māori and Pākehā? Negotiating the experience of the hybrid cultural object* [Master's dissertation, Auckland University of Technology]. Tuwhera Open Access Theses & Dissertations. https://openrepository. aut.ac.nz/bitstream/handle/10292/7710/GrennellN.pdf

Grennell-Hawke (Ngai Tahu, Ngai Mutunga), N., & Tudor, K. (2018). Being Māori and Pākehā: Methodology and method in exploring cultural hybridity. *The Qualitative Report*, 23(7), 1530–1546. https://doi.org/10.46743/2160-3715/2018.2934

130   *Keith Tudor*

Haertl, K. (2014). Writing and the development of the self-heuristic inquiry: A unique way of exploring the power of the written word. *Journal of Poetry Therapy, 27*(2), 55–68. https://doi.org/10.1080/08893675.2014.895488

Hammond, M. (2016). *Therapists' experience of working with shame* [Master's dissertation, Auckland University of Technology]. Tuwhera Open Access Theses & Dissertations. https://openrepository.aut.ac.nz/bitstream/handle/10292/10186/HammondM.pdf

Hiles, D. (2001, October). Heuristic inquiry and transpersonal research [Conference presentation]. Centre for Counselling and Psychotherapy Education Conference, London, UK. http://psy.dmu.ac.uk/drhiles/HIpaper.htm

Hill, J. (2022). *Te whakatere i ngā awa e rua (Navigating the two rivers): A heuristic investigation of Māori identity as a student psychotherapist* [Master's dissertation, Auckland University of Technology]. Tuwhera Open Access Theses & Dissertations. https://openrepository.aut.ac.nz/bitstream/handle/10292/15268/HillJ.pdf

Hudson, M., Milne, M., Reynolds, P., Russell, K., & Smith, B. (2010). Te ara tika guidelines for Māori research ethics: A framework for researchers and ethics committee members. Health Research Council of New Zealand. https://www.hrc.govt.nz/sites/default/files/2019-06/Resource%20Library%20PDF%20-%20Te%20Ara%20Tika%20Guidelines%20for%20Maori%20Research%20Ethics_0.pdf

Kukatai, T., & Taylor, J. (2016). Data sovereignty for Indigenous peoples: Current practice and future needs. In T. Kukatai & J. Taylor (Eds.), *Indigenous data sovereignty: Toward an agenda* (pp. 1–22). Australian National University.

Kumar, S., & Casey, A. (2017). *Work and intimate partner violence: Powerful role of work in empowerment process for middle-class women who experience intimate partner violence. Community, Work & Family.* http://dx.doi.org/10.1080/13668803.2017.1365693

Künkel, F. (1984). *Fritz Künkel: Selected writings* (J. A. Sanford, Ed.). Paulist Press.

Kvale, S. (1994). *InterViews: An introduction to qualitative research interviewing.* Sage.

Lather, P. (1993). *Getting smart: Feminist research and pedagogy with/in the postmodern.* Routledge.

Leuzinger-Bohleber, M., & Fischmann, T. (2006). What is conceptual research in psychoanalysis? *International Journal of Psycho-Analysis, 87*(5), 1355–1386. https://doi.org/10.1516/73MU-E53N-D1EE-1Q8L

Lincoln, Y. S., & Guba, E. G. (1985). *Naturalistic inquiry.* Sage.

Loewenthal, D., & Winter, D. (Eds.). (2006). *What is psychotherapeutic research?* Karnac.

McCann, M. (2022). *Invisible wounds: A heuristic exploration of unintentional racial microaggressions and their relationship to unconscious racialisation* [Master's dissertation, Auckland University of Technology]. Tuwhera Open Access Theses & Dissertations. https://openrepository.aut.ac.nz/bitstream/handle/10292/15067/McCannM.pdf

McLeod, J. (2001). *Qualitative research in counselling and psychotherapy.* Sage.

McLeod, J. (2003). *Doing counselling research* (2nd ed.). Sage.

Meents, J. (2006). *Acres of diamonds: A heuristic self-search inquiry into intuition* [Doctoral thesis, University of Calgary]. PRISM Repository. https://prism.ucalgary.ca/handle/1880/101513

Merry, T. (2004). Supervision as heuristic research inquiry. In K. Tudor & M. Worrall (Eds.), *Freedom to practise: Person-centred approaches to supervision* (pp. 189–199). PCCS Books.

Moustakas, C. (1967). Heuristic research. In J. Bugental (Ed.), *Challenges in humanistic psychology* (pp. 100–107). McGraw-Hill.

Moustakas, C. (1990). *Heuristic research: Design, methodology and applications.* Sage.

Critical heuristics in research 131

Moustakas, C. (2015). Heuristic research revisited. In K. J. Schneider, J. F. T. Bugental, & J. F. Pierson (Eds.), *The handbook of humanistic psychology: Leading edges in theory, research, and practice* (pp. 263–274). Sage. (Original work published 2000)

Munn, Z., Peters, M. D. J., Stern, C., Tufanaru, C, McArthur, A., & Aromataris, E. (2018). Systematic review or scoping review? Guidance for authors when choosing between a systematic or scoping review approach. *BMC Medical Research Methodology*, *18*(143). https://doi.org/10.1186/s12874-018-0611-x

O'Hara, M. (1986). Heuristic inquiry as psychotherapy: The client-centered approach. *Person Centered Review*, *1*(2), 172–183.

Ozertugrul, E. (2015). *Heuristic self-search inquiry into one experience of obsessive-compulsive disorder* [Doctoral dissertation, Walden University]. Walden University ProQuest Dissertations Publishing. https://www.proquest.com/openview/65a1606168471908a d8768f3bea63612/1

Ozertugrul, E. (2017a). A comparative analysis: Heuristic self-search inquiry as self-knowledge and knowledge of society. *Journal of Humanistic Psychology*, *57*(3), 237–251. https://doi.org/10.1177/0022167815594966

Ozertugrul, E. (2017b). Heuristic self-search inquiry into one experience of obsessive–compulsive disorder. *Journal of Humanistic Psychology*, *57*(3), 215–236. https://doi.org/ 10.1177/0022167815592503

Patton, M. Q. (2002). *Qualitative research and evaluation methods*. Sage.

Polanyi, M. (1966). *The tacit dimension*. Doubleday.

Polanyi, M. (1969). *Knowing and being* (M. Green, Ed.). University of Chicago Press.

Polkinghorne, D. (1982). What makes research humanistic? *Journal of Humanistic Psychology*, *22*(3), 47–54. https://doi.org/10.1177/0022167882223007

Rogers, C. R. (1961). 'This is me'. In *On becoming a person* (pp. 1–27). Constable.

Rose, T., & Loewenthal, D. (2006). Heuristic research. In D. Loewenthal & D. Winter (Eds.), *What is psychotherapeutic research?* (pp. 133–143). Karnac.

Schmid, P. F. (2006). The challenge of the other: Towards dialogical person-centered psychotherapy and counseling. *Person-centered & Experiential Psychotherapies*, *5*(4), 240–254. https://doi.org/10.1080/14779757.2006.9688416

Schulz, C. (2015). Existential psychotherapy with a person who lives with a left ventricular assist device and awaits heart transplantation: A case report. *Journal of Humanistic Psychology*, *55*(4), 429–473. https://doi.org/10.1177/0022167814539192

Schwandt, T. A. (1997). *Qualitative inquiry: A dictionary of terms*. Sage.

Sela-Smith, S. (2001). *A demonstration of heuristic self-search inquiry: Clarification of the Moustakas method* [Unpublished doctoral dissertation]. Saybrook Graduate School.

Sela-Smith, S. (2002). Heuristic research: A review and critique of Moustakas's method. *Journal of Humanistic Psychology*, *42*(3), 53–88. https://doi.org/10.1177/0022167802423004

Shantall, T. (1999). The experience of meaning in suffering among Holocaust survivors. *Journal of Humanistic Psychology*, *39*(3), 96–124. https://doi.org/10.1177/0022167899393009

Souba, W. (2011). The language of discovery. *Journal of Biomedical Discovery and Collaboration*, *6*, 53–69. https://doi.org/10.5210/disco.v6i0.3634

Spinelli, E. (2006). The value of relatedness in existential psychotherapy and phenomenological enquiry. *Indo-Pacific Journal of Phenomenology*, *6*(1), 1–8. https://hdl.handle.net/10520/EJC46948

Stark, M. (1999). *Modes of therapeutic action: Enhancement of knowledge, provision of experience, engagement in relationship*. Jason Aronson.

Stevens, C. (2006). A heuristic–dialogial model for reflective psychotherapy practice. In D. Loewenthal & D. Winter (Eds.), *What is psychotherapeutic research?* (pp. 171–181). Karnac.

132 *Keith Tudor*

Sultan, N. (2019). *Heuristic inquiry: Researching human experience holistically.* Sage.

Taft, J. (1973). *The dynamics of therapy in a controlled relationship.* Macmillan. (Original work published 1933)

Totton, N. (2000). *Psychotherapy and politics.* Sage.

Tudor, K. (2010). The fight for health: A heuristic enquiry into psychological well-being [Unpublished context statement for a PhD in Mental Health Promotion]. Middlesex University, London, UK.

Tudor, K. (2016). The argumentative therapist: Philosophy, psychotherapy, and culture [Public inaugural professorial lecture]. Auckland University of Technology, Auckland, Aotearoa New Zealand. Copy in possession of Keith Tudor.

Tudor, K. (2017). The fight for health: An heuristic enquiry. In K. Tudor (Ed.), *Conscience and critic: The selected works of Keith Tudor* (pp. 143–168). Routledge.

Tudor, K. (2018). *Psychotherapy: A critical examination.* PCCS Books.

Tudor, K. (2022). Enjoying critical self-enquiry: Doing heuristic research. In S. Bager-Charleson & A. McBeath (Eds.), *Enjoying research in counselling and psychotherapy.* Springer.

Tudor, K., & Francis, J. (2022). Research and practice: Contributions to the discipline of psychotherapy. *Ata: Journal of Psychotherapy Aotearoa New Zealand, 26*(2).

Wilber, K. (1997). *The eye of spirit.* Shambala.

Williams, N. F. (2020). Going 'beyond the surface' in an app-based group: A heuristic inquiry. *Journal of Humanistic Psychology,* 1–24. https://doi.org/10.1177/0022167820974503

Woolf, V. (1929). *A room of one's own.* Hogarth.

Xiao, Y., & Watson, M. (2017). Guidance on conducting a systematic literature review. *Journal of Planning Education and Research, 39*(1), 93–112. https://doi.org/10.1177/0739456X17723971

10 Keeping it real

Grounded theory for a profession on the brink

Elizabeth Day

Grounded theory is not about the mere testing of existing theories. Rather, it is a creative research method that generates new explanatory theories in order to understand particular experiences in particular contexts. In this way it sits midway between positivism and pure philosophy, balancing the accountability of a transparently engaged method with the open-endedness of ontological enquiry.

Here, the author engages an enquiry into the roots of grounded theory, its branches, and its flowering across a range of disciplines and discursive fields. They show why the generativity of the grounded theory methodology forms a strong basis for researchers in psychotherapy to develop theories from an intersubjective sensibility, while bringing the accountability and credibility that are demanded by the health panopticon of our age.

The term 'research', in the discipline of psychotherapy, usually denotes a generously broad and creative range of ways of being and knowing. The term 'methodology', by contrast, can be received with a hiss, by psychotherapists, for its apparent requirement to move away from immediacy, and its implicit threat of constraint. Taken together, the terms 'research' and 'methodology' are not infrequently assumed in the field of psychotherapy to be an oxymoron. We see this in the false dichotomy of 'clinician' and 'researcher'; a dichotomy asserted more often than not by clinical practitioners. Although these terms designate different pursuits, they are not mutually exclusive. We also see this assumption in the anti-intellectualism that can taint our professional discourses.

In the clinical context we practising psychotherapists work in ways that are woven with presence and intersubjectivity. We learn to be at home with a cultivated uncertainty (Staemmler, 1997), with spontaneity and responsiveness to, in, and from the moment. We will not apply an intervention template to the living substance of the intersubjective field. We develop a wariness of structured approaches and a trained vigilance to fend off the planning tendencies of the mind; of our own and our clients' minds. We have a broad literature and our own practice-based evidence to vouch for the effectiveness of this orienting stance. In a clinical setting this willingness to endure uncertainty and to work in real time with an unfolding process can yield sublime results, opening clients to their own choiceful awareness and subjective agency, generating degrees of safety, relief, restoration, and freedom.

DOI: 10.4324/9781003280859-11

134   *Elizabeth Day*

When we are not looking carefully, however, we can mistake the clinic for the world, and enact our much-vaunted psychotherapeutic process in domains where there is neither contract nor basis to do so. Any of us who have trained psychotherapy students will know the ethical pitfalls of defaulting to a psychotherapeutic—rather than educational—relationship with students during the educational process. This confuses students and can create dependencies. With enough practice years behind us, most psychotherapists start to emerge from the bubble of our own training and come to recognise the different registers in which we operate and navigate our world. When we step into leadership positions—as many of us do—in the profession or the academy, and engage with consumer representatives, training regulators, and government health ministries, as Dorothy (in *The Wizard of Oz*) puts it 'we're not in Kansas anymore'. We're called on to bridge our own discursive fields with those that seek to keep us accountable to specific indicators of quality and of cultural safety.

The invisibility of psychotherapy relative to psychology and other allied mental health practices is a persistent challenge that we grapple with in the profession in many countries. The causality is tricky to unravel here. One of the primary concerns for our profession is the way our research base is perceived to comprise methods that are too low on the research hierarchy and is therefore inadmissible at the tables where funding is negotiated and distributed. Although many of us work in private practice, there are good reasons why our professional and regulatory bodies, at least in Australia and Aotearoa New Zealand, the Psychotherapy and Counselling Federation of Australia (PACFA), the New Zealand Association of Psychotherapists (NZAP), and the Psychotherapy Board of Aotearoa New Zealand (PBANZ), seek to gain traction in public health. These include the ethical requirement to respond to a global mental health crisis and the need to expand the mental health workforce rapidly; the need to address local health inequities by making low-cost services available to under-served populations; and the need to educate consumers about the benefits of psychotherapy, sustain and grow our profession, and ensure equitable remuneration for psychotherapists within the mental health space. There have been ongoing and consistent critiques of the medical model (Ahmed, 2021; Day, 2015; Hogan, 2019; Wampold, 2010) that is currently the dominant discourse in public health; and of the research hierarchy, which is taken to represent all research values but is skewed toward a scientific research orientation, and at the top of which drug companies have influenced the installation of the randomised controlled trial as the 'gold standard' of research. We don't need to fall completely in line with this research hierarchy in order to make headway, yet the struggles for psychotherapy to be visible on the radar of public health in many countries—with all the implications for access to services and for the viability of our profession—signal a complex problem that is not reduced to, but certainly does include, the problem of research.

To take a step back here and consider how psychotherapy comes to know itself, and how it communicates knowledge beyond itself, compels consideration of the borderland between various discourses within clinical spheres of

Keeping it real   135

influence. In particular, we can ask how do we conduct research that matters beyond our field, and how do we cut through with it in order to achieve impact for clients, and resonance if not influence, in public health? How we communicate beyond our bubble to allied fields of psychology, medicine, social work, and public health, while remaining true to our disciplinary bases and praxis, is a pressing question for anyone interested in research in psychotherapy, and the development of the profession.

Grounded theory (GT) has something to say about this. Now the most popular—or at least the most commonly used—methodology in health research (Birks et al., 2019), GT emerged from the social sciences. This is an unusual reversal of the usually unidirectional movement of science-oriented methodologies into disciplines of the humanities, under the pressure from our increasingly quantitative data-driven social and political systems. However, GT was developed in the social sciences to provide a robust qualitative approach to understanding people's subjective experiences of social processes, relationships, and behaviour. The theory generated by GT is co-constructed through an iterative method of eliciting meaning from the ground of the data, which is usually drawn from the subjective utterances of participants. The approach thereby generates a theory that is grounded in the data; producing, by definition, a grounded theory. This methodology balances the accountability of a transparently engaged method with the open-endedness of ontological enquiry.

The explicit depiction of theory as 'grounded' in GT begs the question, what is *ungrounded* theory? And it takes us back to the roots of practice. Here I engage an enquiry into the roots of GT, its branches, and its flowering across a range of disciplines and discursive fields. The generativity of the GT methodology is worth considering as a strong basis for developing theory from an intersubjective sensibility, and bringing the accountability and credibility that are demanded by the health panopticon of our age.

Context

When I started work in academia in Melbourne in the 1980s I was loving my immersive life in the field of literature and cultural theory. The pressing need in my early 20s was to understand my world and engage thoughtfully with it. Although I also studied law for a couple of years I grew weary of the repetitive nature of the readings and the weight of others' thoughts that had to be learned and recited as (relative) truths in the realm of legal decision making. To my mind the law was not sufficiently engaged with questions of existence and meaning making. It applied skills of interpretation but to ends that were neither generative nor creative, nor always just, in my experience. So, abandoning that course of study I took hold of the liberal arts with both hands. Questions of methodology were more implicit in my field back then. Proportionally fewer people enrolled in higher education and even fewer stayed on for Master's, research, much less doctoral. The current student-centred focus that we see in universities, with layered support built in to ensure student success, was an idea that had not yet arrived. So most of us were left to our own devices to enquire and construct according to interest and capacity. In my field we mostly applied a literary hermeneutic or theoretical analysis to our subject matter, through a psychoanalytic, feminist, queer, Foucauldian, materialist, or similar frame of reference. We applied close readings to canonical literature to tease out the power structures that silently enabled the works. We analysed non-canonical pop cultural artefacts to elevate the discursive field within which they sat and to admit the subjective experience of the consumer of popular culture as a newly valid focus for research interest. Identity politics were a still emerging force in the humanities and the demand for methodologically explicit accountability in research in some areas was just over the horizon, keeping in step with the gradual creep of neoliberal ideology and its economic models into the tertiary sector.

Or that is how it seemed. Although I was thoroughly engaged with the wild and creative stream of ideas from classical Western philosophy through to post-structuralist theory that I was grappling with to make sense of my world, I started to feel the disconnect of the rarefied world of pure theory from the ontic realities that the life of the mind perhaps unconsciously fends off. The culture of critique, though necessary, was not sufficient. The gravitational pull of actual lives lived in unequal states of agency and freedom began to exercise me more. The allure and, in equal parts, limitations of psychoanalytic theory propelled me into the direction of intensive studies in consciousness and awareness, into the practice of these, and into embodied and experiential psychotherapeutic training.

From only this much autobiography it will be apparent to you how a methodological process that is both generative of theory, and grounded in context and data, would match my interest, in its fusion of the ontological and the ontic. And so, evidently, my own personal context inevitably infuses my arguments here for a grounded methodology; one that holds the promise of speaking beyond one's own bubble of theoretical constructs to a phenomenon or condition that is unfolding in present time and that can be rendered visible, and communicated compellingly, owing to the credibility of the method used to generate the theory.

In my roles on the research committee of PACFA, as a practising therapist, and as an academic who trains psychotherapists and supervises their research in the tertiary sector in Aotearoa New Zealand, I have a commitment to understanding how *what* we know about our work in human suffering and the change process, and *how* we come to know it, can have traction in the profession and beyond it. Such traction is called for, in support of the viability of the profession and the growing need for mental health services, in a world that seems only to be increasing the determinants of mental ill-health.

In the title of this chapter, I've referred to psychotherapy as a profession 'on the brink'. The 'brink' denotes this time and place of great challenge for the profession. We could *fall* over the edge into irrelevance and be eclipsed by the growth of better understood and funded allied health professions; or we might *leap* over the edge into a period of turbo-charged growth and relevance. The choices we make now, across a range of concerns, will be indicative of which direction we take. And, for sure, the research that we do and how we make it count will form part of this story.

Any research method has a worldview underpinning it. It is axiomatic that the paradigm we use to explore a research question is determined by the specific research question and by what methodology and method are needed to answer the question. However, the research question is itself generated by the researcher from within their explicit or implicit worldview, and this influences the decision. Epistemology and ontology are the philosophical structures that frame research methods. Epistemology is concerned with ways of knowing, and the nature of knowledge. Ontology is concerned with categories of being, existence, and a phenomenal reality that can be registered by consciousness. An objectivist epistemological orientation to the world guides the positivist and concrete thinking predominant in the natural sciences. It aims to objectively quantify phenomena, and this approach currently defines the evidence-based movement in the clinical sciences. An ontological orientation to the world as apprehended subjectively, or intersubjectively, guides much of the thinking in psychotherapeutic literature and training and, by extension, the research we carry out in the disciplines of psychotherapy. This is qualitatively derived knowledge; not limited to materiality and generalisability but more concerned with the rich data acquired through a focus on subjective experience. It engages theoretical dialogue, aligning with strands of continental philosophy, and is closer to what may be termed evidence-informed practice (Dunphy et al., 2019). Within this intersubjective paradigm sit most of the research methodologies used in our field, including hermeneutic and heuristic approaches, case studies, autoethnographies, and narrative and discourse analyses. However, for the most part the research remains niche and rarely cited beyond the field. One strategy toward transdisciplinary dialogue is to engage in research methodologies that have fidelity to the philosophical underpinnings of psychotherapy while having credibility within a wider range of disciplinary fields. GT fits this requirement well.

Grounded theory: An overview

GT is a qualitative approach to research that structures enquiry into subjective experiences of social processes, relationships, and behaviour, generating a theory that is grounded in the data. Bernie Glaser and Anselm Strauss developed the initial version of GT after a long-term study into experiences of death and dying in hospitals. In 1967 they published *The Discovery of Grounded Theory: Strategies for Qualitative Research* to explain the methods they used in the study. Glaser and Strauss were sociologists who, together, were interested in exploring the ontic—local, ordinary, everyday—experiences of those whose voices were not usually considered worthy of research attention. They centred the marginal through identifying and focusing on the intricacies of their

138   *Elizabeth Day*

everyday experiences and co-creating meaning in the process. To this end they wanted to lift research activity from the mere verification of existing theories to the generation of new explanatory theories in order to understand particular experiences in particular contexts, especially in healthcare. Moreover, at that time sociologists with a quantitative bias had been critiquing qualitative research misapplying indicators of quality that pertained only to the quantitative paradigm. This identified a developmental gap in the research field of qualitative studies, with no significant codification of the conduct of qualitative research yet published, and no evaluation of the qualitative approach on its own terms (Charmaz & Thornberg, 2021).

The fields of sociology and anthropology had been formed in large part by qualitative research. However, in the USA in the 1960s quantitative researchers were in the ascendant and argued that without a systematised approach that encoded objectivity, validity, reliability, and replicability, 'only a few talented stars could produce qualitative studies worthy of academic attention' (Charmaz & Thornberg, 2021, p. 310). Disagreeing with this superficial and contemptuous view, Glaser and Strauss 'democratized qualitative inquiry' (Charmaz & Thornberg, 2021, p. 310), ensuring that their GT would enable any researcher to follow the method in order to generate theories. The publication of *The Discovery of Grounded Theory* by Glaser and Strauss launched the systematic methodological approach into the disciplines in the humanities, offering a valid and viable alternative to the more common and positivist cast of quantitative research. A notable innovation in the method was the approach to data collection and analysis as a simultaneous process. Rather than defer the analysis of data until all of the data are collected, this iterative process of analysis enabled further interviews to be conducted, informed by the developing codes and categories, in order to zero in on the most significant issues relating to the phenomenon being explored, as the enquiry progresses.

Glaser was a statistician and Strauss, by contrast, worked with a symbolic interactionist paradigm. Working in collaborative tension these different research orientations found new expression in GT and increased the credibility and trustworthiness of qualitative research (Charmaz, 2006; Charmaz & Thornberg, 2021; Ward et al., 2015). This merging of horizons meant that both objectivist and constructivist methods were considered by them to be admissible in the method. With this wide range within the methodology, it is not surprising that from its first inception to now there have been thousands of published research articles using a GT approach. In that process the method has inevitably evolved through various iterations, with a few key developments, led largely by Strauss and his students. Broad streams of GT are now classifiable as either classical GT (Glaser), post-positivist GT (Strauss et al.) or constructivist GT (Charmaz). Charmaz (a student of Glaser and Strauss) describes GT as both methodology and method (2017) and, indeed, in some studies GT is used not as a methodology but as an analytical method within another qualitative methodology. Straussian approaches tend to be the most commonly adopted of the GT streams, in fields such as education, and also health, largely for the

Keeping it real 139

emphasis on the subjective experience of the participants in the research. The constructivist approach of Charmaz is also gaining in popularity (Stough & Lee, 2021).

Charmaz has adapted elements of GT to match her relativist epistemological stance. Her form of GT integrates important philosophical and political developments in the social sciences and humanities since the 1960s. The principles of contextuality and co-construction of meaning in the work of Charmaz are more consonant with relational psychotherapeutic theory and practice, and for this reason I focus my discussion of GT on her approach. Charmaz describes the approach she has led both as 'constructivist' and as 'social constructionist'. The terms are also used interchangeably in the literature (for an argument against which, see Ward et al., 2015). However, because in one of their most recent articles Charmaz and Thornberg (2021) use the term 'constructivist', I have aligned with their choice in this discussion.

A constructivist GT

Whereas positivism posits an objective reality 'out there' and available to material scrutiny, the position of constructivism is that reality is contextual, historically situated, culturally located, and constructed iteratively from a fusion of individual experience and engagements in the social sphere (Birks & Mills, 2015; Charmaz, 2006; Ward et al., 2015). Constructivism recognises the way knowledge and meaning are co-constructed through discourse and acknowledges multiple realities. In constructivist GT, the researcher is epistemologically aware, treats the literature as contingent, engages in reflexivity, and maintains transparency about their assumptions and processes (Charmaz & Thornberg, 2021). In a constructivist GT process, a theory is co-constructed through the researcher's iteratively derived interpretation of the words of the participants about their experience of the phenomenon being investigated. Multiple participant viewpoints are held within the process of theory construction. GT is therefore a creative methodology: rather than simply testing existing theories and hypotheses, GT generates theories from participants' subjective experience of phenomena. In this way it sits midway between positivism and pure philosophy. The new theory and concepts generated in GT research may influence policy and practice development in the field of study, such as psychotherapy, and in the profession.

GT supports enquiries into how people experience and act in relation to specific phenomena in the context of their daily life (Corbin & Strauss, 2008; Ward et al., 2015). The method proceeds through a systematic approach to collecting, analysing, and constantly comparing qualitative data in order to develop a theory to explain subjective experiences—what is going on—in a slice of social life; a theory drawn from the words of those experiencing the phenomenon (Charmaz, 2008; Ward et al, 2015). Whereas for Glaser and Strauss a theory was considered to be such if it could explain or predict, for Charmaz, interpretation and abstract understanding are prioritised over explanation (Charmaz, 2014).

Method and tenets

GT methods are neither fixed nor prescriptive. Rather, they are orienting tools. The use and adaptation of these tools calls for intentionality and reflexivity. There are, however, critical components that make a research process, by definition, constructivist GT. Birks and Mills (2015) identify these as:

- Initial coding and categorisation of data.
- Concurrent data collection and analysis.
- Writing memos.
- Theoretical sampling.
- Constant comparative analysis using inductive and abductive logic.
- Theoretical sensitivity.
- Intermediate coding.
- Selecting a core category.
- Theoretical saturation.
- Theoretical integration.[1]

I cover these in a general way below. First, though, I discuss the preliminaries of a research process including methodological self-consciousness, the place of the literature review in constructivist GT, and interviewing participants.

At the very start of a constructivist GT process the researcher establishes methodological self-consciousness (Charmaz, 2014). This involves recursive self-reflection about how their worldviews imbue the research process and influence the participants. It requires awareness of the often privileged role of a researcher relative to participants, and a commitment to working with participants co-constructively, rather than objectifying them within the research process. This awareness is familiar to therapists and parallels our intersubjective relational work with clients.

Most research commences with a literature review to engage with the current findings and debates in the research area and to identify gaps in the literature that the research seeks to address. In classical GT Glaser discouraged the conduct of a literature review in order to minimise researcher preconceptions, and to sustain open mindedness for the inductive enquiry, given that the theory was to emerge from the data. In a constructivist GT, the recognition that preconceptions exist and form part of the process has shifted the position on the literature review. A constructivist GT process starts with a literature review, but takes the literature to be provisional. It may elucidate significant parts of the developing theory and help bring them to light, but it does not swamp the theory. For Birks et al. (2019) the identification of the researcher's assumptions from the start helps to ensure that theoretical sensitivity, rather than bias, informs the research. The researcher's reflexivity and transparency throughout the research process enable mediation between the literature review, the data, and the analysis of the data.

Participants are usually recruited via purposive sampling because in GT the aim is to interview people who are engaged in a social experience of some kind. So random sampling is neither required nor adequate to meet this aim. Charmaz (2006) describes conversational interviewing as preferable to merely informational interviewing in order to source rich data, through fostering dialogue and reciprocity.

The researcher is embedded in the research, their assumptions are articulated, and the unfolding iterative process of data collection and analysis is traced via memos. In this way GT parallels the intersubjective processes of psychotherapy, in that the researcher is immersed in the words and worlds of the participants, and mediates between the field (in which the theory is grounded) and wider readerships who have a shared language for making sense of this research.

The approach to data analysis in GT has been arguably its principal innovation, in the concurrence of data collection and analysis. Whereas in most research methods data analysis commences only when data collection is completed, in GT data are analysed as they are being gathered, through a process of theoretical sampling, to inform the interview direction and sampling for new participants. To this end the researcher performs a light, modifiable coding of the first few interviews to identify ideas and concepts based on data to hand. From this analysis they determine what data are now needed to fill out the picture. During the coding process the researcher writes memos about the codes and any thoughts or questions they have about them, or comparisons between codes and units of data. Memos become increasingly analytical in the course of the research, tracing the development of the thinking and of the theory.

> Once you have coded the data from your purposive sample and written memos about your first impressions, it is time to make a decision about where and how to collect or generate the next tranche of data. In other words, where to sample next is based on the developing theory.
>
> (Birks et al., 2019, p. 4)

Additional participants are thus sampled theoretically, based on what they can add to the data already gathered (Birks & Mills, 2015; Charmaz, 2014). This allows the researcher to branch out the enquiry as new categories are constructed from the data (Birks & Mills, 2015; Kvale & Brinkmann, 2009). As interviews progress, the researcher can direct the interview questions to open up and develop the main categories. As the researcher's theoretical sensitivity to concepts develops through the interview and data analysis processes, they iteratively return to initial codes and concepts with fresh understandings (Birks et al., 2019).

This process of constant comparison brings layers of meaning and insight in support of the developing theory, until theoretical saturation—sufficient data to form a credible theory—is reached. Data collection is finalised once there is theoretical saturation of categories (Charmaz, 2014; Ward et al., 2019). Throughout the research process, the GT researcher constantly makes comparisons between data codes and, later, between codes and categories, and

142 *Elizabeth Day*

between the categories themselves. They then compare their final category with the literature (Charmaz & Thornberg, 2021, pp. 308–309.). The iterative data gathering and analysis process offers four advantages. It prevents researchers from gathering data 'in a superficial and random way … feeling overwhelmed due to a huge amount of unanalyzed data … being unfocused for lengthy periods and … uncritically adopting the participants' view or stock disciplinary categories' (Charmaz & Thornberg, 2021, p. 318).

Through interpretation and analysis, the main categories are drawn together to form a major category, or what Glaser, Corbin, and Strauss termed the 'core concept' of the research (Charmaz & Thornberg, 2021, p. 318). You can tell it is a main category because looking back through the data, the main category was 'the most significant and frequent code, and was related to as many other codes as possible and accounted for more data than other categories' (Charmaz & Thornberg, 2021, p. 319). Through the use of memoing of ideas along the way and the use of diagramming to clarify the emerging hierarchies of ideas, and their relationships to each other, the theory starts to take shape and the research is complete.

Indicators of quality in GT

Since its origins in the 1960s, the evolving versions of GT have been evaluated by different criteria according to their epistemological and ontological foundations. For constructivist grounded theory there are four criteria for quality in GT: credibility, originality, resonance, and usefulness (Charmaz, 2006, 2014; Charmaz & Thornberg, 2021). Credibility requires sufficient and relevant data to enable a depth and thoroughness of analysis, and researcher reflexivity and methodological self-consciousness. Originality is shown through new insights or new ways to conceptualise an existing problem, and through establishing its significance. Resonance is evident where the constructed concepts represent the participants' experience as well as providing insight beyond that group. Usefulness relates to the effects of the research: it helps to illuminate elements of their experience for participants, and may influence policy, practice, and research directions.

The main aim of GT is to produce a theory grounded in data. The newly constructed theory is situated and validated in dialogue with related existing theories (Charmaz, 2014). This increases the explanatory force of the new theory and increases its transferability to other contexts (Birks & Mills, 2015).

GT is attractive to new and emerging researchers, as well as more experienced researchers, because it offers both a flexible and coherent framework for exploring a research question (Birks et al., 2019). There is plenty of literature on the methodology to guide the process, though it is most effectively carried out with supervision from a researcher with experience in the methodology. Its focus on the what and how as well as the why of a phenomenon (Birks et al., 2019) brings GT closer philosophically to a contextual and provisional notion of reality. This pairs well with the intersubjective orientation of psychotherapy, making GT sympatico for research in this profession.

Grounded theory: Examples

Here I offer three examples of how GT is used by some of my doctoral students in psychotherapy at Auckland University of Technology (AUT). I refer to these as examples of a good fit between research question and research method/ology. I include as a fourth example my own research collaboration that, though not a fully GT process, used GT methods for data analysis.

1. Glenn Lucini's doctorate is titled 'At the Coalface of Mental Health: Exploring the Experiences of Psychologists in the Aotearoa New Zealand Health Care Service'. Glenn is investigating how psychologists maintain or use the therapeutic alliance in the context of institutional processes in public health settings. Glenn offers this rationale for the research:

> Many psychologists place a high priority on their capacity to build and sustain an alliance with their clients. However, in modern health care settings multiple factors can compromise clinicians' capacity to build effective therapeutic alliances. The impact of clients' socio-economic and demographic vulnerabilities for clinical relationships in health care delivery are well established; but a relatively unexplored factor is the impact of the expectations and ideologies of the institutions practitioners work in.
>
> (Lucini, 2018)

To best address this question, Glenn has chosen a constructivist-informed GT methodology. He justifies this because the research explores alliance building 'as a socially constructed process—underpinned by institutional power dynamics and the interplay between multiple realities' (Lucini, 2018).

Glenn aims for wider utility of the work and this forms part of his choice of methodology:

> This study aims to contribute insights and suggestions to a rapidly evolving contemporary health care model in New Zealand. The study hopes to shed light on how institutions and psychologists can work, learn, and support each other in ensuring the implementation of a relationship-focused culture of health care.
>
> (Lucini, 2018)

As this research nears completion, the focus has morphed as a result of early stage theoretical sampling. It promises to offer a credible, original, and resonant theory with utility beyond this specific participant cohort. These are indicators of quality in constructivist GT research (Charmaz & Thornberg, 2021).

2. Brigitte Viljoen's doctoral research explores human experiences of artificial intelligence (AI) social robots and how this may inform our psychosocial futures. She explains that her interest in this area developed from her Master's dissertation in which she explored the use of social media by millennials and its impact on their attachment experiences. This work identified online social

media use 'as a potential barrier or a defence against engagement, a loss of reality and transference displacement' (Viljoen, 2019). Brigitte references Turkle, the founding director of the MIT Initiative on Technology and Self, who notes that 'a robotic face is an enabler … It encourages us to imagine that robots can put themselves in our place and that we can put ourselves in theirs' (Turkle, 2011, p. 85). She wants to know what's going on psychologically in these exponentially increasing human/AI interactions: 'It appears the impact of the technological evolution is unknown as we are in the midst of it' (Viljoen, 2019).

In order to capture something of significance and utility from this unfolding process she engages an ontological stance of symbolic interactionism as an orientation for understanding the experiences of her participants as they are unfolding. Within that approach she has chosen to use a Charmazian GT method because 'it is a fluid, interactive, and open-ended method and is useful with the study of social interactions and experiences, and aims to explain a process' (Viljoen, 2019). Her aim in the use of this method is 'to build a theory that explains processes and actions in relation to the research question, with the anticipation that the theory generated in this research may be useful to other contexts' (Viljoen, 2019). The research is more than halfway completed now and is shaping up to offer significant value to current debates in AI and in psychological therapies, among other fields, locally and internationally.

3. Jane Tuson's PhD is structured around an enquiry into how the training and practice of psychotherapy impacts the lives of the psychotherapist's significant others. She explains:

> What is of interest to me is how both the work and the preparation for the work (i.e., the education/training psychotherapists undertake) reverberate through the lives of people close to us. I hypothesise that there are ways that being intimate with a psychotherapist have a very real consequence that thus far have barely been investigated. I wonder how partners, children and parents of psychotherapists perceive our work and how might these perceptions influence and shape their own lives.
>
> (Tuson, 2020)

She anticipates that the work may not only benefit significant others, in supporting greater understanding of their own lived experiences, but also inform training providers and regulators in the ways that the training ripples out through various communities:

> Understanding the perspective of partners, children, parents or other intimately connected people could be useful as a means of celebrating the cascading benefits of psychotherapy as a career choice, and/or for pre-empting negative consequences in the work life of a therapist and those they care about.
>
> (Tuson, 2020)

Keeping it real 145

In her research proposal, Jane memoed her presuppositions and deepened her theoretical sensitivity to the research area through a literature review. Understanding that her enquiry is contextually bound, she chose to explore it within an interpretivist paradigm and was initially unsure whether to use GT or interpretive phenomenological analysis. She decided on GT for its utility:

> I am guided by whom I wanted to engage with the research, particularly educators and trainers of psychotherapy who can influence better outcomes for the interpersonal relationships of psychotherapists. Grounded theory would mean that this research may ultimately have greater utility as it could 'develop theoretical explanations of the relationships among categories of data as the research proceeds' (Osborne, 1994, p. 181) effectively developing a theory from the ground up that could be a useful tool in any psychotherapeutic training programme.
>
> (Tuson, 2020)

Within GT, Jane opted for a Charmazian constructivist approach, because it 'resonates with my intersubjective and relational leanings as a psychotherapist' (Tuson, 2020).

Still in development, this research brings sensitivity to the experience of families of psychotherapists in training and promises to influence the development and delivery of curriculum, to take in wider circles of relatedness, in psychotherapy and other intensive training programmes.

4. My colleague Kerry Thomas-Anttila and I, toward the end of the first year of the COVID-19 pandemic, set out to learn about the experiences of our Master of Psychotherapy students as their clinical work moved from in-person to online during lockdown periods. Due to time constraints—we wanted the results to inform our curriculum and teaching practice as soon as possible—we produced a quick-turnaround research project using a mixed-methods approach and analysing qualitative data using GT methods.

We purposively sampled our Master's students who were providing psychotherapy online to clients at our university health clinic. Twenty-six (72%) of the 36 invited students responded, and completed a 10-question online survey including closed- and open-ended questions. Rather than aiming to generate a theory from the data, we wanted to find a narrative that best captured the experiences of trainee psychotherapists working clinically online for the first time (Day & Thomas-Anttila, 2021a). We split the questions and coded separately using gerunds to generate nouns from verbs in the data. Charmaz (2017) argues for the use of gerunds for coding because the focus on actions rather than on concrete statements helps prevent conceptual leaps before the analysis is completed.

After initial coding of separate research questions, we checked each other's coding against the data. Throughout this analysis phase we met to discuss co-emergent meanings, to enquire into what might be being described in the data,

146 *Elizabeth Day*

and what we might be missing. Constant comparison was used to establish the relationships between data, properties, and codes, resulting in a synthesis of the co-constructed meanings in the data.

Through the process of developing open codes, linked by axial codes (Day & Thomas-Anttila, 2021b), we generated a selective code or core category that provided our narrative: our students experienced 'technological, spatial, and relational challenges in transferring their clinical work to the online space during lockdown due to the pandemic' (Day & Thomas-Anttila, 2021a, p. 108). Students preferred in-person clinical work, but are willing to engage online and 'to do this well they expressed a need for comprehensive, guided experiential training and practice to develop skilful online therapeutic presence' (Day & Thomas-Anttila, 2021a, p. 108).

We didn't set out to produce a grounded theory as such, and we didn't follow the GT method fully, but we used a GT method of data analysis to support rigour and generate meaning from the data. In so doing we identified some critical elements of the students' experience that helped to inform our teaching in the following year, to support them to offer effective clinical work online, and to feel confident in that process.

These examples of the work of my post-graduate students, and of my own work with Kerry, show some of the range of options for undertaking GT research in our field. As a thinker trained in post-structuralist cultural theory last century, and in psychodynamic, intersubjective, and embodied psy-chotherapies this century, my focus is more on Charmaz's constructivist approach to GT, rather than Glaser or even Strauss and Corbin. However, if it is a good fit for exploring the research question, any form of GT could be justified for research in the field of psychotherapy.

Conclusion

I started this chapter by signalling the challenges to the viability of the profession of psychotherapy and of the role of research to address this. Some research approaches that are already considered well-suited to our profession generate quality findings but fail to cut through to other allied fields. To dialogue and have impact in a wider transdisciplinary space we do need to look further afield to genres of research that bridge disciplinary domains, while answering our research questions effectively. Systematic literature reviews are currently understood to be more compelling to a wider research-literate readership. However, GT, in all its forms, makes an excellent match for research in psy-chotherapy for its interest in and capacity to track and theorise what is going on in social interactional spaces and events. GT has significant traction in the fields of health, social sciences, education, and beyond, as a methodology that when well pursued generates credible results: results that have utility beyond the discursive field of the researcher. Now that's at least worth a conversation, don't you think?

Note

1 Stough and Lee (2021) provide a similar list based on their systematic review of the literature in the field of education research. Interestingly the majority of the 210 articles they reviewed used a Straussian or mixed approach to GT. So, there may be a core set of elements starting to settle that can map across the range of GT approaches.

Acknowledgements

My thanks to Glenn, Brigitte, and Jane for permission to discuss their research while it is in process.

References

Ahmed, S. A. (2021). The medical model and its application in mental health. *International Review of Psychiatry*, *33*(5), 463–470. https://doi.org/10.1080/09540261.2020.1845125

Birks, M., Hoare, K., & Mills, J. (2019). Grounded theory: The FAQs. *International Journal of Qualitative Methods*, *18*. https://doi.org/10.1177/1609406919882535

Birks, M., & Mills, J. (2015). *Grounded theory: A practical guide*. Sage.

Charmaz, K. (2006). *Constructing grounded theory: A practical guide through qualitative analysis*. Sage.

Charmaz, K. (2008). Constructionism and the grounded theory method. In J. A. Holstein & J. F. Gubrium (Eds.), *Handbook of constructionist research* (pp. 397–412). The Guilford Press.

Charmaz, K. (2014). *Constructing grounded theory* (2nd ed.). Sage.

Charmaz, K. (2017). The power of constructivist grounded theory for critical inquiry. *Qualitative Inquiry*, *23*(1), 34–45. https://doi.org/10.1177/1077800416657105

Charmaz, K., & Thornberg, R. (2021). The pursuit of quality in grounded theory. *Qualitative Research in Psychology*, *18*(3), 305–327. https://doi.org/10.1080/14780887.2020.1780357

Corbin, J., & Strauss, A. (2008). *Basics of qualitative research: Techniques and procedures for developing grounded theory* (3rd ed.). Sage.

Day, E. (2015). Psychotherapy and counselling in Australia: Profiling our philosophical heritage for therapeutic effectiveness. *PACJA*, *3*(1) https://pacja.org.au/2015/07/psychotherapy-and-counselling-in-australia-profiling-our-philosophical-heritage-for-therapeutic-effectiveness-2

Day, E., & Thomas-Anttila, K. (2021a). In person online: What trainee psychotherapists discovered about online clinical work. *Ata: Journal of Psychotherapy Aotearoa New Zealand*, *25*(1), 99–115. https://doi.org/10.9791/ajpanz.2021.07

Day, E., & Thomas-Anttila, K. (2021b). Zoomed out: Trainee psychotherapist perspectives on online clinical work during the COVID-19 pandemic. *PACJA*, *9*(1). https://pacja.org.au/2021/04/zoomed-out-trainee-psychotherapist-perspectives-on-online-clinical-work-during-the-covid-19-pandemic-2

Dunphy, K., Bloch-Atefi, A., Day, E., Mornane, A., O'Neill, G., & Snell, T. (2019). *Evidence-informed practice statement*. PACFA. https://www.pacfa.org.au/common/Uploaded%20files/PCFA/Documents/Evidence-Informed-Practice-Statement-May2019.pdf

Glaser, B., & Strauss, A. (1967). *The discovery of grounded theory: Strategies for qualitative research*. Aldine.

Hogan, A. J. (2019). Social and medical models of disability and mental health: Evolution and renewal. *CMAJ, 191*(1), 16–18. https://doi.org/10.1503/cmaj.181008

Kvale, S., & Brinkmann, S. (2009). *InterViews: Learning the craft of qualitative research interviewing* (2nd ed.). Sage.

Lucini, G. (2018). At the coalface of mental health: Exploring the experiences of psychologists in the Aotearoa New Zealand Health Care Service. [Unpublished Confirmation of Candidate Research Proposal (PGR9)]. Graduate Research School, Auckland University of Technology, Aotearoa New Zealand.

Osborne, J. W. (1994). Some similarities and differences among phenomenological and other methods of psychological qualitative research. *Canadian Psychology/Psychologie canadienne, 35*(2), 167–189. https://doi.org/https://doi.org/10.1037/0708-5591.35.2.167

Staemmler, F.-M. (1997). Cultivated uncertainty: An attitude for gestalt therapists. *British Gestalt Journal, 6*(1), 40–48.

Stough, L. M., & Lee, S. (2021). Grounded theory approaches used in educational research journals. *International Journal of Qualitative Methods, 20*, 1–13. https://doi.org/10.1177/16094069211052203

Turkle, S. (2011). *Alone together*. Basic Books.

Tuson, J. (2020). How does the training and practice of psychotherapy impact the lives of the psychotherapist's significant others? [Unpublished Confirmation of Candidate Research Proposal (PGR9)]. Graduate Research School, Auckland University of Technology, Aotearoa New Zealand.

Viljoen, B. (2019). Exploring what is happening with regards to Millennials' experience of AI avatars and social robots and how will it inform our future? [Unpublished Confirmation of Candidate Research Proposal (PGR9)]. Graduate Research School, Auckland University of Technology, Aotearoa New Zealand.

Wampold, B. E. (2010). The research evidence for common factors models: A historically situated perspective. In B. L. Duncan, S. D. Miller, B. E. Wampold, & M. A. Hubble (Eds.), *The heart & soul of change: Delivering what works in therapy* (2nd ed., pp. 49–81). American Psychological Association.

Ward, K., Hoare, K., & Gott, M. (2015). Evolving from a positivist to constructionist epistemology while using grounded theory: Reflections of a novice researcher. *Journal of Research in Nursing, 20*(6) 449–462. https://doi.org/10.1177/1744987115597731

Ward, K., Hoare, K., & Gott, M. (2019). Mastering treatment for sleep apnoea: The grounded theory of bargaining and balancing life with continuous positive airway pressure (CPAP), in the context of decisional conflict and change theories. *FQS, 20*(3), 13. https://www.qualitative-research.net/index.php/fqs/article/view/3137/4443

11 Researching from the inside

Using autoethnography to produce ethical research from within psychotherapy practice

Sarah Helps

In this chapter I review the development of autoethnography and describe how it can be used within psychotherapy research. As is common in autoethnographic publications, I both show *and* tell, demonstrating how autoethnographic approaches can spotlight moments in the process of psychotherapy that are complex, relational, small, and mighty, that invite the reader to explore what resonates with their own practice. Because of the importance of doing no harm, of privileging the needs of our patients in anything we write that involves them, ethical considerations have to thread throughout any auto-ethnographic inquiry. Ultimately, I argue that, when written with dynamic, reflexive, relational, and ethical care, autoethnographic accounts can powerfully contribute to the development of better, more transparent psychotherapeutic research and practice.

In this chapter, I draw on three brief episodes from my practice. I have selected the examples because they started to 'glow' to me (see MacLure, 2013), helping me understand something about how I practice that might be of benefit to others. The episodes come from my work as a practitioner-researcher within private and public mental health services for children and their families in the UK (and hence, as I work mainly within the National Health Service, I choose to use the word patient). Each episode belongs within a much bigger piece of therapeutic work, but looking at them as individual episodes enables a slowed-down viewing from different angles, to illuminate aspects that cannot usually be noticed. The episodes are part of a larger collection that explores what I have learnt from my patients.

Coming to autoethnography

I never go into a psychotherapy session thinking that I might write about what happens; my mind is focussed on what I can do in the service of my patients. But psychotherapists are ethnographers: we are careful observers of our own and others' experiences. We are also biographers in that we co-construct and trace the contours of our patients' lives, tracking and mapping how they got to wherever here is and where they would like to go. We are evidence-based practitioners, drawing from theory and empirical research as well as the

DOI: 10.4324/9781003280859-12

150 *Sarah Helps*

moment-to-moment experience of the therapeutic encounter. We journey alongside our patients, examining small fragments of experience alongside grander narratives. We can also be researchers. Thus, autoethnography offers a mechanism through which to braid our theoretical, clinical, evidence-examining, and relational skills to produce practice-near academic research.

When I first started doing research about mental health and psychotherapy, I took the detached stance of a scientist-practitioner. Perhaps like a traditional ethnographer, I observed my research subjects with respect, curiosity, and fascination, but without consideration of how my presence affected their participation. I did not for example consider how being a young woman, a trainee clinical psychologist, might impact on the staff who engaged with me in a busy accident and emergency department, and how my identitarian articulations (Vila et al., 2021) influenced the stories they told me. I was focussed on them and their experiences as if these were totally separate from me.

I came across autoethnography in the mid-2010s, when identifying a method of inquiry for my systemic psychotherapy practice-near doctoral research exploring what actually happens in the delicate flow of conversation between people in psychotherapy. As a trainer as well as a clinician, I had become as interested in 'them' and 'their experience' as I was in me and my trainees' experiences as a way of providing and improving psychotherapeutic services. Autoethnography seemed congruent with my clinical practice. I particularly liked autoethnography's use of reflexivity and its ongoing invitation to focus on what I-the-therapist bring to the encounter. Autoethnography fitted as a way of making transparent my affect, and my inner dialogue—that usually hidden process of deciding at each moment how to make the next move in therapeutic conversations—but also as a way of showing how all the different parts of me—the institutional contexts and rules, the therapeutic modality trainings, societal discourses and my very being—contribute to each conversation. It provided me with a rigorous methodology to research my psychotherapy practice from within.

Below, in italics, you will find snippets of autoethnographic writing. These are not full autoethnographic accounts, but are offered as a sort of amuse-bouche, intended to tickle your taste-buds and show the power of autoethnographic inquiry.

Locating autoethnography within a methodological landscape

Ethnography and ethnomethodological approaches to inquiry stem from the disciplines of sociology and anthropology, and traditionally involve a researcher going into 'the field', observing social life, observing how people make shared sense of their situation, then leaving the field and making some interpretation of their observations and notes, which are then written up and published (Garfinkel, 1967; Goffman, 1981). These methods have been highly influential across the social sciences, particularly as qualitative research methods have moved more to the mainstream (Denzin, 2010).

Researching from the inside 151

Autoethnography as a recognised method of inquiry emerged in the 1980s in response to concerns about ethnographic 'othering', about colonial, imperialistic observation, about research conducted mainly by white people going out to somewhere 'foreign' and bringing back stories of the exotic and 'otherly' (Ellis et al., 2011). It offered some ways of looking inwards to connect the experience of the researcher-self with the exterior world, and was considered particularly helpful to the researcher-practitioner who wanted to systematically explore their own experiences in relation to broader cultural and contextual experience (Ellis et al., 2011). Ellis & Bochner (2000, p. 742) defined autoethnography as 'autobiographies that self-consciously explore the interplay of the introspective, personally engaged self with cultural descriptions mediated through language, history, and ethnographic explanation.'

Autoethnography provides a broad methodological starting point for an inquiry that focuses on telling stories from the inside where the researcher is both the researcher and the researched, enabling the reader to *feel* along with the writer (Ellis, 2007; Ellis & Bochner, 2000). Autoethnography involves telling a story, commenting on and critiquing culture and cultural practices, and embracing researcher relationality and vulnerability so as to compel a response from the reader. It is frequently embedded within a social justice framework, working to challenge harmful cultural beliefs and practices.

Of course, social experience does not exist in a vacuum and 'every story of the self is a story of relations with others' (Bochner, 2017, p. 76). Autoethnography, situated within a post-modern, social constructionist epistemology, is increasingly seen as a relational, dialogical, collaborative method (see Chang et al., 2016; Ellis & Rawicki, 2017). The issue of 'auto', addressing whether experience is solely our own, has been explored in collective, collaborative, and duo-ethnographies (see, for example, Esnard & Cobb-Roberts, 2018; Holman Jones, 2021; Moreira & Diversi, 2012; Sawyer & Norris, 2012).

Gail Simon pushes on from the 'auto', referring to relational ethnography as a method of inquiry useful within systemic psychotherapeutic practice. She writes: 'I am not telling "my" tale in isolation from others. Even when I am researching "my own" practice relationships from within living moments, the shaping of my research endeavor and its telling will be influenced by many others, directly and indirectly involved with it' (2013, p. 33).

Particular attention has also been paid to the 'ethno' in relation to cultural othering or other-being (Stanley & Vass, 2018) by working to ensure decolonising practices.

The data analysed for autoethnography can be prospective or retrospective, although permission-seeking when working retrospectively is more complex (Tolich, 2010). The data might be observations or diary extracts, they might concern a single experience, or might involve events that happen over a prolonged period with deep dives into sparkling or sharp moments. The content of autoethnographies can involve traumatic or negative experiences or positive and mundane experiences. The data are always focussed on the experience of the researcher set within a cultural, institutional, and societal context.

152 *Sarah Helps*

Below I explore two kinds of psychotherapy autoethnography: firstly, that which focuses on psychotherapists' lived experiences, and secondly, writings from within moments of therapeutic practice.

Psychotherapists writing autoethnographies about themselves

Writing autoethnography can 'strip away the veneer of self-protection that comes with professional title and position … to make ourselves accountable and vulnerable to the public' (Denzin, 2003, p. 137). This can be professionally vulnerable-making (Edwards, 2021; Helps, 2017). Based on both our physical and digital presence, we reveal much about our identities which speak to that which cannot be visibly known.

Psychotherapists have used autoethnography to share different aspects of their lived experiences which entangled with therapist roles. For example, Fiona Stirling (2020) explored whether to show her self-harm scars within the counselling room. She noted that in the very act of autoethnographic writing, she made a choice to show this aspect of herself in the knowledge that once it is 'out there' anyone—clients, supervisors and supervisees, colleagues—could see it. Leah Salter (2015, 2017) explored how naming lived experiences that were similar to those of the women with whom she was working contributed to a more transparent, collaborative, and equal therapist–client relationship. I have written about sharing my status as an adopted person and how I have shared this otherwise invisible aspect of my identity when building a collaborative working relationship with adopted people (Helps, 2018).

Are there some lived experiences that we psychotherapists should not share through autoethnography? Given my role and professional codes of practice, are there some stories that, if my patients were to know about them, might be unhelpful to the therapeutic relationship? Are there some stories we as practicing therapists cannot write about under our own names because of the reputational risk that could be caused? Or do we write them for ourselves and our own development and ensure that they do not move into the public domain? How might you feel placing your published autoethnography about your experience of X in your waiting room so your clients can read it before their sessions with you?

Just as we write our clinical notes on the basis that patients might read them, we should assume our patients, during or after their contact with us, might read our publications, either because we choose to share them as part of therapeutic engagement or because, in doing their due diligence in choosing a therapist, patients will search our digital footprints. In doing so, both our published writings and our academic, course-produced writings can often be found.

How can we now envisage what future ripples our current writing might cause? We can never know the impact of our writing on the reader. We need to remain open to how the effect might be different to what we intend, how the effect might be immediate or much delayed, and we need to be prepared to discuss this with our patients.

Writing from within psychotherapeutic practice

Psychotherapy autoethnographies have shown different viewpoints about what happens throughout a psychotherapeutic intervention (Siddique, 2011). Published accounts offer therapist experiences (Meekums, 2008; Rober & Rosenblatt, 2017; Speciale et al., 2015; Speedy, 2013), therapist experiences of being a patient (Fox, 2014), and the experiences of researchers who have moved between the two positions (Lorås et al., 2022; Råbu et al., 2021). Therapists have also co-produced autoethnographies—perhaps better described as duoethnographies—with our patients, where an account is collaboratively produced (see, for example, Rose & Hughes, 2018).

At the end of last session, in response to her nudge, I promised Z faithfully that I would send along an invoice for our most recent sessions. But more than a week has gone by, and I haven't done so. Yesterday and again this morning I went to my laptop to produce the invoice, but my fingers became frozen, my mind wandered, and I drifted away from the task.

It's been a decade since I started working with Z and she described the traumatic images that had got stuck fast in her mind, which I helped unstick with EMDR (Eye Movement Desensitisation and Reprocessing) as one strand of the weave of our work together. Even now, writing these words on the page, I can picture the image created in my mind based on her account: I can feel the fabric of my chair and its wooden arms as I sat with her as she silently processed the sticky images.

Z often sits on my shoulder when I am working with other people. Her wry smile appears in my mind when patients ask for my advice. A while ago, when working with her and her son, we joked about how maybe they should have a picture of me on their mantelpiece so I could keep an eye on them between sessions, to interrupt the arguments they sometimes found themselves in. I've started to think it's Z who keeps an eye on me.

I worry about the boundaries of our therapeutic relationship, about the meaning of not sending invoices in a timely way, juxtaposed with the swift and fluid way that we start each therapeutic conversation no matter how long the gap between sessions. Z knows I'm writing about her. More than knowing, Z has read this chapter and has consented for my account of some of our work to be included. I could not write about her without her consent; this would be dishonest and would break something important between us. If I wrote about me and her without her knowledge, then the benefit of the writing would be all mine: that doesn't fit with the collaborative, mutually constructed way in which I work.

It's curious that the relational dynamics of the transaction of payment within psychotherapy have not been well explored (Herron & Sitkowski, 1986). It's also curious that long-term systemically informed therapeutic work evolves in so many unexpected ways (Chimera, 2020). Despite being experienced, I think I am still learning as much about 'doing' therapy with Z as I think she is gaining from the process of the work.

This episode is partly about Z but is mostly about me. Autoethnography provides a mechanism to demonstrate the stuff of therapy and the workings of the therapeutic relationship from the perspective of the therapist.

Writing about me in relation to them: Respectful, responsible, and ethical researching from within psychotherapy practice

Gail Simon (2012) notes that in writing autoethnographically inspired pieces from within systemic practice, a space can be created to slow down, reflect, and make visible that which cannot be caught in the usual flow of interaction. She suggests that writing from within moments of practice enables the hidden world, the internal dialogue of the therapist, the thoughts and feelings that whirl through every practice moment to be made visible to others, so inviting readers to explore these processes for themselves. Writing about therapeutic conversations and therapeutic processes in this way thus places ordinary practice experiences under scrutiny, and makes transparent that which is usually invisible in the service of improving one's own practice and contributing to the development of others' practice.

The ethics of telling one's own story and the consequences for implicated others are well described (e.g., Andrew, 2017). Even with formal consent, to braid the story of the other with the story of the self is a complex and ethically sensitive process. Below, I suggest some important areas to consider when writing autoethnography about and within psychotherapeutic practice.

Ethics I: Do good, not harm

The clinical and research relationship between therapist and patient is protected by professional codes of practice. Whatever form of research psychotherapists engage in, we need to adhere to these rules and codes to research with care, accountability, and safety, always prioritising the needs of the patient.

Above all, our professional codes of practice require us to do good, primarily ensuring the wellbeing of our patients as well as the greater benefit of those who might read our work and learn from it (Tudor and Grinter, 2014). Balancing the needs of these two groups and evaluating whether we might do or have done harm by our writing requires a dynamic and continuous questioning of ourselves, and an ongoing observation of the way in which the material lands with those about whom we have written.

Ethics II: Procedural, relational, and dynamic

Societal views of what is acceptable in the name of research, and what ethical research looks like, evolve over time. Procedural ethics refers to the series of required institutional steps taken—or, arguably, hoops jumped through—to obtain approval to carry out a study, ensuring research subject, researcher, and host institution are all safe. This field has grown in recent decades in the wake of abuses to humans and animals conducted in the name of research.

Institutional ethics review bodies often decline to review autoethnographies because they assert that there is no *human subject* (Forber-Pratt, 2015) in autoethnographic research, seeming to omit the fact that in being both object-of-research and researcher, the researcher is potentially doubly vulnerable compared to an 'other/ed' subject. In her autoethnographic writing, Trisha Greenhalgh helpfully addresses this by considering what she describes as existential ethics, a way of framing whether the wounded storyteller is sufficiently protected from harm in their writing (Greenhalgh, 2017).

Static procedural ethical permission is never sufficient when researching from within therapeutic practice, and a dynamic, relational approach, where the relationship between psychotherapist and patient, in the context of their work together, is required throughout the research relationship (Bondi & Fewell, 2016). This is relational ethics (Ellis, 2007), and involves the process of constantly considering the relationship between researcher and researched and prioritising both this and the needs of the other throughout the research process.

Ethics III: Consent

In any psychotherapeutic academic submission or published account where there is an imbalance within the professional relationship—such as that between therapist and patient—it is important to describe how permission from all identifiable 'others' has been negotiated and obtained and how the researcher is being protected throughout the research period (Simon, 2018).

So, if we want to write about the detail of our work with our patients in a way that could make visible or identify the patient, then consent is needed from the patient. Obtaining consent from patients is an ongoing process requiring consideration through all stages of the research project until publication (Ellis, 2007; Tudor & Grinter, 2014).

Autoethnographers and other qualitative researchers have described how patients are very often eager for their stories to be shared (Bondi & Fewell, 2016; Helps, 2017). Such tellings can powerfully give voice to marginalised voices and can also start to rebalance the power and benefit within the psychotherapy relationship.

If researching from within a current therapeutic relationship, it is important to consider how asking for consent to write about your work with a patient will affect your relationship with them. How will you explain that you are writing about them? How might asking for this permission change the way that the work unfolds? Will the risks of requesting consent outweigh the risks of not doing so? Should you negotiate permission to write at the start of a piece of work or wait until the end? Providing retrospective consent is complex across all kinds of research because the 'data' of what happened and how it was recorded might have been different had the research frame been known. An alternative perspective is that retrospective consent preserves the therapeutic relationship and privileges the work.

Jonathan Wyatt (2021) writes of his client, Frank, and clearly notes that he sought and gained Frank's permission to publish the piece. But what about the supporting characters? What about the administrative staff who are small but

156 *Sarah Helps*

central characters in his unfolding narrative? It is not clear from the account whether permission to be included in the story was sought or obtained from these women.

Ethics IV: Making more anonymous

In autoethnographically researching my psychotherapeutic practice, I can't not implicate my patients. As Jane Speedy (2013) suggests, the partial or fragmentary identities of client, therapist, and researcher cannot be held separately, and an exploration of their weave through each other is undoubtedly helpful. As above, prioritising the wellbeing and anonymity of our patients is the highest context and we can sometimes write about our practice using strategies that adhere to patient confidentiality, such as anonymisation.

It was late on Friday evening when she returned to her shared office and took her shoes off, partly to ground herself by scrunching her toes on the nylon carpet and partly because London was amid a heatwave and the hospital rules requiring close-toe shoes at all times were driving her nuts.

The sound of the helicopter whirling away from the hospital was loud and made the windowpane shake. Her tears had almost stopped, and her breathing was returning to a more ordinary rhythm. She knew she'd done a good job of supporting the parent tell their child— the child who'd been brought in to the hospital on that helicopter after such an awful accident—that their other parent had died. She knew she'd been present, attentive, compassionate, firm. She was content she'd used physical touch as well as words, that she'd very swiftly built a therapeutic alliance, and then drawn on the evidence base to help the parent understand the importance of responding truthfully to the child's questions.

And she was utterly wrung out. How could she jump on her bike and go to the pub to meet her husband and her own son and play happy?

She knew about recovery from work, she had excellent supervision, she had great support from her team. And in that moment, she could not scoop herself up from the chair to make the next move. In that moment, all the techniques of creating boundaries between work and home flew out the window, sucked along in the slipstream of the helicopter. What she really needed was a hug, like the one that she had just given to the parent and the child and the staff doing the physical care. But she was just so pleased that psychological care was valued alongside physical care, that the hospital so solidly believed in looking after mind and body of children and families.

The parent I had in my heart and mind as I wrote this episode has not given consent for me to write about them. The situation I described is not unique: if it were then I would not write about it because it would be too easy for the family to identify themselves and for others to identify them. But I was certainly writing from within a specific moment of huge emotion and complex therapeutic practice. So, was I writing about them? Or was I writing about me? Would the parent recognise themselves despite the actions I have taken to anonymise the episode?

I have removed gender from the extract and have altered the day of the week the extract took place as a way of maintaining confidentiality and

Researching from the inside 157

anonymising the piece. Did you become curious about what wasn't there as you read? Did you assume a gender for each parent or for the child? Did you wonder about culture, class, religion? About geography? Did your mind go to what you read in the news that might connect with this story? In removing detail to ensure confidentiality, what gets lost?

I have also written in the third person, in effect distancing myself from the account while still maintaining verisimilitude and integrity.

But do the benefits of storying this episode outweigh the risks? If a therapist reads the extract and reflects on their own practice, feels a resonance, is reminded of similar struggles within their own practice, feels that it's more OK to *feel* within their work than they had previously given themselves permission to do, do the ripples of that benefit outweigh any potential damage to the parent?

And where is the balance between manipulating details to tell an anonymised story and altering details so much that the story becomes a fiction? How can we tell an authentic story *and* protect the integrity of the source material? If we amalgamate multiple patients or de-identify them by stripping away the context, by changing important personal characteristics, we will be telling a *different* story. It might be an evocative story but is it still an authentic account? If I say that someone is male when they are female or trans or white when they are Black, then the story I tell might not make sense. The balance between telling a fiction and presenting a factual account needs careful thought.

Overall, in researching using autoethnography, I want to be true to myself in representing the meaning of the words of myself and others in the context in which they were originally spoken. While I want to utilise a 'pragmatic truth' (McNamee, 1995), I also want to hold tight to the 'truth' of my experience.

What difference does autoethnography make?

All research has to make a useful contribution to its field. There are many different forms of autoethnography and thus many ways to evaluate whether autoethnography is 'good'. Good autoethnography can be evocative, it contains clear analysis, linking the 'data' with societal discourses.

Tracy's (2010) eight markers of high quality in qualitative research (a worthy topic, rich rigor, sincerity, credibility, resonance, significant contribution, ethics, and meaningful coherence) and Simon's (2018) criteria for quality in systemic practitioner research (research about and from systemic practice, methods that fit with the practice of systemic work, research that is situated within practice, maintaining focus on relational ethics, maintaining focus on relational aesthetics, reflexivity, coherence, and contributions) go some way in guiding the researcher to produce high-quality reflexive research. These criteria are of strong relevance to autoethnographic research.

Adams (2012) goes a slightly different way and writes of the benefits and joys of autoethnographies: writing through pain, confusion, anger, and uncertainty, illuminating nuances—complexities—of cultural phenomena; creating

158   *Sarah Helps*

accessible and engaging texts; generating insider knowledge; granting a person the ability to (re)claim voice on a taboo or silenced topic; and making life better. These fit well with the overall endeavour of psychotherapy.

Taking these to the psychotherapy field, a good psychotherapy auto-ethnography will likely be engaging to the reader and will help the reader—whether psychotherapist, patient, or interested 'lay' person—understand something of the process and dilemmas of psychotherapy; it will contain an authentic account that is ethically written, clearly privileging both the care of the patient who is implicated and the wellbeing of the researcher; it will contribute to better psychotherapy practice. Tracing the line between the auto-ethnography and better practice is a challenge still to be elucidated.

Some conclusions: Research using the frame of autoethnography within psychotherapy

You were the first family I met in my first job as a newly qualified clinical psychologist, working in Camberwell in the mid-1990s. You had three children as well as the one that had been referred to the clinic. Your little one must be pushing 30 by now. I had no children then. You lived on the 'wrong' side of the local estate, on the estate where it was unsafe for children to play out. I lived along the scruffy-but-grand leafier street, less than ten minutes' safe walk from the clinic.

My boyfriend worked nights, so I was often up early to see him when he got home and then in clinic by 8. You had no help getting your little boys up. Yet you were all always there bang on time. 9am on a Friday morning. Your boys loved the wooden rocking horse in the corridor—so out of place in a hospital, a big, fancy toy in the middle of a poorly furnished, airless corridor. You listened to every word I said and remembered it and came back the next week having thought about it, questioning me about what I meant. I prepared carefully for every conversation as though I 'knew' what we needed to talk about and was blown away by how the conversations never went according to my plan.

You've stayed with me all these years, and when I returned to work in the same corridor in a different role after two decades, I started to map all that you had taught me, about privilege, about being a good-enough parent, about resilience, about respectful challenge, about how people take up psychotherapeutic services. When I had my own three boys, I realised with a jolt just how hard you had worked to get to sessions on time: I wondered why you had never questioned the time of appointments (perhaps, I now see, you did not see yourself as having the power or authority to question me?). You taught me as much as some supervisors, some managers, some colleagues. You taught me about valuing what you have, about compassionate patientship, about commitment and bloody-mindedness to give our kids something better than we had ourselves. Thank you for making me a better therapist.

Psychotherapy is all about relationships and its effectiveness is concerned with how the very special nature of the therapeutic relationship can help patients find ways to live more comfortably. Autoethnography is a powerful self-story-telling method that fits very well for psychotherapy process research through which the researcher can write reflexively from within practice, discourse, and

Researching from the inside 159

context in the service of improving their own and others' practice, social justice, and as an act of resistance and solidarity (Beazley, 2022; Salter, 2017).

Autoethnography can provide a flexible frame through which to examine what the therapist does and how they do it, and what influences them at every turn. Writing into our practice, and writing stories about our practice, can also help us understand ourselves; it can be seen as a form of radical self-supervision (Helps, 2021) that can enhance and deepen the connection between therapist and patient and generate knowledge about the use of our own experiences in the service of the patient.

It offers a frame of how to write about our practice of psychotherapy, from within our experience of that practice, using visceral, evocative, and analytic ways of writing to connect with others. Embracing the arts-based leaning of autoethnography, the way that autoethnography is written, to tell powerful and feeling-full stories, is as important as the choices made about what to write about.

Because our work as psychotherapists centrally involves privileging the wellbeing of the other, we must think very carefully about what we share and how. Brilliant psychotherapists can be wounded healers, have had lived experience of trauma: how we choose to display our selves in our research writing needs careful consideration, not so we present ourselves as smoothed-out, edited fictions constrained by normative discourses but so we continue, while engaging authentically, to privilege the needs of the patients with and for whom we work.

Within systemic and relational psychotherapies, there is a strong push to level the epistemic playing field, to work collaboratively and transparently, showing our working-out in the service of the work. Autoethnography provides a helpful vehicle through which to do this.

The responsibility to produce methodologically rigorous research involves shared and overlapping responsibilities between all parties: the author, their supervisor, the host institution, and any publisher. Even if we cannot run our projects through an ethics committee or institutional review board, we need to engage with relational and procedural ethical practices throughout the work. As a developing field, we can encourage institutional review boards to see the review of autoethnographies as within their frame, to safeguard not only the researcher but also the others with whom their stories intersect.

Choosing to do autoethnography is an immersive process that turns the lens towards the researcher, attracting researchers who are keen to explore their own actions and interactions. It attracts researchers with a desire to decolonise, to write reflexively and transparently, to see themselves as part of the creation of research data, and to see themselves as doing justice within research. It attracts researchers who are interested in the small stuff, the detail, in the intricate ways in which people interact. It attracts researchers who want to understand their experiences in the context of societal pulls. It necessitates finding allies to support you and challenge you and critique your methods and analyses.

160 *Sarah Helps*

It involves artistry with words and the creation of a really good story that makes a difference.

References

Adams, T. E. (2012). The joys of autoethnography: Possibilities for communication research. *Qualitative Communication Research, 1*(2), 181–194. https://doi.org/10.1525/qcr.2012.1.2.181

Andrew, S. (2017). *Searching for an autoethnographic ethic.* Routledge. https://doi.org/10.4324/9781315397948

Beazley, P. (2022). An autoethnographic exploration of a lone-mother trainee systemic therapist. *Journal of Family Therapy, 44*(4), 445–461. https://doi.org/10.1111/1467-6427.12394

Bochner, A. P. (2017). Heart of the matter. *International Review of Qualitative Research, 10* (1), 67–80. https://doi.org/10.1525/irqr.2017.10.1.67

Bondi, L., & Fewell, J. (2016). *The power of examples: Practitioner research in counselling and psychotherapy.* Red Globe Press.

Chang, H., Ngunjiri, F., & Hernandez, K.-A. C. (2016). *Collaborative autoethnography.* Routledge. https://doi.org/10.4324/9781315432137

Chimera, C. (2020). Olena's battle for utopia. In A. Vetere & J. Sheehan (Eds.), *Long-term systemic therapy* (pp. 43–68). Palgrave Macmillan. https://doi.org/10.1007/978-3-030-44511-9_3

Denzin, N. K. (2003). *Performance ethnography: Critical pedagogy and the politics of culture.* Sage.

Denzin, N. K. (2010). Moments, mixed methods, and paradigm dialogs. *Qualitative Inquiry, 16*(6), 419–427. https://doi.org/10.1177/1077800410364608

Edwards, J. (2021). Ethical autoethnography: Is it possible? *International Journal of Qualitative Methods, 20*, 1–6. https://doi.org/10.1177/1609406921995306

Ellis, C. (2007). Telling secrets, revealing lives. *Qualitative Inquiry, 13*(1), 3–29. https://doi.org/10.1177/1077800406294947

Ellis, C., Adams, T. E., & Bochner, A. P. (2011). Autoethnography: An overview. *Historical social research/Historische sozialforschung, 36*(4), 273–290. https://www.jstor.org/stable/23032294

Ellis, C., & Bochner, A. P. (2000). Autoethnography, personal narrative, reflexivity: Researcher as subject. In N. K. Denzin & Y. S. Lincoln (Eds.), *Handbook of Qualitative Research* (2nd ed., p. 733–768). Sage.

Ellis, C., & Rawicki, J. (2017). Remembering the past/anticipating the future: A professor from the white working class talks with a survivor of the Holocaust about our troubled world. *Qualitative Inquiry, 24*(5), 323–337. https://doi.org/10.1177/1077800417741387

Esnard, T., & Cobb-Roberts, D. (2018). *Black women, academe, and the tenure process in the United States and the Caribbean.* Palgrave. https://doi.org/10.1007/978-3-319-89686-1

Forber-Pratt, A. J. (2015). 'You're going to do what?' Challenges of auto-ethnography in the academy. *Qualitative Inquiry, 21*(9), 821–835. https://doi.org/10.1177/1077800415574908

Fox, R. (2014). Are those germs in your pocket, or am I just crazy to see you? An autoethnographic consideration of obsessive-compulsive disorder. *Qualitative Inquiry, 20*(8), 966–975. https://doi.org/10.1177/1077800413513732

Researching from the inside 161

Garfinkel, H. (1967). *Studies in ethnomethodology*. Prentice-Hall.

Goffman, E. (1981). *Forms of talk*. Blackwell.

Greenhalgh, T. (2017). Adjuvant chemotherapy: An autoethnography. *Subjectivity*, *10*(4), 340–357. https://doi.org/10.1057/s41286-017-0033-y

Helps, S. (2017). The ethics of researching one's own practice. *Journal of Family Therapy*, *39*(3), 348–365. https://doi.org/10.1111/1467-6427.12166

Helps, S. (2018). Telling and not telling: Sharing stories in therapeutic spaces from the other side of the room. In L. Turner, N. Short, A. Grant, & T. Adams (Eds.), *International perspectives on autoethnographic research and practice* (pp. 55–63). Routledge. https://doi.org/10.4324/9781315394787-4

Helps, S. L. (2021). Developing supra-vision using naturally occurring video material within supervision. In M. O'Reilly & J. Lester (Eds.), *Improving communication in mental health settings*, 240–255. Taylor & Francis. https://doi.org/10.4324/9781003024330-13-16

Herron, W. G., & Sitkowski, S. (1986). Effect of fees on psychotherapy: What is the evidence? *Professional Psychology: Research and Practice*, *17*(4), 347–351. https://doi.org/10.1037/0735-7028.17.4.347

Holman Jones, S. (2021). Autoethnography and the importance of working collectively. *International Review of Qualitative Research*, *14*(2), 217–220. https://doi.org/10.1177/1940844720978765

Lorås, L., Lindeman, S., Breden, A., & Hansen, H. A. (2022). Being a therapist, becoming a researcher: A collaborative autoethnography on the experiences of novice researchers. *European Journal for Qualitative Research in Psychotherapy*, *12*, 1–12. https://ejqrp.org/index.php/ejqrp/article/view/140

MacLure, M. (2013). Researching without representation? Language and materiality in post-qualitative methodology. *International journal of qualitative studies in education*, *26*(6), 658–667. https://doi.org/10.1080/09518398.2013.788755

McNamee, S. (1995). Research as rationally situated activity: Ethical implications. *Journal of Feminist Family Therapy*, *6*(3), 69–83. https://doi.org/10.1300/j086v06n03_05

Meekums, B. (2008). Embodied narratives in becoming a counselling trainer: An autoethnographic study. *British Journal of Guidance & Counselling*, *36*(3), 287–301. https://doi.org/10.1080/03069880802088952

Moreira, C., & Diversi, M. (2012). Betweeners speak up: Challenging knowledge production through collaborative writing and visceral knowledge in decolonizing times. *International Review of Qualitative Research*, *5*(4), 399–406. https://doi.org/10.1525/irqr.2012.5.4.399

Råbu, M., McLeod, J., Haavind, H., Bernhardt, I. S., Nissen-Lie, H., & Moltu, C. (2021). How psychotherapists make use of their experiences from being a client: Lessons from a collective autoethnography. *Counselling Psychology Quarterly*, *34*(1), 109–128. https://doi.org/10.1080/09515070.2019.1671319

Rober, P., & Rosenblatt, P. C. (2017). Silence and memories of war: An autoethnographic exploration of family secrecy. *Family Process*, *56*(1), 250–261. https://doi.org/10.1111/famp.12174

Rose, N., & Hughes, C. (2018). Addressing sex in occupational therapy: A co-constructed autoethnography. *The American Journal of Occupational Therapy*, *72*(3). https://doi.org/10.5014/ajot.2018.026005

Salter, L. (2015). From victimhood to sisterhood: A practice-based reflexive inquiry into narrative informed group work with women who have experienced sexual abuse.

European Journal of Psychotherapy & Counselling, 17(4), 402–417. https://doi.org/10.1080/13642537.2015.1095215

Salter, L. (2017). Research as resistance and solidarity: 'Spinning transformative yarns'—a narrative inquiry with women going on from abuse and oppression. *Journal of Family Therapy, 39*(3), 366–385. https://doi.org/10.1111/1467-6427.12172

Sawyer, R. D., & Norris, J. (2012). *Duoethnography*. Oxford University Press. https://doi.org/10.1093/acprof:osobl/9780199757404.001.0001

Siddique, S. (2011). Being in-between: The relevance of ethnography and auto-ethnography for psychotherapy research. *Counselling and Psychotherapy Research, 11*(4), 310–316. https://doi.org/10.1080/14733145.2010.533779

Simon, G. (2012). Relational ethnography: Writing and reading in research relationships. *Forum Qualitative Sozialforschung/Forum: Qualitative Social Research, 14*(1). https://doi.org/10.17169/fqs-14.1.1735

Simon, G. (2018). Eight criteria for quality in systemic practitioner research. *Murmurations: Journal of Transformative Systemic Practice, 1*(2), 40–62. https://doi.org/10.28963/1.2.5

Speciale, M., Gess, J., & Speedlin, S. (2015). You don't look like a lesbian: A co-auto-ethnography of intersectional identities in counselor education. *Journal of LGBT Issues in Counseling, 9*(4), 256–272. https://doi.org/10.1080/15538605.2015.1103678

Speedy, J. (2013). Where the wild dreams are: Fragments from the spaces between research, writing, autoethnography, and psychotherapy. *Qualitative Inquiry, 19*(1), 27–34. https://doi.org/10.1177/1077800412462980

Stanley, P., & Vass, G. (Eds.). (2018). *Questions of culture in autoethnography*. Routledge. https://doi.org/10.4324/9781315178738

Stirling, F. J. (2020). Journeying to visibility: An autoethnography of self-harm scars in the therapy room. *Psychotherapy and Politics International, 18*(2), e1537. https://doi.org/10.1002/ppi.1537

Tolich, M. (2010). A critique of current practice: Ten foundational guidelines for autoethnographers. *Qualitative Health Research, 20*(12), 1599–1610. https://doi.org/10.1177/1049732310376076

Tracy, S. J., (2010). Qualitative quality: Eight 'big-tent' criteria for excellent qualitative research. *Qualitative inquiry, 16*(10), 837–851. https://doi.org/10.1177/1077800410383121

Tudor, K., & Grinter, C. (2014). Informing consent for the publication of case material: Principles, considerations and recommendations. *Ata: Journal of Psychotherapy Aotearoa New Zealand, 18*(1), 51–65. https://doi.org/10.9791/ajpanz.2014.05

Vila, P., Ford, M., & Avery-Natale, E. (2021). Ahmaud Arbery: Murder as the outcome of an assemblage's enactment. *Social Identities, 27*(6), 729–745. https://doi.org/10.1080/13504630.2021.1975536

Wyatt, J. (2021). Frank and the gift, or the untold told. In T. E. Adams, S. Holman Jones, & C. Ellis (Eds.), *Handbook of autoethnography* (pp. 79–88). Routledge. https://doi.org/10.4324/9780429431760-8

12 (Re)searching poetically

Poetic inquiry in psychotherapy

Emma Green

> Poetry (here I hear myself loudest)
> is the human voice,
> and are we not of interest to each other?
> (Excerpt from *Ars Poetica #100*, Eliza-
> beth Alexander, 2005)

The poem, like love, is consciousness made flesh. It quietly wakes us: across brain, across skin, the wet line of the tongue.

(Anne Michaels, 1995)

Methodological frameworks provide vital scaffolding for researchers. However, they can become rigid. Poetry and poetical thinking (Freeman, 2016) can help researchers flex outside and around more established ways of thinking. This chapter briefly outlines a philosophical foundation for poetic inquiry, through the tradition of hermeneutic phenomenology. It explores how these approaches lend themselves to one another, and illustrates this through the author's own 'found' poems (Green, 2020). A found poem (American Academy of Poets, n.d.) comprises text borrowed from another source, repurposed, and often rearranged. For researchers in the fields of psychotherapy and counselling, poetic inquiry creatively unsettles and disrupts familiar ways of doing research, of being in and seeing the world, bringing forth new, potential understandings, and allowing the unexpected to emerge in fresh and vibrant ways.

Poetic inquiry (Prendergast, 2009) encompasses the diverse use of poetry as/in/for research (Faulkner, 2017). The poetic invites interactive, embodied, felt responses, creating or making 'the world in words' (Leggo, 2008, p. 167). Poetic inquiry lends itself to hermeneutic phenomenology beautifully, and vice versa, because both share the common aspiration of being able to express human experiences in ways that evoke recognition, emotion, and new possibilities in the reader.

Catching a tiger by the tail

In the very essence of poetry there is something indecent:

DOI: 10.4324/9781003280859-13

164　*Emma Green*

> a thing is brought forth which we didn't know we had in us,
> so we blink our eyes, as if a tiger had sprung out
> and stood in the light, lashing his tail.
> (Excerpt from *Ars Poetica?* Czeslaw Milosz, 1988)

What is this thing brought forth in us through the essence of the poetic? How ready are we to face this indecent thing unfurling from within and without, the hot breath of the tiger on our faces as we stand, mouths open, blinking at the beast? What might this powerful creature offer to us as researchers, and how might we best approach this indelicate animal in all its wildness?

Like the tiger, poetic inquiry is undoubtedly at once beautiful, powerful, and indelicate, offering us ways to (re)present rich, nuanced understandings but perhaps, like the tiger, we would do well to respect its inherent resistance to domestication. No matter how firm our grip on the tiger's tail, the tiger belongs wholly to itself and is unlikely to respond well to our vain attempts at ownership or mastery. Poetry can say things without saying them, can astonish, delight, and shock. It might make us quiet, might make us weep, might make us human. The poetic opens an imaginal space, a slippery space for play, possibility, ambiguity, and abandon; a revealing of fresh and surprising ways of thinking about phenomena which can enliven qualitative research. With its roots penetrating deep into the fertile soil of hermeneutic phenomenology, poetic inquiry can help us make meanings and reveal experience. Concerned with understanding our shared, interconnected, embodied existence, hermeneutic phenomenology often (re)turns to the poetic for language capable of expressing and evoking the richness and nearness of lived experience.

> Language can do all this
> The poem awakens
> a secret life
> in words
> that had seemed
> to be used up
> and worn out,
> and tells us of ourselves.
> In language the world
> presents itself.

Drawing up from the roots

Hermeneutic phenomenology as qualitative research methodology has grown from the traditions of hermeneutics and phenomenological philosophy. Starting from the premise that our most basic experience of the world is already full of meaning, it seeks 'to touch the mystery of this place', looking for 'a glimpse of deeper meanings sequestered in time and cultural distance' (Brady, 2005). Enmeshed in the world as we are, we experience it as meaningful *because* our world exists prior to any of our attempts to understand, explain, or account for it. In research terms, the purpose or intention of hermeneutic phenomenology might be thought about as bringing to light the meanings of lived experience, in turn allowing us to reflect upon it. Such a practice attempts to describe phenomena as they are, *before* theory and abstraction. Such an attempt is always tentative, imperfect, and never complete.

Philosophical phenomenology traces back to the early beginnings of philosophy as a discipline but was catalysed by the work of Edmund Husserl, who suggested that we are *always, already* in the world and that our experience of the world is the only thing about which we can be certain (Husserl, 1913/1999). Husserl urged that we begin with our experiences, expressed in his oft-quoted insistence on returning to the things themselves, rather than relying on abstractions or theories to explain those things.

For Husserl, phenomenology provided a way to study the 'pre-given' world of pure experience, before theory and abstraction. Immersion in this pre-reflexive world, before categorisation or conceptualisation, allowed for the opportunity to study those things often taken for granted, or dismissed as common sense, thus providing a way to uncover new and/or forgotten meanings and penetrate more deeply into 'reality' (Husserl, 1913/1999).

Heidegger, Merleau-Ponty, Sartre, and Levinas would later challenge and expand Husserl's ideas, developing and extending the philosophical understandings of hermeneutic phenomenology. The ontological turn recognises a shift in human understanding(s). There is an exposing of the notions that there is a single 'natural' or 'real' world to be perceived 'underneath' different cultural assumptions. Instead, there is a multiplicity of worlds and worldviews (see, for example, Law, 2004, Law & Lien, 2013). The ontological turn radically shifts the concept of human understanding from the theatre of intellectual exercise to the realm of existential concern. Heidegger in particular helped transform our relationship to understanding in moving us away from mere conceptualisation and explanation toward the fundamental structure of *Dasein* (there/being) (1962/2008). Originally a student of Husserl, Heidegger was concerned with a hermeneutics of facticity (1962/2008). This is the hermeneutical situation in which we find ourselves, 'the concrete, pregiven world in which and by which we are formed, with all of its difficulties and impasses' (Caputo, 2000, p. 42). This ontological turn and the inextricability of being from situatedness, along with Heidegger's contribution to the development of phenomenological thought in this regard, is now widely recognised (Laverty, 2003).

Following Heidegger, Gadamer's work subtly shifted the Heideggerian focus on being toward a focus on language and the other, with whom we find ourselves in conversation or dialogue. This other is no longer merely an object for the subject, but 'someone to whom we are bound in the reciprocations of language and life' (Gadamer, 1994, p. xi). For Gadamer, 'understanding is no method but rather a form of community among those who understand each other' (p. xi). Gadamer conceived of this as a new dimension, not merely another field of inquiry, but as constituting the 'praxis of life itself' (p. xi). It

166 *Emma Green*

was Gadamer who would highlight the absolute inextricability of interpretation and understanding, which is, 'the original character of the being of human life itself' (1975/2013, p. 230). In other words, as soon as we attempt to move towards understanding, we are interpreting, pulling what we are attempting to know into our horizon. As researchers, the need to remain open, even with the inevitable gravitational weight of this pull, becomes clear.

The word 'hermeneutic' derives from the Greek, *herménuenō,* meaning 'to interpret'. Hermeneutics has a long tradition of interpreting religious and sacred texts that can be traced back to pre-Christian times (Laverty, 2003). As early as the fourth century, theological scholars such as St Augustine used the term *ars hermeneutica* to indicate the art of interpreting canonical texts (Grondin, 1994). In a more contemporary sense, hermeneutics represents an arm of continental philosophy dealing with interpretation and the inherent linguistic and historical context in which we find ourselves (Grondin, 1994). Very simply, hermeneutics could be described as 'the discipline that deals with principles of interpretation' (Kaiser & Silva, 1994, p. 15). As a discipline, hermeneutics has been developing over the last two centuries, notably through the work of Schleiermacher in a theological context (see Bowie, 1998), Dilthey (2010) in a historical context, and Heidegger (1962/2008) with regard to ontology, but it was Gadamer who focused on language and turns hermeneutics back to the task of interpreting philosophical tradition (Silverman, 1991) and human experience. Gadamerian hermeneutics provides for a way of being in the world that is concerned with making meaning, of 'trying to understand one's self and others in a common world' (Schuster, 2013, p. 12). The question is of *how* we orient ourselves *toward one another* as we attempt to come to understanding. Whilst we may share a common world it is also true that we see the world *we* see (and experience the world *we* experience) because of how we are shaped by our world. This is Gadamer's notion of 'prejudice' or 'fore-understanding'. Gadamer (1975/2013) requires the hermeneutic phenomenologist to scrupulously examine their own understandings, in order that they might gain insight into how they orient towards the other.

Understanding, disclosing, and the poetic word

All understanding begins with interpretation as I bring myself to the process of understanding. In approaching a text, artwork, poem, interview transcript, or rather, in being addressed by it, I immediately want to begin to make sense of it, I seek to *understand* it. To do this, I summon my own thoughts in response to the material before me. The swirl of thoughts, ideas, and associations evoked by the material before me mingles with my pre-existing ideas and a meaning-making process has begun. *Coming to an understanding* is therefore inextricably connected with language since it is language that discloses meaning (Gadamer, 1989). The poetic word, or poetical thinking (Freeman, 2016), reveals something to us that prose might otherwise obscure. The poetic opens up and reveals, even as it condenses. For Gadamer (1989), the event of the poetic word discloses an 'infinity of unspoken meaning' (p. 427).

dɪsˈkləʊz/
verb
To disclose
is to
expose to view
lay bare.
To be
in the process of
bringing to light
the stone house that rests
just below the carpet of pines
in the valley of thick green.
Disclosing
is
the work of
breaking
open.
Making the house's secrets
known.

Uncovering,
unlocking,
revealing.
What was once hidden
is now seen.
The light shines from the window
even as the door slowly opens
in invitation.

For Gadamer, the power of language is in how it calls forth things from their concealment (Tate, 2016), the world presents itself to us through language, and never more so than through the poetic word (Tate, 2016). This is the raw beauty and power of the tiger at work. Language discloses reality, simultaneously revealing it as it summons it (Gadamer, 1986). The poetic represents a particular aspect of language. One might be relatively unaware of how everyday language functions to disclose reality but, for Gadamer, it is through poetry that we see language at work 'in the process of disclosing' (Vessey, 2010, p. 170). This is why Gadamer can claim that 'poetry language stands out as the highest fulfilment of that revealing which is the achievement of speech' (1986, p. 112). The poem's meaning is its own and the poetic word, unable to be captured or expressed in prose, speaks for itself (Gadamer, 1986). The poem creates something in our imagination and we each see the house created for us in a green valley, each to our own. We do not seek verification as to whether a poem is true or whether the stone house is real. The poet summons a house for us, calling into being a house for each of us. The image of the house is real and alive in our imagination, unique to the imaginer. We do not question the 'truth' of the poem, or the poet's purpose (Gadamer, 1986). The poetic has this unique ability to both condense meaning, to distil something essential; at the same time as it opens a spaciousness for thinking and feeling. There is a truth in the poetic word (Gadamer, 1986) in that it is self-fulfilling.

> **Unsaid and to be said**
> **In words we are at home.**
> realisation of meaning
> finite possibilities of the word
> oriented toward the infinite
> expressing what is unsaid and is to be said
> all this is found
> **intensified**
> in the poetic word
> an event
> wide ocean of beautiful utterance
> expressing its own relationship to being
> disclosing
> infinity of unspoken meaning.

Poetic language is not fulfilled by anything beyond itself, it is 'self-fulfilling … in that it bears witness to itself' (Gadamer, 1986, p. 110). The poem allows us to experience 'nearness' (p. 114). For Gadamer, the 'truth of poetry consists in creating a hold upon nearness' (p. 113). We can taste the woody pine resin, see the mist rising from verdant valley, stroke tentative fingers over cold stone walls, even as we anticipate the warmth of a fire within. As Tate (2016), interpreting Gadamer, has suggested, 'it is through language that we have a world in which we feel at home, it is in poetry that we experience its abiding nearness' (p. 182). This is the brush of the tiger's breath on our cheek, the anticipation of smoky air as we near the house. Poetry, poetic language, and poetical thinking then have a special place with regard to hermeneutic phenomenology and qualitative research. The poetic word brings the world, and thereby the other, closer.

Nearness and experience

Gadamer (1975/2013) suggested that 'everything experienced [*Erlebte*] is experienced through oneself [*selbsterlebtes*]' (p. 60). What is experienced 'belongs to the unity of *this* [emphasis added] self and thereby contains a distinctive and irreplaceable relation to the whole of this one life' (p. 60). The translation of *Erlebte* from the German is 'experienced', the past tense of the verb, and *selbsterlebtes* translates as personal experience. In other words, one's experiences are not meaningful simply because one lived through them and experienced them; rather, that which is experienced as meaningful is made so by the 'reflective glance' (Schutz, 1972, p. 71). It is this reflective glance that constitutes meaning. The reflective glance is comprised of the pre-understandings which constitute this 'oneself'. The work of hermeneutic phenomenology attempts to bring light to, and reflect on, the meanings of these experiences. The poetic is perfectly placed to slip inside, laying bare meanings that might otherwise remain obscured.

Poetry *as* inquiry and (re)presentation

Poetry as/in/for research

> tapping into
> universality
> a radical subjectivity
>
> where personal experience
> and research
> create anew
> from the particular
>
> The particular
> becomes universal
> as we relate
>
> embody
> experiencing
> the work,
> the word,
> as our own.

Melissa Freeman (2016) writes that poetical thinking aims to 'reveal experience as it is experienced, not as it is thought' (p. 75). This statement shows the kinship with phenomenology and other methodologies that seek to disclose meaning. This is a kind of thinking that 'reaches beyond a search for knowledge or meaning into the sensual, afferent and efferent, difficult-to-grasp, or to put into words, experiential world' (Freeman, 2016, p. 73). Thinking poetically can potentially provide new ways of seeing and knowing that are particularly useful in the uncovering of lived experience, but like our grip on the tiger's tail, we are in the realm of the efferent, we have to be willing to hold our understandings and meanings lightly.

A language that attempts to reveal or bring light to the meanings of lived experience must be a language that resounds with a phenomenological sensibility (Henriksson & Saevi, 2009). Henriksson and Saevi (2009) suggest that hermeneutic phenomenology 'needs an expressive language to "write the lived experience" rather than to simply write "about" the lived experience' (p. 35). I would argue that the same could apply to research projects that fall into auto-ethnography, heuristic, or even more critical, post-modern methodologies. For Henriksson and Saevi, this represents 'an event in sound' (p. 35); not only will we hear the tiger's roar, it will be a resonant rumble felt in the chest, known in the body.

Gadamer makes a special case for the language of poetry because there is a way in which everyday language conceals itself. For Gadamer, the poem presents us with access to a secret life, renewing words which had seemed worn out. Something we do without thinking, language reveals and discloses and is, at the same time, self-concealing or perhaps self-forgetting (Gadamer, 1975/2013). That is, we are often unaware of how language calls the world into being; it is a process not often in our conscious minds.

For Gadamer, what is brought forth through the language of the poem stands before us in the 'openness of its unconcealment' (Tate, 2016, p. 157). This idea of unconcealment comes to us from *Alatheia*, Greek goddess of the spirit of truth. In Greek philosophy, the word 'aletheia' represents truth or disclosure. Gadamer's use of aletheia has been translated as 'openness' (Nicholas Walker's translation in *Relevance of the Beautiful and Other Essays*, [Gadamer, 1986, p. 108]) and 'disclosure' (Joel Weinsheimer's translation in *Truth and Method*, [Gadamer, 1975/2013, p. 494]). Drawing on Heidegger's notion of 'unconcealedness', Gadamer (1986) brings our attention to the relationship between truth and shining. Since shining means 'to make that which the light falls upon appear', shining requires something to shine upon (Gadamer, 1975/2013, p. 498). This speaks to something essential at the heart of research methodologies that seek to reveal meaning. The poetic becomes both the invitation and the means to tentatively dwell with the things we are trying to shine light upon, allowing that we might surface them, even as they are concealed from us in their everydayness.

Poetical thinking keeps 'understanding in flow', expanding and challenging the imagination, 'creating what is not yet thought possible' (Freeman, 2016, p. 86). Linking poetry to the hermeneutic circle or spiral, Richardson (1997) suggested 'a poem is a whole that makes sense of its parts; and a poem is parts that anticipate, shadow, undergird the whole' (p. 143). Here is a back and forth, a descent and upsurging of meaning, that allows new understandings to emerge.

As the poet Rita Dove (1994) suggests, poetry might be thought about as 'the art of making the interior life of one individual available to others' (p. 25). This not only illuminates something essential about the capaciousness of poetry, but also the way in which poetic inquiry fits beautifully with the aims of hermeneutic phenomenology, autoethnography, and heuristic research amongst others, and more broadly, with psychotherapy and counselling praxis and research. The poetic lends itself to this revealing process, this making interior life available to others, that both heightens our attunement and sensitivity to the clinical work and to the uncovering work of (re)searching.

Laurel Richardson (1997) notes that 'lived experience is lived in a body, and poetic representation can touch us where we live, in our bodies' (p. 143). Poet Jay Parini (2008) highlighted poetry 'as a language adequate to our experience', suggesting that 'poetry allows us to articulate matters of concern in such a way that they become physical, tangible and immediate' (p. 25). What better way, then, to bring forth lived experience, to make it tingle with aliveness for the researcher, participants, and readers? The possibilities of how one might draw from the wellspring of the poetic word are limitless. For example, creating poetry from the data (transcript material) could become part of the process of data analysis and act as a way to (re)present data (for further examples, see Green et al., 2021).

Data analysis as dwelling and reverie

Durs Grünbein (2010) suggests that poetry opens up 'branches of the otherwise intractable psychic cave system that runs through the bodies of all humans [becoming] a resourceful imagination audaciously pushing forwards into still unsecured galleries' (p. 90–91). Smythe and Spence (2012) describe the importance of dwelling with the data, of allowing oneself to be immersed in that which one is seeking to analyse and understand. Romanyshyn (2013) has described a 'loitering in the vicinity of the work' (p. 223) where the researcher welcomes what presents itself in the moment. There is a sense in which we might be 'not so impatient to engage the work in any conscious way, not so quick to irritate the work into meaning' (p. 223); instead, we 'linger in reverie' (p. 223). The poetic word can facilitate this lingering in reverie, or dwelling with the data, because poetry allows us to touch the sensual, the felt-sense, and to enter imaginal spaces that facilitate the research journey in new and surprising ways. The poetic gives us courage, both imaginal and real, to reach towards that which we do not yet know.

Rigour and some considerations for the poetic inquirer

As qualitative researchers, we are prompted to consider the robustness, credibility, and rigour of our research endeavours. Rather than ask 'is this a good poem?', we might ask instead 'what is this poem good for?' (Vincent, 2018). Fernández-Giménez and colleagues (2019) have noted that good poetic inquiry and good poetry are not necessarily the same thing. The authors suggest that good poetic inquiry will be both evocative and provocative. It will disrupt hierarchies and humanise research by centring participants' lived experience. It will amplify participant voice and evoke emotion, whilst fostering researcher flexibility and encouraging collaborative research.

Patricia Leavy (2015) argued that *vigour* is a term that might better replace rigour in the evaluation of credibility in arts-based research projects. Whilst readers of this chapter may not be explicitly considering an arts-based study per se, making use of poetry and poetic inquiry to extend one's research imagination requires a move away from more traditional evaluations of research integrity.

172 *Emma Green*

Sandra Faulkner (2017) emphasised that poetic inquirers are 'seeking to represent research participants in ways that honour their stories, that create social change and new ways of being while speaking to issues of presentation and research participation' (p. 227). She suggested that poetic inquiry be evaluated on 'the demonstration of artistic concentration, embodied experience, discovery/surprise, conditionality, narrative truth, and transformation' (Faulkner, 2017, p. 224). She argued that 'poetic criteria' fall somewhere between those criteria that would typically be used to evaluate scientific and artistic works. I include Faulkner's poetic criteria in more detail below because they provide those new to poetic inquiry with some thoughtful questions to consider in their use of poetry and the poetic.

Artistic concentration

Does the poetic inquiry work show careful attention to details such as punctuation, titles, figurative language, and word choice? Does the work evoke feeling? How does the poetry work to 'refresh language'? (Parini, 2008, p. 25).

Embodied experience

Does the reader feel with, rather than about, the work? Is the poetry an experience for the reader (rather than reading about an experience)? The imagery used in the poetry transforms, bringing something nebulous into being, into the realm of the expressed (Hirshfield, 1997). Does the poetry succeed in bringing experience to immediacy; that is, as something able to be experienced by the reader?

Discovery and surprise

Does the poetic inquiry work to show the reader something that might have been familiar in new and surprising ways? Does the poetry inspire and express wonder? How might an experiencing of poetic language in unexpected ways allow for discovery?

Conditionality and narrative truth

There is a recognition of the work as partial, as conditional. The work rings true (the phenomenological nod) but is not necessarily 'the truth' (or The Truth). Rather it is *a* truth, *a* way into the work.

Transformation

Does the poetic inquiry provide new insights? At the end of the poem how am I changed? What do I know now that I did not know before?

(Re)searching poetically 173

For Faulkner (2017), these poetic criteria connect with evaluating what poetry can do 'as/in/for social research' (p. 208). The considerations can further be used to stimulate researcher reflexivity. In addition to Leavy's (2015) vigour, Faulkner's criteria lend weight to the use of poetry, and stimulate thinking as to *how* poetry is used in research, in contrast to criteria such as rigour, trustworthiness, and credibility, which quantitative research has tended to prioritise.

Parting thoughts

Poetry evokes a felt response as we read or hear, encouraging embodied and aesthetic ways of knowing, as well as creativity, deep contemplation, and pleasure (Hurren, 2018). As well as the layers of meaning evoked, there are the layers of meaning we bring (our fore-understandings or prejudices); these mingle with what the poem summons in us. As Freeman (2016) suggested, because poetical thinking expands and challenges the imagination, new understandings can unfold as we allow the poetical to work on and in us, meaning that poetic inquiry holds possibilities for researcher, participants, readers, and practitioners. Thus, poetical thinking, and poetry itself, can open up research in exciting and revealing ways, inviting us into the sensual to explore the 'still unsecured galleries' (Grünbein, 2010, p. 91) of our contexts and research imaginations.

References

Academy of American Poets. (n.d.). *Found poem.* https://poets.org/glossary/found-poem

Alexander, E. (2005). *American sublime.* Graywolf Press.

Bowie, A. (1998). *Schleiermacher: Hermeneutics and criticism and other writings.* Cambridge University Press. https://doi.org/10.1017/CBO9780511814945

Brady, I. (2005). Poetics for a planet: Discourse on some problems of being in place. In N. K. Denzin & Y. S. Lincoln (Eds.), *The SAGE handbook of qualitative research* (3rd ed., pp. 979–1026). Sage.

Caputo, J. D. (2000). *More radical hermeneutics: On not knowing who we are.* Indiana University Press.

Dilthey, W. (2010). *Wilhelm Dilthey: Selected works, volume IV: Hermeneutics and the study of history* (R. A. Makkreel & F. Rodi, Eds.). Princeton University Press.

Dove, R. (1994). What does poetry do for us?*University of Virginia Alumni News,* January/February, 22–27.

Faulkner, S. (2017). Poetic inquiry: Poetry as/in/for social research. In P. Leavy (Ed.), *Handbook of arts-based research* (pp. 208–230). Guilford Publications.

Fernández-Giménez, M. E., Jennings, L. B., & Wilmer, H. (2019). Poetic inquiry as a research and engagement method in natural resource science. *Society & Natural Resources, 32*(10), 1080–1091. https://doi.org/10.1080/08941920.2018.1486493

Freeman, M. (2016). *Modes of thinking for qualitative data analysis.* Taylor & Francis.

Gadamer, H-G. (1986). *The relevance of the beautiful and other essays* (R. Bernasconi, Ed., N. Walker, Trans.). Cambridge University Press.

Gadamer, H-G. (1989). *Truth and method* (J. Weinsheimer, Trans.). Sheed and Ward.

174   *Emma Green*

Gadamer, H-G. (1994). Foreword. In J. Grondin (Ed.), *Introduction to philosophical hermeneutics* (J. Weinsheimer, Trans.). Yale University Press.

Gadamer, H-G. (2013). *Truth and method* (J. Weinsheimer & D. G. Marshall, Trans.). Bloomsbury Academic. (Original work published 1975)

Green, E. (2020). *Women's experiences of looking and being looked at*. [Doctoral thesis, Auckland University of Technology]. Tuwhera Open Access Theses & Dissertations. http://hdl.handle.net/10292/13743

Green, E., Solomon, M., & Spence, D. (2021). Poem as/and palimpsest: Hermeneutic phenomenology and/as poetic inquiry. *International Journal of Qualitative Methods, 20.* https://doi.org/10.1177/16094069211053094

Grondin, J. (1994). *Introduction to philosophical hermeneutics* (J. Weinsheimer, Ed. & Trans.). Yale University Press.

Grünbein, D. (2010). *The bars of Atlantis: Selected essays* (J. Crutchfield, M. Hoffman, & A. Shields, Trans.). Farrar, Straus and Giroux.

Heidegger, M. (2008). *Being and time* (7th ed.). Harper and Row. (Original work published 1962)

Henriksson, C., & Saevi, T. (2009). 'An event in sound': Considerations on the ethical-aesthetic traits of the hermeneutic phenomenological text. *Phenomenology & Practice, 3* (1), 35–58. https://doi.org/10.29173/pandpr19820

Hirshfield, J. (1997). *Nine gates: Entering the mind of poetry*. HarperCollins.

Hurren, W. (2018). What's a good poem for? Pedagogical connections between good poetry and social studies. *Canadian Social Studies, 50*(1), 1–11.

Husserl, E. (1999). *The idea of phenomenology* (L. Hardy, Trans.). (Original work published 1913)

Kaiser, W. C., & Silva, M. (1994). *An introduction to biblical hermeneutics: The search for meaning*. Zondervan.

Laverty, S. M. (2003). Hermeneutic phenomenology and phenomenology: A comparison of historical and methodological considerations. *International Journal of Qualitative Methods, 2*(3), 21–35. http://dx.doi.org/10.1177/160940690300200303

Law, J. (2004). *After method: Mess in social science research*. Routledge. https://doi.org/10.4324/9780203481141

Law, J., & Lien, M. E. (2013). Slippery: Field notes in empirical ontology. *Social Studies of Science, 43*(3), 363–378. https://doi.org/10.1177/0306312712456947

Leavy, P. (2015). *Method meets art: Arts-based research practice* (2nd ed.). Guilford Press.

Leggo, C. (2008). Astonishing silence: Knowing in poetry. In G. J. Knowles & A. L. Cole (Eds.), *Handbook of the arts in qualitative research: Perspectives, methodologies, examples, and issues* (pp. 165–174). Sage.

Michaels, A. (1995). Cleopatra's love. In T. Lilburn (Ed.), *Poetry and knowing: Speculative essays and interviews* (pp. 177–183). Quarry.

Milosz, C. (1988). *The Collected Poems 1931–1987*. Ecco Press.

Parini, J. (2008). *Why poetry matters*. Yale University Press.

Prendergast, M. (2009). 'Poem is what?': Poetic inquiry in qualitative social science research. In M. Prendergast, C. Leggo, & P. Sameshima (Eds.), *Poetic inquiry: Vibrant voices in the social sciences* (pp. i–xlii). Sense. http://dx.doi.org/10.1163/9789087909512

Richardson, L. (1997). *Fields of play: Constructing an academic life*. Rutgers University Press.

Romanyshyn, R. D. (2013). *The wounded researcher: Research with soul in mind*. Spring Journal Books.

Schuster, M. (2013). Hermeneutics as embodied existence. *International Journal of Qualitative Methods*, *12*(1), 195–206. https://doi.org/10.1177/160940691301200107

Schutz, A. (1972). *The phenomenology of the social world*. (G. Walsh & F. Lehnert, Trans.). Northwestern University Press.

Silverman, H. J. (1991). Introduction. In H. J. Silverman (Ed.), *Gadamer and hermeneutics: Science, culture, literature*. Routledge.

Smythe, E., & Spence, D. (2012). Re-viewing literature in hermeneutic research. *International Journal of Qualitative Methods*, *11*(1), 12–25. http://dx.doi.org/10.1177/160940691201100102

Tate, D. L. (2016). Hermeneutics and poetics: Gadamer on the poetic word. *Estetyka i Kyrtka/The Polish Journal of Aesthetics*, *43*(3), 155–185.

Vessey, D. (2010). Dewey, Gadamer, and the status of poetry among the arts. In P. Fairfield (Ed.), *John Dewey and continental philosophy* (pp. 161–173). Southern Illinois University Press.

Vincent, A. (2018). Is there a definition? Ruminating on poetic inquiry, strawberries and the continued growth of the field. *Art/Research International: A Transdisciplinary Journal*, *3*(2), 48–76. https://doi.org/10.18432/ari29356

13 Putting ourselves in the picture

Phototherapy, collaborative writing, and psychotherapy research

Jane Speedy and Jonathan Wyatt

In this collaborative inquiry into collaborative writing approaches to psychotherapy research, following the artist Jo Spence (1986), we bring ourselves into the picture. We first set the context with our own histories as therapists and scholars, together with the history of therapy regarding research 'about' rather than 'with' and thus 'them' not 'us'. We then undertake phototherapy and writing as collaborative inquiry. We each choose photos from our lives to engage with: one as children, one in our young adult years (late teens and 20s), and one from now, in our 60s. We consider these images and the stories that surround and arise from them, and we co-respond. We explore the possibilities this collaborative inquiry might have for re-thinking and re-framing psychotherapeutic research in these fragmented, atomised, polarised, fragile times.

Beginnings

Hi Jono,

So how are we going to do this? To tell you the truth, much as I wanted to write collaboratively with you, and much as this writing is going into a folder labelled 'writing with Jono' and stored under 'favourites' in an especially magenta font, my heart *sank* when you first said you were editing a book about 'therapy research'. Libraries, and indeed my own bookshelves, are cluttered with books written by the oh-so-stable and mentally healthy therapists. They're written 'about'—even when fictionalised, like Yalom's excellent *Love's Executioner and Other Tales of Psychotherapy* (2012), or ostensibly written 'with', like the account of Mary Barnes' *Journey Through Madness* by Joseph Berke and Mary Barnes (1979). They are those unfortunate 'others': those poor people, other than us and unlike us insightful 'experts in the field'. Those others needed 'helping', poor creatures with 'mental health difficulties' we are helping to solve. From where I'm sitting, we have both been guilty of this dodgy entitled politics of therapy in the past, even when we have thought we were implicating ourselves and our own lives and losses and worlds in our collaborative inquiries (see Speedy, 2007; Wyatt, 2008).

I've always been against the 'health as opposed to illness' model of psychotherapy. I've always seen myself as an educator and have regarded therapy

DOI: 10.4324/9781003280859-14

Putting ourselves in the picture 177

as a form of inquiry/learning about our 'selves' and how we operate/are operated upon in our worlds. Hence I am a narrative therapist and Professor of Education, in a School of Education—from the Latin *educare* means to bring forth—but I notice you are a Professor of Qualitative Inquiry in the School of Health, so perhaps you disagree? Perhaps for you, psychotherapy is the talking 'cure' for 'illness'? I don't think so, somehow. My goodness, I'm having to put practically all my words in inverted commas …

Jane xx

Hi Jane,

Writing to/with you feels like a blast from the past. It takes me, in particular, to us writing in a triad with Ken, the three of us exploring our experiences of the joint doctoral thesis Ken and I wrote under your supervision (Gale et al., 2010). 'Under' (my first scare quotes) doesn't feel right, though. 'Together with' would be a better description of your supervision; or even 'together with you and your supervision', which might suggest you wrote the thesis with us, which in a sense you did. We've written together with others since but not as a pair. Never just as a pair.

Our counselling and psychotherapy department at Edinburgh was originally also in the School of Education. It joined (along with Nursing Studies and Clinical Psychology) in late 2000s the then newly formed School of Health in Social Science, a few years before I moved to Edinburgh. I don't know the details of that story. Like you, I find the discourse of 'mental health' (and illness) that therapy gets wrapped up in problematic, for the reasons you give, and I'd feel more at ease in an education department. In interviews with applicants to join our counsellor education programme—and yes, we call it an 'education' programme—we ask people to talk with us about their experiences in a 'helping' role. That question always troubles me. I wrote a recent chapter about autoethnography and therapy (Wyatt, 2021) and the problems with the claims that either of them 'helps'.

The problem with 'helping' is ethical, political, and ontological. To be more precise, the problem is with helping *as purpose*, in seeing the therapist or writer as the *one who helps*. It's a power move, a trespass, and the dynamic … becomes one where we (as the 'helpers') see ourselves as 'agentic and responsible and altruistic' and the 'helped' as grateful recipients of our expertise and generosity (Tamas & Wyatt, 2013, p. 62). However, helping (if it happens, which it may not) is not something someone 'gives' or 'does' to someone else but something that arises within the relational process, in the encounter between therapist and client, between writer and text and reader, and back, in the flow and space between them. Helping might happen but if it does it will not be because 'we' help (Wyatt, 2021, p. 84).

I'm wanting this chapter, and how we explore collaborative writing as an approach to inquiry in this field, to disrupt those assumptions about therapy being something we (the well, the sorted, the worked-out) do to make others

178 *Jane Speedy and Jonathan Wyatt*

(the ill, the chaotic, the all-over-the-place) more like us; and to disrupt similar assumptions that haunt research dynamics.

Jono/Jonathan xx

Photos from the family album

Jane

So let's have a go then shall we? Writing collaboratively with people who were originally my clients (Speedy, 2005a, 2005b) appeared to move 'seamlessly' from facilitated teams of witnesses to each other's lives to co-writing, but that was partly because of a long gap between the two relationships which was never really interrogated in the co-writing until recently (Speedy et al., in press). Our (yours and my) collaborations go way back. We killed me off once (deeply Freudian). Except it was me, not you and Ken, who wrote my own obituary, do you remember? (Gale et al., 2014).

Perhaps, since you've just been to see the Jo Spence exhibition in Bristol (held 2020/2021), we could continue our work together doing artful collaborative inquiries into our own lives? Never mind our clients. Let's investigate how *our* own lives and identities are being produced by, and are producing images of us, as a form of creative, collaborative, relational inquiry. Perchance, borrowing from Martin and Spence (see Spence, 1986), you and I could adopt their approach of facilitating each other, collaboratively over a period of time about how we present ourselves in our everyday worlds through seeking to 'understand how photo-graphs operate in the construction of age, class, identity and notions of beauty' (Richard Saltoun Gallery, 2020). In the 1970s and 1980s, Martin and Spence used phototherapy to work through, as the Gallery notes:

> their own personal histories and traumas; their feelings; their relationships with their bodies and the idealized female (or in your case, male); the emotional roots to patterns of eating; and battles against working-class roots. Spence later used photo therapy as a tool to document her fight against cancer.
>
> (para. 2)

I imagine already, just thinking casually about the family photo album in my dresser drawer in Wales, that both our accounts will be riven with issues of class, culture, and gender …

It is spring 1961. Here I am aged seven, in a bridesmaid's dress that was made by my mum for Aunty Mary and Uncle Darrel's wedding (Figure 13.1). I was going to be a bridesmaid for the first time, and very conscious of the honour bestowed on me. This black and white photo was taken by a professional wedding photographer before the ceremony, lest we all get our frocks in a mess later. My mum kept this photo, alongside one of my brother as a page boy at the same wedding, in an album filled with images of our childhood. The next two pages featured Chris as Robin Hood, and me as the Virgin Mary, in our respective last-year-of-primary-school

Figure 13.1 Jane at seven years old (photograph: Francis Frith).

productions. In the photograph I am gazing, adoringly, off to the right, at Aunty Mary, in all her early 1960s merengue-shaped bridal finery, complete with a stiff white tulle veil. I thought she looked like a princess.

I hated my dress. It was made of stiff, scratchy organdie, underpinned by several scratchy sticky-outy taffeta petticoats. Quite apart from the discomfort of all this itchy stuff, I thought the silly puffy sleeves and big bow at the back made me look like a twit—and I said so.

There is another photograph of me that same spring, not included in the family album, wearing my black-watch tartan dungarees, also made by my mother, and my favourite item of clothing ever (I still regret their passing), with my brother's Cub cap perched at an angle on my head. I am sticking my tongue out at the photographer (my dad). My poor mum had spent hours making that wretched, itchy dress. My brother Chris was the page boy at the same wedding. He was wearing a pair of grey, short trousers and a white shirt. He looked (and probably was) comfortable.

I never wore that dress again. I don't suppose Aunty Mary did, either.

Jonathan

This is a photograph of a photograph (Figure 13.2). My mother has this, alongside others—of our late father, our weddings, our children, and their

Figure 13.2 Jonathan at six or seven.

weddings and children—on the windowsill of her room in her residential home. I took this photo when I visited her a few weeks ago. I think it's the reflection of my facemask, which we were still required to wear (along with plastic apron and gloves) at the time of my visit, in the lower centre of the image. I took off a glove to hold her hand. Doing so was against the rules, but she and I both decided that rule needed breaking.

I sit for the photographer, wearing a shirt and tie. My hair is neatly parted on the right, which has never been where it falls on its own. I keep my hair short these days (because there isn't much of it) but when I had more hair it fell to the left, which is fitting.

I look across my shoulder to the right. My gaze seems to look over my sister, Nicola, who is in turn looking to her left past older brother, Simon, who gazes ahead beyond her. We are each looking somewhere, but not at each other. Our mum or dad would have been there at the sitting. Maybe it's one of them we're responding to. I like to think it's my dad I'm looking at. He's pulling a face—sticking out his tongue, pulling his ears, or both, which he was wont to do; but maybe he wasn't there and I'm only doing what I'm told: 'Smile for the camera, Jonathan.'

I don't know for sure how old I am. I am, respectively, four and five years younger than my sister and brother. (I was an accident; they tease me still.) I think I must be six in this image, maybe seven.

The photograph is staged, contrived. Perhaps even the smiles are contrived. The image is professional, the background formal. I am dressed as if for a wedding or for church or for school. I would not have chosen to wear this. I'm

Putting ourselves in the picture 181

dressed for presentation. It's an 'official' portrait of one family's children, a white, (upper) middle class, English, Surrey, comfortable, 1960s family's children. None of the country's or the world's politics of the late 1960s seem present. I would perhaps have gone home after this occasion, which I would have chafed at, and sung along to one of my favourite gramophone records at that time, a blue disc, 'Black Sambo', a story with songs. I and my parents, I assume, were oblivious to its politics: its shameful, casual racism.

We are all, each of us, at this age at or on our way to boarding school. If I'm right about my age it's about a year before I left home. One or both parents would have been at the sitting, but neither is involved in the photo; benign, proud, but invisible. A shaded, distant presence.

Jane

It is late summer in 1971. Here I am aged 16 (Figure 13.3). This photograph is taken by my father, outside our house in the front garden. It is, as usual, slightly out of focus. I made this maxi-dress myself out of an Indian bedspread. It had a hood at the back of the neck. I based the design on a dress I had seen in Biba, and I thought I looked great. My mum hated this dress, and, most especially, hated my tendency to wander around the town in it, in bare feet. Mum

Figure 13.3 Jane at 17 years old (photograph: Michael Speedy).

specifically asked Dad not to get my dirty feet in this photograph. Nonetheless it is my mum I am looking, and smiling wryly, at, over to the left of this photo. We were all out in the garden taking photographs of each other to mark the occasion. In the driveway to the left of my mum, the car was packed.

In the next photograph in this series, the one I took of my mum, she is carrying a Tupperware box full of sandwiches for the journey. My parents are about to drive my brother off to Cambridge for the first time. He was the first person in our family to go to university. At that point he was the only person. We were all very proud of him. I was about to be left on my own at home all weekend, and was trusted not to burn the house down. (I did not burn the house down, but I did have a party, which was a secret because I've always been very good at clearing up, until the neighbours snitched on me!) This 'photo-shoot', then, was a great family occasion. These photographs are all in that same family album, towards the back, before all the degree ceremonies and my generation's round of weddings/not weddings …

Jonathan

It's 1978. I am 17 (Figure 13.4). I have just tried surfing for the first time and survived. It's South Australia, a beautiful beach at Middleton, near Adelaide.

Figure 13.4 Jonathan, aged 17 (photograph: Carolyn Markey).

Putting ourselves in the picture 183

I've left school and am travelling round Australia with my friend, Robin, and we're the guests of his family's relatives, the Markeys, staying for a few days at their 'cottage' (though it was/is more rustic, more rudimentary, than that term suggests) on the beach. I'd been watching the surfers and felt compelled, so my hosts drove me to hire gear and said off you go.

This was not a beginner's surfing beach. I had no clue. I was a liability—one surfer had to bail out of his ride because I was in the way. Here, out of the water and safe, I'd been in no more than half an hour, paddling out through the huge waves (which had looked so manageable from above) beyond the breaks before tumbling back into the shore. I'm relieved to be on the beach, relieved to be alive.

Carolyn is taking the picture. She's the same age as me, perhaps a little younger. Robin is there too. They're both laughing, I remember, at my escapade. Though I had the gear for another day I didn't try again.

Carolyn and I are still friends. Two years ago, I was back in Australia for the first time since this picture was taken and we stayed with her in Middleton. I didn't surf.

I spent five months in Australia in 1978. I remember it as a long, sometimes lonely, time. I think I see that, as well as the euphoria of survival, in this photo. Soon after this part of the trip, half-way through those five months and becoming tired of being with Robin, I went off on my own. I was happier without the tension between us but, if I had been honest with myself, I was also homesick and lovesick. I was happiest in my tent, writing letters to family and friends at home and to Geraldine, whom I'd met in Perth. I told her I'd go back to Perth before flying home but didn't.

Jane

It is winter 2021. Here I am at 66 (Figure 13.5). No dress in this photograph, taken by my partner in West Wales, where I live part-time. It is Sarah that I am looking and smiling at. I was wearing jeans I think, beneath my t-shirt and cardigan, on a bright, windy, wintry day. I am really, really, happy in this photograph, taken by Sarah. I am sitting in my favourite place in the world, in the company of my favourite person, on the bench beside St Non's chapel, looking out across the Irish sea. This was the first day that I had made the trip myself, along the back lanes out of St David's, and out towards the coast, on my new mobility scooter, not driven in a car by somebody else. This photograph is taken 25 years after my mum, the keeper of the family albums and archives, had died, so it is not in any album, anywhere, except digitally, on my phone and computer.

Jonathan

This is St Andrew Square, Edinburgh (Figure 13.6). I'm 60. Edinburgh has been my home for eight years. I'm looking south in the middle of the day one Saturday in April, 2021. COVID-19 lockdowns continue, and cafés are not yet

Figure 13.5 Jane at 66 (photograph: Sarah Hall).

Figure 13.6 Jonathan at 60 (photograph: Tess Wyatt).

Putting ourselves in the picture   185

open to drink inside, so we have bought take-out coffees and we sit here in the early spring sunshine. There's enough of a chill to keep on my scarf but enough warmth to take off, and sit on, my coat. My eyes are closed, taking this in: the 'set' of coffee, sunshine, and company. The photographer is Tess. She is there, with me, and I am with her. We are together. I am feeling, I would say, happy. This is what I am taking in.

Postscript to photo album musings

Jane

What I notice in all these images of me, taken 60 years apart, is that I have my head slightly, wryly, to one side in all of them, and that, despite a plethora of different styles and lengths and up-dos and down-dos betwixt and between times, I appear to have, more or less, the same haircut in all three photographs.

Nowadays, since my stroke, which was ten years ago, physiotherapists are always trying to get me to stand up straight and not lean over to one side, but perhaps I have always taken a slightly lopsided view of my world? Life 'at a slant', to quote Emily Dickinson. 'Tell the truth but tell it slant', Emily advised us in the early 1860s:

> Tell all the truth but tell it slant —
> Success in Circuit lies
> Too bright for our infirm Delight
> The Truth's superb surprise.
>   (Franklin, 1998, stanza 1263)

Poem 1263 from Emily Dickinson was not published until after her death, like most of her poetry. In this poem she seems a precursor of Donna Haraway (Haraway, 1988) and other future feminist writers and theorists, predicting a 'situated' sense of truth and knowledge—just as I am situated differently and relationally in these photographs, by both myself and the different photographers. All family albums are 'situated' and tell the truth at a particular slant, even—or, perhaps, especially—those on my iPhone.

I notice that in each of these photographs, taken for different reasons at different times by different people, I am pictured gazing and smiling lovingly at a woman I love: my favourite auntie, my mum, and my life partner.

I also notice that the clothes I wear get more and more comfortable as time goes by. This is a reflection of the 'packaging' of women, 1950–2020, but also of my own attitudes towards frocks, formality, and to what constitutes a 'family occasion'.

Jonathan

Yes, the images of me too, all those decades apart, convey their relational and cultural situatedness. In the first, there is the six- or seven-year-old, smiling

186 *Jane Speedy and Jonathan Wyatt*

resolutely, looking beyond the picture frame at nothing in particular, his siblings alongside but separate. He is soon to leave home for boarding school. In the second there is the would-be intrepid 17-year-old adventurer and traveller.

Both these images speak of the intersection of whiteness and class—who, after all, has had the cultural capital and financial resources either to go to boarding school or travel from the UK at 17 to spend five months in late-1970s Australia? They also suggest, perhaps, a performance of a particular masculinity: straight and cis, and one short on intimacy and long on (premature, quasi-) independence, all the while yearning for the former and tired of the latter. The 17-year-old, one might imagine, has more insight into these relational and cultural politics than the seven-year-old, of course, but I can tell you he remains largely oblivious.

The final image, the 60-year-old, gives less away, it seems to me. His eyes are closed, he's not looking at the camera, and he may not even be aware there's a photo being taken. His thinning grey hair, which needs a cut (hairdressers remain closed during this phase of the COVID-19 pandemic), and the sunlight blanching his face, make him seem tired. There is, perhaps, ambiguity in his gender performance (the bright-coloured top, the knotted scarf).

Jane

What I most noticed as a difference comparing our photo-stories was how peopled yours are, whereas I am alone in mine. Your two siblings appear in yours, and you speak of them, whereas I had cut my brother out of both photo one and photo two. I have written quite often about Chris's suicide (e.g., Speedy, 2005a) just as you have written often about your father's death (e.g., Wyatt, 2008), and I didn't really want this chapter to be about Chris and how defining his suicide has been. Splicing two family photos in half, however, is quite a dramatic gesture, and here I am writing about that all over again. Hard to cut him out. Hard to keep him in, and not to notice how much he had changed between eight and 18—I remember, intensely, the discomfort he felt at 18. The weight of getting into Cambridge, and of family expectations.

As I see the two photo-stories, this feels like quite a betrayal, cutting him out of the frame. Family photo albums are about so much more than who is in the photo; they are about who took the photos, where they are taken and displayed, and who is not in the photos, or the album, even. Eventually, since the 19th century at least, family photos become the 'official' family stories. The photo album becomes the memory-keeper. Langford (2001) even describes the family album as the 'afterlife of memory'. If you were not in the photo, were you even there, we ask?

For Jo Spence, the co-founder (alongside Rosy Martin) of 'phototherapy', photography was extended out of the envelope of a documentary and/or artistic endeavour to become a therapeutic medium. As I now sit here, mid-pandemic, looking at and reading your photo-stories and placing them alongside mine, I am hugely, rightly, envious of Jo and Rosy, engaging in this process in each other's presence. I wish you were here in the room, sitting with me. When you first sent me your writing, I felt your presence, but now I come to respond, I keenly feel your absence. In her work in the 1970s, curtailed by her early death from cancer in the middle of her 'final project', an unfinished body of work, in 1992, Jo Spence began to ask how ordinary people could 'use photography to represent themselves and take control of their own visual narratives?' (Richard Saltoun Gallery, 2020, para. 3).

And here I stand before you, my stomach churning, as I compare our photographs, apparently 'out of control' of my own visual narrative. Looking at my three photographs I am acutely aware of presenting as a woman at various ages and stages, and of the various ways I am dressed. In the commercial portrait of the 'sweet' little girl in the party frock, I had no control over my visual narrative. I could, now, collage my black-watch tartan dungarees with the darned knees over the party frock. Indeed, I feel sure Jo Spence would encourage me to do so … so here are Chris and I, both sitting comfortably restored—him in shorts and me in my tartan dungarees …

I sit here now, at 67, very satisfied with my graffiti-ed version of the 'Chris and Jane' portrait (Figure 13.7), and wonder what my life would be like, would have been like, if I had gone to that wedding in tartan *dungarees? And what my life would be like now if I still had a smiling older brother watching my back?* But the afterlife of these memories is just a moment, and in my memory I had to watch his back a good deal more than he had to watch mine. I know from some of

Figure 13.7 Chris and Jane.

our conversations, and some of your other writings, that my 'adult sibling envy' is misplaced. I tend to sugar-coat my memories of Chris, and highlight the closeness, rather than the tensions in our relationship.

I also had a childhood sugar-coated version of boarding school, since in all the best adventure stories, such as 'The four Marys' in *The Bunty* (a British comic for girls, published by Thomson & Co, 1958–2001) or Enid Blyton's (1947) *The Twins at St Clare's,* the child heroes of the stories all went to boarding school, thus escaping the world of adult/parental control—and subsequently got into incredible scrapes and escapades, exhibiting great bravado and derring-do. My version of boarding schools as an adult has been altered drastically by my experience as a counsellor with the young (mostly male) students at a rather toffee-nosed British university, struggling to understand and survive the aftermath of their experiences of being abandoned by their parents at an extremely young age to the systemically punitive, and often physically and sexually abusive, British public school system.

Jonathan

This is the first time I've seen an image of your brother, I think. I feel I have come to know him, a little, through your writing, especially that one about how you continue to spend your birthday with him (Speedy, 2005a), in which you've also written with your clients about their own loss and grief. I find myself looking at him here, wanting him to speak, wanting to read his gaze and his smile. I am noticing his closeness to you, both of you smiling. He is suddenly here with you, here in our writing together, present with us in a way he wasn't earlier. A truth, told slant.

There are absences from my photographs too. I've mentioned them: my mum and dad from the childhood photo of my siblings and me, travel companion Robin and host Carolyn from the lone surfer image, life partner Tess from the recent one. They are each out of shot, behind the camera, or not present. The various relational forces, the absent presences, have different hues, different intensities: my father likely at work in London (despite my fantasy he may be making me laugh), my mother likely cajoling, encouraging, both of them knowing I would leave soon for boarding school; Robin distant, our friendship struggling by that time in our trip; Carolyn warm, welcoming, enjoying my mix of terror and relief, gently laughing with (at) me, belonging in this picture; and Tess, simply, deeply, there. Still there beside me, after all this time, after everything.

Writing and making memories as collaborative inquiry

Jane

I realise how important it has been to engage in this work collaboratively, how vital it is to have you, and your childhood and family, in my mind's eye, as I

Putting ourselves in the picture   189

engage with these images from both our lives. I don't know how we are going to limit this writing to a short chapter. Each set of photo comparisons could fill a whole book, and even though I knew it would happen, and I was expecting to be moved by these stories, I am astonished at how full of feelings I am for us, and for all the selves we were, that have made their absence felt, that we might have been and might yet therapeutically restore. Perhaps, borrowing from Martin & Spence (Spence, 1986, p. 68) you and I could counsel each other over a period of time about how we presented ourselves in the everyday world through our personal styles: 'make-up, fashion, body gesture, facial expression'?

Jonathan

I am thinking and feeling with these images of ours, the stories we tell around them, and the responses we have to both our own and each other's. They are, in turn, a story, one story, today's, in June, 2022, of a journey towards psychotherapy, psychotherapy research, and collaborative writing. They are images and stories about an absence of, a search for, and (at times and in the end) a presence of, intimacy and connection. Love, even.

Eve Sedgwick (1998) suggests that psychotherapy is a 'dialogue on love'. Therapeutic change is not possible, she argues, either in isolation nor through conforming to therapy's procedures and rules, nor through, for its own sake, pain. Meaningful, sustained, therapeutic change involves joy, she writes:

> I don't know how to say it properly: I've gotten hold of an intuition that if things can change for me, it won't be through a very grim process. It won't happen as I always used to imagine in the old days, by delivering myself up for good at the door of the Law. I used to take one deep masochistic breath and determine I was ready to surrender to the disciplinary machine—in enough pain to have to do it—but then of course I didn't know how to, and couldn't sustain my resolve anyway; and nothing about the therapy would work. Now it seems that if anything can bring me through to real change, it may be only some kind of pleasure.
>
> (p. 617)

Psychotherapy is not like heading off to boarding school and putting up with it without resistance. It's the pleasure of being seen by, of being with, the other: Shannon, Sedgwick's psychotherapist, whom she witnesses, unbeknownst to him, replacing the grass divot she dislodged when she slipped on a bank. He is in the place where she once was, tidying up after her; an intimate, impersonal gesture. 'I love that his care for me was not care for *me*' (Sedgwick, 1998, p. 631).

Psychotherapy is like the pleasure of being with, and being seen, on a sunny April Edinburgh morning, take-out coffee in hand, the pain, sadness, and loss of what surrounds and precedes that moment present but held. Like the pleasure too of being in your favourite place in the world, having made the journey yourself, not without struggle, for the first time in years. And like the pleasure, too, of crafting words with and alongside others, of 'writing *with*' (Diversi et al., 2021):

> I sense this writing *with* in terms of new becomings. I love the potency of this beautiful not yet known. I know, that as I write, something new is always emergent in this writing process that is generative of the substance of me, you, us, we, them, they, those …
>
> (p. 303)

You and I had an idea, a concept (that we would follow Martin and Spence), but we did not have a 'research plan'. Following Richardson (1995) and many others since, we wrote together to see what emerged; and we have been writing *with* throughout: with each other, with others' writing, with photographs, with memories, with place and space. We have written together, to each other, each other present throughout, as a process of inquiry (Richardson, 1995; Speedy & Wyatt, 2014); and we have been writing with images—colour, shape, texture—and where their 'sensory loadings' (Gale et al., 2013, p. 272), their 'material/relational/vibrational inter-weavings' (Speedy et al., 2022, p. 107), take us. The writing-imagi(ni)ng has enabled something to happen.

Jane

I have enjoyed writing this inquiry with you, Jonathan. I was a bit miffed at first when you did not instantly respond to my calls, and then became amused when your feathers ruffled up because I took a while to respond to your 'highlighted' alterations. But now, towards the end of these negotiations, I feel a renewed intimacy; a rekindled sense of friendship. I am falling, once more, in love with this process of writing with you. ('You'. There; I edited that. I first of all wrote 'in love with us'.) In love with all these versions of you.

In each of your photographs I can see the little boy, the scared/relieved adolescent/the tall middle-aged man I first saw, standing in the doorway of my collective biography workshop at the 2004 British Association of Counselling and Psychotherapy research conference, listening intently/the current iteration in his sixties/there. You are each present in each iteration, as I am in mine.

Writing, and sharing images, as a method of inquiry with and to you has regained an intimacy that has been lost between us over the course of the past decade. Writing into this space has moved me from a space next to you and alongside you as a colleague, towards this closer, loosely connected, vibrant, intimate, collaborative space in between us. This writing together has an intimacy and a vibrancy. This has a transsubjective lack of edges. It is a *vibrant matter* (Bennett, 2010). This writing matters. Suddenly, you vibrantly, intensely, matter to me. You the little boy, the adolescent, the man entering middle age who became my PhD student, and the man sitting in the sun in his sixties.

Putting ourselves in the picture 191

You, and all the selves you were, and are about to become. This closeness is, for me, a becoming-kin; a becoming the many Jonathans you are and will be.

I realise as I am writing this, that I am writing against the grain, or at least very close to the grain, of many traditional versions of therapeutic and research endeavour. Closeness, intimacy, love, vibrancy, lack of edges, and friendship, although considered *bona fide* ethical methods, or even foundations of certain notions of qualitative inquiry (see Diversi & Moreira, 2009; Kirsch, 2005; Tillman-Healy, 2003), such criteria are anathema to traditional hierarchical models of healer/patient relationships.

My argument here, in advocating collaborative writing/image-sharing as a method of inquiry in psychotherapy, not only between therapists and therapy educators, but also between therapists and clients, is an argument for a democratisation, and a flattening of the hierarchies that have been constructed within many psychotherapeutic relationships based on outdated medical models (ostensibly a 'necessary' by-product of the professionalisation journey amongst psychotherapists and counsellors). Collaborative writing processes frequently lead to different, more egalitarian, and creative genres of relationship, more vibrant and lively spaces in between people, and different, more intimate, and proximal ethical practices amongst participants (see Diversi & Moreira, 2009; Speedy, 2012; Speedy et al., 2010).

Such a movement, in terms of research practices, seems completely in keeping with approaches to therapy as an endeavour that allows us to jointly engage with people in inquiring into their lives and how they want to live them. This was, after all, how we described our work to each other at the beginning of this paper. This is a movement 'towards' and 'in-between', rather than 'about' the people who consult therapy practitioners, just as this paper is a movement between and towards us.

References

Bennett, J. (2010). *Vibrant matter: A political ecology of things*. Duke University Press.
Berke, J., & Barnes, M. (1979). *Two accounts of a journey through madness*. Pelican.
Blyton, E. (1947). *The twins at St Clare's*. Methuen.
Diversi, M., Gale, K., Moreira, C., & Wyatt, J. (2021). Writing *with:* Collaborative writing as hope and resistance. *International Review of Qualitative Research*, *14*(2), 201–312. https://doi.org/10.1177/1940844720978761
Diversi, M., & Moreira, C. (2009). *Betweener talk: Decolonizing knowledge production: Pedagogy and praxis*. Routledge.
Franklin, R. (1998). *The poems of Emily Dickinson*. Harvard University Press.
Gale, K., Gallant, M., Gannon, S., Kirkpatrick, D., Malthouse, M., Percy, M., Perrier, M., Porter, S., Rippin, A., Sakellariadis, A., Speedy, J., Wyatt, J., & Wyatt, T. (2013). Inquiring into red/red inquiring. *Humanities*, *2*(2), 253–277. https://doi.org/10.3390/h2020253
Gale, K., Speedy, J., & Wyatt, J. (2010). Gatecrashing the oasis? A joint dissertation play. *Qualitative Inquiry*, *16*(1), 21–28. https://doi.org/10.1177%2F1077800409349758
Gale, K., Speedy, J., & Wyatt, J. (2014). Negotiating the storms of collaborative writing: The obituary as method of inquiry. In J. Speedy & J. Wyatt (Eds.), *Collaborative writing as inquiry* (pp. 66–77). Cambridge Scholars.

192 *Jane Speedy and Jonathan Wyatt*

Haraway, D. (1988). Situated knowledges: The science question in feminism and the privilege of partial perspective. *Feminist Studies, 14*(3), 575–599. https://doi.org/10.2307/3178066

Kirsch, G. (2005). Friendship, friendliness and feminist fieldwork. *Signs, 30*(4), 2163–2172. https://doi.org/10.1086/428415

Langford, M. (2001). *Suspended conversations: The afterlife of memory in photographic albums.* McGill-Queens University Press.

Richard Saltoun Gallery. (2020). *One hundred percent women exhibition: Jo Spence.* https://www.richardsaltoun.com/saltoun-online/jo-spence-photo-therapy

Richardson, L. (1995). Writing-stories: Co-authoring 'The sea monster', a writing-story. *Qualitative Inquiry, 1*(2), 189–203. https://doi.org/10.1177%2F107780049500100203

Sedgwick, E. K. (1998). A dialogue on love. *Critical Inquiry, 24*(2), 611–631. https://www.jstor.org/stable/1344181

Speedy, J. (2005a). Failing to come to terms with things: A multi-storied conversation about poststructuralist ideas and narrative practices in response to some of life's failures. *Counselling and Psychotherapy Research, 5*(1), 65–74. https://doi.org/10.1080/14733140512331343949

Speedy, J. (2005b). Collective biography practices: Collective writing with the unassuming geeks group. *British Journal of Psychotherapy Integration, 2*(2), 29–38. http://www.ukapi.uk

Speedy, J. (2007). *Narrative inquiry and psychotherapy.* Palgrave.

Speedy, J. (2012). Collaborative writing and ethical know-how: Movements in the space around scholarship; the academy and the social research imaginary. *International Review of Qualitative research, 5*(4), 349–356. https://doi.org/10.1525%2Firqr.2012.5.4.349

Speedy, J., Bainton, D., Bridges, N., Brown, T., Brown, L., Martin, V., Sakellariadis, A., Williams, S., & Wilson, S. (2010). Encountering 'Gerald': Experiments with meandering methodologies and experiences beyond our 'selves' in a collaborative writing group. *Qualitative Inquiry, 16*(10), 894–901. https://doi.org/10.1177/1077800410383130

Speedy, J., Davies, B., Gannon, S., Kirkpatrick, D., Laidler, C., & Linnell, S. (2022). Arctic terns: Writing and art-making our way through the pandemic. *Cultural Studies ↔ Critical Methodologies, 22*(2), 107–121. https://doi.org/10.1177%2F15327086211072265

Speedy J., & the Unassuming Geeks (in press). *Letters to Chris: An autoethnographic, epistolary inquiry.* Routledge.

Speedy, J., & Wyatt, J (Eds.). (2014). *Collaborative writing as inquiry.* Cambridge Scholars.

Spence, J. (1986). *Putting myself in the picture: A political, personal and photographic autobiography.* Camden Press.

Tamas, S., & Wyatt, J. (2013). Telling. *Qualitative Inquiry, 19*(1), 60–66.

Tillman-Healy, L. (2003). Friendship as method. *Qualitative Inquiry, 9*(5), 729–749. https://doi.org/10.1177/1077800403254894

Wyatt, J. (2008). No longer loss: Autoethnographic stammering. *Qualitative Inquiry, 14*(6), 955–967. https://doi.org/10.1177%2F1077800408318324

Wyatt, J. (2021). Frank and the gift, or the untold told: Provocations for autoethnography and therapy. In T. E Adams, S. Holman Jones, & C. Ellis (Eds.), *Handbook of autoethnography* (pp. 79–88). Routledge.

Yalom, I. (2012). *Love's executioner and other tales of psychotherapy.* Basic Books.

14 From post-qualitative inquiry towards creative-relational inquiry in (and beyond) the education/ training of therapists

Fiona Murray

This chapter is a tale of two halves. Firstly, it follows the research journal of a trainee therapist at the University of Edinburgh, as she embarks on a post-qualitative inquiry (Lather & St. Pierre, 2013). We (I and you, the reader) follow her uncertain process and tentative decision-making and share in her joys and fears as she meets this approach for the first time. Then, reflecting further on this, we step towards thinking about creative-relational inquiry (Wyatt, 2018) as an alternative to post-qualitative inquiry, noting some points of difference between the two approaches.

Conventional qualitative research methodology can be thought of as becoming as predictable as positivist social science (Guttorm et al., 2015). Post-qualitative inquiry is a sharp departure from this convention. It discards methodology altogether. Post-qualitative inquiry (often abbreviated to 'post-qual') is provocative, and St. Pierre (2020a) wants students to know from the beginning that their methodological choices are political.

I will start by giving a kind of in-a-nutshell answer to the question, 'What *is* post-qualitative inquiry if it isn't a methodology?'—as if that was possible or even ontologically 'correct' in the sense that a more pertinent question would be to ask what it *does*. Post-qualitative inquiry does not seek to represent or find meaning that already exists a priori to inquiry but, instead, seeks to experiment, speculate, and imagine something new.

St. Pierre (2020b) writes:

> Post-qualitative inquiry offers a critique of conventional humanist qualitative methodology and marks a turn toward post-structural and posthuman inquiry. It also takes account of the new empiricisms emerging with the ontological and material turns in the humanities and social science.
>
> (p. 163)

Therefore, to *do* a post-qual, you exchange a 'picked from the shelf' methodology with a philosophy of immanence (Deleuze & Guattari, 1980/2013). Through reading post-structural theory, you will begin to put the concepts to work, figuring out your techniques and next steps from the inside of your own project.

DOI: 10.4324/9781003280859-15

194 *Fiona Murray*

St. Pierre (2020b) continues, 'Post-qualitative inquiry is an invitation to think and do inquiry outside normalized structures of humanist epistemology, ontology, and methodology' (p. 163). Therefore, it also becomes clear that to do post-qual we also need to think with a new onto-epistemological arrangement (Barad, 2007) that de-centres the human.

You might wonder how an onto-epistemological arrangement that does not centre the human can be applicable to the field of therapy (that is, psychotherapy and counselling)? Isn't therapy *all about the human* after all? But again, this would be asking the wrong question. *Applying* to fields is what conventional methodology does. Application 'has less to do with invention than [it does] mastery and control' (Massumi, 2002, p. 17), whereas experimenting with concepts is about doing, inventing, and creating.

Rather than try to *explain*, I will *experiment* with how it works in the field, by writing some notes on a counselling session to see what I can notice differently, that is, onto-epistemologically differently, about the links between practice and research.

In the counselling room …

I sit and close my eyes as I wait for my clients to arrive. No matter how long I practice, I find the unknown difficult. I think here about how as counsellors we already work without a method (Jackson, 2017) or methodology. We know the dangers of method. We use theory and concepts to guide us in our practice. This is how St. Pierre wants us to approach research, through our knowledge of (post-structural) theory rather than following a kind of paint by numbers approach.

I am waiting for my clients Ash, H, and Grey to arrive. Ash and Grey arrive together but H is online. We have a hybrid session. (The field of counselling has had to quickly adapt to a more-than-human relationality that is mediated by technology during the pandemic; embracing post-human theory may help us to think about technology relationally.) They are a polycule of sorts who have come for relationship counselling. Ash and Grey met H on Feeld. (Now, many more intimacies are technologically mediated, thus bringing more forms of relationship diversity into the counselling room, and post-qualitative inquiry asks us to consider the more-than-human.)

There is some antagonism in the throuple. Over time, Grey and H didn't find they were very compatible so now both Grey and H mainly have a relationship with Ash separately from each other, though occasionally they sleep together as a three. (Of little importance to the work, it is nevertheless pertinent to say that all three clients were assigned female at birth and now two are non-binary trans people. An onto-epistemology that thinks beyond the human is that it doesn't necessarily mean *not* interested in the human, but that it is interested in a different *description* of what it means to be human than our current baseline. Part of the politics of post-human inquiry is to think of the human as white cis man and any divergence is perhaps more-than-human.)

Towards creative-relational inquiry 195

The problem is that H lives in a different city and is now a carer, which means that they can't travel much to visit anymore. Instead, Ash has to fly to see H, but Grey is not enjoying the new arrangement. They are getting annoyed with the expense of the flights as Ash and Grey are nesting partners and are more entangled financially. But also, H is an activist on sustainability and the amount of flights Ash is taking is 'really pissing them off'. (Another reason to decentre the human is that we are living under the threat of climate change caused by humans. The new materialisms [another body of theory that informs post-qualitative inquiry] critiques conventional research methodology as anthropocentric.) As we wait for H to join us online, Ash, with a hint of sarcasm, says, 'I really enjoy paying good money to sit around waiting for my favourite metamour'.

As we leave the counselling room, I feel reminded that we do not practice in a vacuum. We live between times of huge technological advancement that has changed the way we relate and a climate emergency that makes the world and the field within precarious (Braidotti, 2019).

Comment

I don't bring this polycule example as a way of being woke (a slang term referring to being socially aware, for more on which see Kanai and Gill, 2020), but because it is important that we are not educated by our clients around gender, and sexual and relationship diversity. Currently, and rightly, I have noticed at the University of Edinburgh, and on the professional programme I train on, that there is true pressure from our students to equip them for working in a knowledgeable and aware way about new ways of living and loving.

Post-qualitative inquiry, like therapy itself, is a demanding approach. It demands that we think differently ontologically, and that we do so without a clear methodology—and, because of the speed at which the world we live in is changing, that we do so quickly. Therapy—its practice, education/training, and research—must respond to the politics that it lives in, must respond to change in order to be sustainable, that is, to keep being relevant to new ways of relating and living.

Post-qualitative inquiry

In this part, through research journal entries, I present the trail of one student who comes to embody a post-qualitative approach to her research. I say embody because St. Pierre (2017) writes that 'the post-qualitative researcher must *live* the theories' (p. 2). I take us through her fictional research diary (containing the kind of fiction that can contain more truth than fact sometimes does) of a student on a research course at the University of Edinburgh.

This student is a composite of students who is embarking on post-qual-inspired work. I nod enthusiastically with Manning (2021) when she puts

196   *Fiona Murray*

forward that we should call students co-conspirators because we learn and adventure together. For this reason, I will refer to the student(s) as co-conspirator(s). Underneath each journal entry, I aim to add a more educative response to speak to the kind of questions that may come up when considering a post-qualitative approach.

Week 1

I started BCR (Between Counselling and Research) today. It's a qualitative research course. It's pretty philosophical. My Master's is in psychology. You could say I'm a stats girl. I'm all kinds of uncertain. Maybe I could do a mixed-methods study.

Our co-conspirator writes that she is a *stats* [statistics] *girl*. She *became* a *stats girl* because that is what she was taught to be. St. Pierre (2019) writes, 'If you learn quantitative methodology, you'll likely use that methodology in your research and teach it to your students. We learn what we're taught, and then we teach what we know.' (p. 4). I don't stand outside of that box as I teach what I learned too. The difference is you can't really *teach* post-qual, only its principles.

On the first day of the course, our co-conspirators are asked to throw out words that they associate with research. They say immobilising words like '*analysis*', '*coding*', '*generalisability*', '*measurement*', and other affectless words so void of intensity that they leave me numb.

Week 2

In class today we were invited to stay open to what approach we may take during the course. I will try to loosen my attachment a little to stats.

Also, my seminar group has decided to set up a reading group. Our tutor suggested we read 'Thinking with Theory in Qualitative Research' (Jackson & Mazzei, 2012) because it will help us get to know some different post-structural philosophers. He said that it would help us challenge our assumptions.

Reading post-structural theory early on in the research process is pertinent because post-qual requires a 'long preparation' (St. Pierre, 2017, p. 604) that involves the deep reading of post-structural thinkers. To impress on our co-conspirators the importance of this I share this quote of St. Pierre's (2018): 'Reading is key, but no one can read for you, and people who read a lot can always tell when others don't' (p. 13). This raises a nervous chuckle, and that is just in me. *Have I read enough to write this, to teach this?* But though there is truth in the statement, the way of knowing if enough has been read is not necessarily the understanding shown, but the questions being asked and importantly, a key sign is that the next step of what to do emerges. It is advantageous to approach the reading lightly, without trying to capture a single meaning as that would be ontologically futile. Deleuze and Guattari didn't share the same understanding of the concept of intensity that they both wrote about together (Smith, 2012).

Towards creative-relational inquiry   197

Our co-conspirators' idea to set up a reading group is a good one. Recently, Boltd and Powell (2022), guest speakers at the Centre for Creative-Relational Inquiry (2022) advised their audience 'good friends would never let you read Deleuze alone'.

Week 3

I feel a bit wrecked today after class. It was my turn to present my research idea. I thought it was well conceptualised and that I identified an important gap in the literature that it would fill. I expected my tutor to notice how tight it was but no, he just looked at me confused for freakin' ages—and then he asked me why I even cared!

I could feel myself well up but realised it wasn't because of his unexpected response but because he was right. He asked me what I am passionate about and what I care about. I said I didn't know.

I am passionate about making music with others. I am a violinist. But is this relevant?

Today I was introduced to the power of example (Bondi & Fewell, 2016). I felt really inspired—but can I do that? Is it even research?

Our co-conspirators often find it difficult to work out if where they are moving towards can legitimately be called research. It may be helpful to think of *inquiry* instead. Post-qual is inquiry because it starts with philosophy; it is experimental, speculative, playful. Manning (2021) tells us that philosophy is what inquiring children do, driving us forward by pushing thought to places that are 'edgy and exciting' (online). Just as qualitative approaches to research don't start with a hypothesis to be tested, inquiry doesn't start with a static and well-formed question but, instead, a playful and provoking question-*ing* that is constantly in motion, generating more questions. If we can truly understand this kind of 'childing' (Kohan, 2014, p. 81) to be something that doesn't mean without adulting, and can still carry rigour, then we may open our rigid structures of thinking about what is possible.

Week 6

Heartgasms! I loved this week's readings on autoethnography. It is surprising and thrilling to think that I can actually write about myself! Is my story worth hearing? Is it really valuable? Does my voice carry knowledge? I want to give this a go. This stats girl has never been so excited to climb into her earth-suit and do something truly embodied.

In our reading group, we have read two chapters already. Barad (2007) writes about onto-epistemology. It makes me think about the limits of human knowing. Reading her work is so difficult but I am enjoying the challenge and strangely enjoying the not-knowing, the feeling that knowledge is not there to be captured or colonised. We thought as a group we might also try some writing next week.

In this entry, our passionate co-conspirator is standing in some tensions. She is moved into autoethnography and also enjoying the challenge of the post-structural thinkers. The authors that she reads in her reading group also write papers that critique autoethnography (Jackson & Mazzei, 2008). So, what she is

198 *Fiona Murray*

moved by, and what she is reading are not necessarily onto-epistemologically coherent. The ontological turn sets ontology free from the sovereignty of epistemology. This is because epistemology might be explained as a human hyphen between ontology and methodology. But what she is reading is decentring the human that her chosen methodology arguably centres. St. Pierre (2017) writes that her students

> often email … after they've designed a humanist qualitative study and collected data in the field and ask, for example, how they can use a Deleuzian concept like the rhizome in their autoethnography or what they should do with their face-to-face interviews which they now realize don't make much sense in post-qualitative inquiry. I respond that it may be too late to salvage those studies, though the students seem to already know that.
>
> (p. 604)

Week 9

Today we heard about post-qualitative inquiry. I need to swear. Wtf? After all of this, they are saying don't bother with methodology at all?!

I am gutted! I so wanted to embrace subjectivity and write my autoethnography. I mean I was getting the sense from the post-structural reading group that I may not be able to use the 'I' in any unambiguous way but I didn't think I would need to abandon ship. They are saying that I can still do autoethnography but can I really now that I know what I know? Does this mean we can't tell our stories anymore? Am I right that now focussing on our internal data is not only navei gazing but is also too anthropocentric? I feel some guilt too. Was I 'bad' for even wanting to do this in the first place? Is methodology old fashioned? I feel kind of betrayed. I thought it was revolutionary and pretty radical. They say 'Post'. This means 'after' right? Does this mean this 'new' stuff we've been learning is 'old' stuff? Does post-qual have more capital now? What does the best student do?

We tell our co-conspirators that they will genuinely be supported to use any (non)methodology they want. We tell them that the 'post' of post-qual can mean the engagement with the posts such as post-structural and post-humanist theories rather than necessarily something that comes after qualitative methodologies. We tell them that it would feel withholding for us not to bring contemporary debates to them and that we want them to make informed choices.

I pause here in the writing as I become aware of a certain irony that I am experiencing and writing through. Although I often expect students to enjoy the academic freedom of a non-methodological approach, I note that for some, the freedom offered is not necessarily trusted, and that students fear they will be led to failure. I am also aware of my sense of almost trying to *convince* some (students) that, to a certain extent, this is a battle that has already been fought and won by those like St. Pierre, Manning, and Barad who now provide a citational field. St. Pierre (2020a) says that it is often our co-conspirators that scare themselves. She writes that, generally speaking, if supervisors and examiners have a sense that the work is done well—which seems to mean well-informed through deep engagement with theory, and well-written—then most will accept something being done differently. I remind them of the week they read about 'writing as a method' and talk about how St. Pierre (2007) has made these ontological shifts before them.

Our co-conspirator asks political questions around the idea that post-qual may be the right choice because it is in vogue. This reminds me of a colleague who said that the language of new materialisms and post-humanism is exclusionary and reserved for the party on the rooftop: it is and can be problematic. On the one hand, we need a new language because the one we already have is exclusionary, but it is still the one that even those who are excluded know and follow; as Truman writes (2022): 'I have ongoing concerns … of how some of what circulates as post-qualitative research manifests within the neoliberal concept ecology it seeks to unsettle' (p. 142). For further critique of this, see, for example, Rosiek et al. (2019) and Pillow (2020).

Week 14

I am still writing and sometimes from the 'I' though I am working out ways to bring this in and fade this out through various musical phases.

Every time I am playing the violin and am making music with others, I can hear theory. The theory is penetrating my bones and the horsehair of my bow. It makes the world sound different. I recorded some music to incorporate into my thesis.

By week 14, our co-conspirator seems to have embodied the approach, is working with the nuances, and is finding her next steps forward. She has set off on a musically playful post-qual jaunt.

After we present post-qual in our research course, we bring our co-conspirators the concept of *creative-relational inquiry* (CRI) to play with next. It makes sense for CRI to come after post-qual in the learning as it would be fair to say that CRI would not exist if it hadn't been for the emergence of post-qual out of the social sciences. Whitehead (1929/2010) writes that 'there is nothing which floats into the world from nowhere' (p. 244). In the next part I step tentatively in thinking about the subtle ways in which CRI is slowly becoming singular.

Towards creative-relational inquiry

The 'ontological turn' decentres the human as knower and flattens our assumptions about knowing (epistemology) by prioritising the entanglement between the human and the more-than-human. There are many other propositional and experimental approaches that have emerged in response to this turn (Rosiek et al., 2019; St. Pierre, 2018). The concept of *research-creation* (Manning, 2016; Springgay & Truman, 2019) has been a key entrance into

200 *Fiona Murray*

these debates for me as it draws centrally on process philosophers such as Alfred North Whitehead and William James. As Manning (2008) puts it: 'Research-creation works at this in-between of immanence and actuality where multiplicities converge into affirmations' (p. 24). The trajectory you think with will depend on the kind of questions that you are asking. I often ask questions around how creative work actualises, potentially because of my difficulties with completing a task!

Here, I seek to find the *thisness* of CRI. I look into the becoming-discreteness of CRI, but do so while holding on to Manning's (2021) assertion that, by seeking to speak to the discrete, we can 'amplify differences that are really similarities and this can put them into an antagonism' (30:26). Together, working against the heterogeneity of methodology, many trajectories create a larger citational pool for those engaging with experimental approaches. It is not unusual for our co-conspirators to draw heavily on post-qual literature while claiming they are 'doing' a CRI.

So, what matters in the articulation of CRI? Gale (2020) writes of creative-relational worldings where it is possible to 'come as you are' (p. 98). This picks up on an openness, but worldings can also be difficult to think of as they can be both 'everything and nothing at the same time' (Malone & Murris, 2022, p. 144). CRI is hard to define as it is not an encyclopaedic concept with an identity (Smith, 2012). As Deleuze liked to say: 'I am nearly incapable of speaking in my own name [en mon nom]' (Deleuze & Lapoujade, 2007, p. 65). There is no phenomenology of a concept. Smith (2012) confirms that 'in this sense, Deleuze's critique of the identity of the self or ego has as its exact parallel a critique of the identity of concepts' (p. 63).

It is possible to trace creative-relationality as a concept through the people it has moved through. Massumi (2015b) first used the term 'creative-relational' before Wyatt (2018) added the *Inquiry*. More recently, a special edition of *Departures in Critical Qualitative Research* (de Andrade et al., 2020) explores the different ways in which CRI has been picked up and conceptualised. However, soon after its initial elaboration and development, the archiving of a concept quickly becomes redundant as it travels more widely and in different directions. CRI is now CRIs (plural) with multiple singular differentials and continuous variations. For instance, instead, I can try *anarchiving*, which Massumi (2016) suggests 'is not documentation of a past activity. Rather, it is a feed-forward mechanism for lines of creative process, under continuing variation' (p. 6). So, rather than seeking the eternal, I shall experiment in a creative process in the come-as-you-are-here-and-now, setting a clock for two minutes and plugging the creative-relational into the writing as a feed-forward mechanism. This is exactly the task that our co-conspirators do in our research class.

A creative-relational anarchiving

As I write, I have an image of Ash, Grey, and H beckoning me back into the session where they are already living the creative-relational experiment. They are daring me to

Towards creative-relational inquiry 201

practice it with, through, and for them by thinking differently about my current under-
standings of relationships, and thinking creatively-relationally with them on how the
polycule works. The sentence from before, when Grey with a hint of sarcasm said, 'I
really enjoy paying good money to sit around waiting for my favourite metamour' is a
*lure for feeling (*Whitehead, 1929/2010*), felt now as a proposition that is lodged in my*
throat, awaiting its own expression. Grammarly, my vital writing platform, points out to
me that 'metamour' is an unknown word, a new concept. I click 'add to dictionary'.
The same red line appears under 'throatlump' (I don't think throatlump will take
off, so I don't add it to the dictionary, and live with the red line that it sits on
declaring its lack of acceptance). I will follow this metamour thread, seeing it as my
next step. I am drawn to the paradox of Grey's antagonism towards their metamour
alongside my feeling that metamour is actually a beautiful word. In ethical non-
monogamy, your metamour is your lover's other lover. I guess it means 'withlove'
(another red line). How can withlove (without the need for a space) be an unknown
concept? With that question Manning (2021) appears in my mind's eye as I
remember writing above about her advice not to dwell too much on the differences
that put us into antagonism. Was she now saying instead being 'withlove'? Grey's
antagonism towards H is now bringing creative-relationality to the idea of the dif-
ferent trajectories being metamours, sharing troubled love, withlove and withtrouble.
Sharing a love of philosophy? Lovers of the theory? Lovers of childing, sharing our
values, sharing our practices of experimenting, worlding, inquiry, lovers of working
and living and making music together? How can we conceive of a creative-relational
metamouring?

Time up

Below, as a way of thinking through CRI's discreteness, I name three *withloves*
I apply to CRI: metamouring with theory, metamouring with our co-conspirators on the Master's programme, and metamouring with practice by writing in collusion with other practices.

Metamouring with theory

Research diary week 16

This week we were introduced to creative-relational inquiry. We had to plug the concept
into our writing and see where it took our projects. It didn't matter what theory we were
thinking with or if we were planning on using conventional methodologies or not. We
just came as we were.

CRI has no other starting point rather than the concept itself. It doesn't
require a philosophy of immanence. Denzin (2016) writes:

> Over the last two decades, poststructuralists have fought hard to claim an
> interpretive space for inquiry which questioned norms of objectivity,
> emphasized complexity, subjective interpretive processes, performance …

202   *Fiona Murray*

> These understandings, like obdurate structures, ought not to be compromised. They are knots in our interpretive handkerchief.
>
> (p. 14)

This fighting hard may be why St. Pierre (2019) writes that to do a post-qual, 'you must study poststructuralism—that's required' (p. 6).

This is very monogamous and not necessarily what I might think of as a practice of metamouring that allows you to bring other loves and to have relationship diversity, or creative-relationality. However, I have found St. Pierre's definiteness around this very enabling because, when it was very new and the idea of not using methodology at all seemed so daunting, her clarity and what I felt as force, rendered me capable (as Haraway, 2016, puts it) of making the ontological shifts required and I had and developed a borrowed confidence. St. Pierre's work contributed to the establishment of the knots or remembrances in the interpretative handkerchief to which Denzin refers—and, as Denzin (2016) also writes in the same paper, 'we need a bigger tent!' (p. 14).

Vagle and Hofsess (2016) write about possibilities of bringing phenomenology and post-structural theory together for 'qualitative researchers interested in playing (or experimenting) with entangled connections among seemingly disparate philosophies, theories, and methodologies' (p. 334). However, in response, Springgay and Truman (2017) write:

> Counter to St. Pierre's (2016a, 2016b) arguments, Mark Vagle and Brooke Hofsess (2016) ask questions about the productivity of bridging phenomenology with post-qualitative methodologies, insisting that a playful 'putting together' of phenomenology and Deleuze and Guattarian concepts provoke a post-reflectivity. However, our own new materialist and speculative conjectures about methodologies and methods are more in line with St. Pierre's convictions that reflexivity (humanist) and radical empiricism (more-than-human) are incommensurate.
>
> (p. 206)

There is nobody there to say what creative-relational inquiry can or cannot do before experimentation. For Deleuze and Guattari (1994), to sense the concept as an experimental tool is to suggest that concepts 'are not pieces of a jigsaw puzzle but rather the outcome of throws of the dice' (p. 35). It is worth adding that the metamouring situation of Ash, Grey, and H is currently not working well and whether or not matters will be resolved is not yet known. It is not so much that everything will work, as it is that no one knows beforehand. Writing about immanent critique, Massumi (2015a) observes that

> as its name implies, cannot purport to apply already-established criteria of correctness or necessity to the field of collective action. It cannot operate in the imperative, based on a prior political programme or already structured set of moral precepts. It cannot justify itself by appealing to

Towards creative-relational inquiry 203

established principles. It immanently enacts its own principle, which is one with its exemplary movement.

(p. 106)

Many of our co-conspirators draw on psychoanalytic theory. There are tensions between working with the psyche and post-structural theory but, as Seigworth (2021) says, 'we do not yet know what a body can do but nor do we yet know what consciousness can do'. Therefore, it seems important that we do not create a 'cancel culture' that closes down experimentation. Boldt (2020) is a therapist who draws on contemporary relational psychoanalysis in experimental combination with the concepts of Deleuze and Guattari. She writes: 'And while I recognize that post-human studies do not privilege the human in the flow of affect, as a therapist, my concern is both human experience—my clients' and my own—and how we are affected by things that exceed the human' (p. 232).

So far, CRI appears to be open to creative relations with its theoretical metamours. No one, other than the concept itself in any particular encounter, can know if it is pushed beyond its limits of what it can do.

Metamouring with Master's co-conspirators

Research diary week 16 (continued)

I feel today like I made a bit of leap after doing some writing in class. I want to keep writing from where I left off.

A quick conversation prior to writing this chapter:

FIONA: What do you think CRI actually does?
JONATHAN: (Wyatt, a colleague, looks both confused and thoughtful before saying): I think it does this … (Jonathan starts to move his arms like he is ushering someone past).
FIONA: (slowly nods and confirms): Yes, it does do that.

CRI does not require the same *long preparation* that post-qual inquiry does. It is as demanding as a co-conspirator needs it to be to pass their particular programme. It needs to be done well and the work must be convincing that there has been involvement with the literature enough to satisfy Master's level work. Master's students who have completed dissertations that picked up on the creative-relational at Edinburgh (and there have now been a few), have been convincing. It is important that, if conventional qualitative methodology is becoming predictable, then we must find a way to make or create work that departs from this conventionality and is accessible to our Master's co-conspirators. It is those who are on the Master's programme that make up the majority of the research course. Thus, we need an approach to research that Master's students are able to pick up quickly (as they have

204 *Fiona Murray*

shorter timescales than doctoral students), and that is aligned to the principles and values of post-qualitative inquiry.

Though many of our Master's co-conspirators still want to embrace more traditional methodologies, CRI is made accessible to them by providing a momentum by starting with a concept. This is not the same as using a pre-conceived methodology as concepts are 'not waiting for us ready-made, like heavenly bodies. There is no heaven for concepts. They must be invented, fabricated, or rather created and would be nothing without their creator's signature' (Deleuze & Guattari, 1994, p. 5). It is the students' particular working of the concept that is interesting. In class, they leave with writing, momentum, and usually a desire to keep writing. The doctoral students have more time to do and develop this, but CRI nurtures all processes, paying attention to concrescence (to grow together or become, for more on which see Whitehead, 1929/2010), nudging them along, with flailing arms, across metamouring programmes, working together, promoting accessibility, and hopefully rendering each other capable (Haraway, 2016).

A metamouring of practices

I meet Mingxi (their real name), my doctoral co-conspirator, on Teams for what I am about to find out will be a creative-relational research supervision session. She hasn't sent me any writing to read for this month and she has permitted me to share this and that with you [the reader]. I will assume that I have her permission to also tell you that she hasn't yet sent me much writing. She is just starting her project and I know that she is finishing her counsellor training, which takes priority. I trust her process wholeheartedly and know that she will return to her training's metamour. I fathom we will meet anyway, touch base, keep research in her thoughts, and figure out a next step or two. (As an addendum, I was correct to trust Mingxi, who has turned into a prolific writer.)

Mingxi is one of the people that carried out the creative-relational writing exercise in the research class and she tells me when we meet that she thought she would just continue writing during our session, with her screen shared, and me as witness to the words taking form in real-time. It feels like an adventure to be together in this unpredictable edge.

I watch as she types a letter onto the page, followed hesitantly by another, and another. It is slow and stuttered writing, that is very recognisable to me. As many of her words are deleted as survive until she deletes the little survivors too.

And we are back to blank.

I wonder if writing is Mingxi's practice or if she has others. I have slowly come to think of writing as my practice, but I don't find it easy to start either and often end up back to blank.

It strikes me how vulnerable the process is, each letter a little sigh. I become acutely aware of my role in her process and wonder how I can move with her in time, creatively, and relationally, moving together.

In writing with Mingxi, I had a sense of a greater pedagogical potential still to be discovered in the way we can nurture our co-conspirator's processes. This took me back to Jonathan's waving arms that now don't only mean a movement away from stillness, or stagnancy, but also a moving through the academic gates that privilege writing even though theory itself does not advocate for any particular application to any particular practice.

Therefore, something distinctive about CRI is that it provides momentum through writing, but it does so in collusion with other practices, with a valuing of them as legitimate ways of thinking and knowing. It does so with the understanding that everyone must submit writing even if this is not their intuitive way. Writing is privileged in the academy even though as, like St. Pierre (Richardson & St. Pierre, 2005) and Wyatt (2018) and also Mingxi, I, too, am happy writing on the whole, and although I can also draw, I know that I would never have completed a doctorate if it had to be submitted as a single piece of art that stood up against other pieces of art because it simply would crumble. CRI works to enable processes of the unhappy or at least less happy writer, by helping move them into writing and to become good enough writers, even excellent writers, that can stand up against others who can claim more easily that the work *wrote itself*.

The concept itself makes space for the collusion of different creative practices and capacities to be in relation to each other and even if a thesis must be submitted in words, it can involve those words to be engaged in the discussion of other immobilising practices and artful ways of working. It is a pedagogical concept in the sense that it says 'here is your entry into the conceptual' to those who think more naturally with affects and percepts.

Research diary week I have no idea anymore!

The tutor facilitator roles for 'Between Counselling and Research' have been advertised for next year. I am thinking I could apply. It's been two years now since I did the course. I still don't really know where I am going, I am still in process, but I think I kind of know what I am doing.

There are no more educative comments as I am currently in the same place as this co-conspirator, still in process, working it out, withlove.

References

Barad, K. (2007). *Meeting the universe halfway: Quantum physics and the entanglement of matter and meaning* (2nd ed.). Duke University Press Books.

Boldt, G. (2020). On learning to stay in the room: Notes from the classroom and clinic. In A. Nicollini, N. Lesko, B. Dernikos, & S. McCall (Eds.), *Mapping the affective turn in education: Theory, research, and pedagogy* (pp. 229–245). Routledge.

Boltd, G., & Powell, K. (2022, May 13). Making connections: Processes of relating in therapy and inquiry [Speech]. Centre for Creative-Relational Inquiry, University of Edinburgh, UK.

Bondi, L., & Fewell, J. (2016). *Practitioner research in counselling and psychotherapy: The power of examples*. Red Globe Press.

Braidotti, R. (2019). *Posthuman knowledge*. Polity.

Centre for Creative-Relational Inquiry. (2022). *Homepage*. https://www.ed.ac.uk/hea lth/research/centres/ccri

206   Fiona Murray

de Andrade, M., Stenhouse, R., & Wyatt, J. (2020). Some openings, possibilities, and constraints of creative-relational inquiry: Introduction to the special issue. *Departures in Critical Qualitative Research*, *9*(2), 1–15. https://doi.org/10.1525/dcqr.2020.9.2.1

Deleuze, G., & Guattari, F. (1994). *What is philosophy?* Columbia University Press.

Deleuze, G., & Guattari, F. (2013). *A thousand plateaus: Capitalism and schizophrenia*. Bloomsbury Academic. (Original work published 1980)

Deleuze, G., & Lapoujade, D. (2007). *Two regimes of madness: Texts and Interviews 1975–1995* (revised ed.). Semiotext(e).

Denzin, N. K. (2016). Critical qualitative inquiry. *Qualitative Inquiry*, *23*(1), 8–16. https://doi.org/10.1177/1077800416681864

Gale, K. (2020). Writing in immanence. *Departures in Critical Qualitative Research*, *9*(2), 92–102. https://doi.org/10.1525/dcqr.2020.9.2.92

Guttorm, H., Hohti, R., & Paakkari, A. (2015). 'Do the next thing': An interview with Elizabeth Adams St. Pierre on post-qualitative methodology. *Reconceptualizing Educational Research Methodology*, *6*(1), 15–22. https://doi.org/10.7577/rerm.1421

Haraway, D. J. (2016). *Staying with the trouble. Making kin in the Chthulucene*. Duke University Press.

Jackson, A. Y. (2017). Thinking without method. *Qualitative Inquiry*, *23*(9), 666–674. https://doi.org/10.1177/1077800417725355

Jackson, A. Y., & Mazzei, L. A. (2008). Experience and 'I' in autoethnography. *International Review of Qualitative Research*, *1*(3), 299–318. https://doi.org/10.1525/irqr.2008.1.3.299

Jackson, A. Y., & Mazzei, L. A. (2012). *Thinking with theory in qualitative research*. Routledge.

Kanai, A., & Gill, R. (2020). Woke? Affect, neoliberalism, marginalised identities and consumer culture. *New formations: A journal of culture/theory/politics*, *10*(2), 10–27. https://doi.org/10.3898/NewF:102.01.2020

Kohan, W. (2014). *Childhood, education and philosophy: New ideas for an old relationship*. Routledge.

Lather, P., & St. Pierre, E. A. (2013). Post qualitative research. *International Journal of Qualitative Studies in Education*, *26*(6), 629–633. https://doi.org/10.1080/09518398.2013.788752

Malone, K., & Murris, K. (2022). Worlding. In K. Murris (Ed.), *A glossary for doing postqualitative, new materialist and critical posthumanist research across disciplines* (pp. 144–145). Routledge.

Manning, E. (2008). Creative propositions for thought in motion. *INFLeXions*, *1*. https://www.inflexions.org/n1_manninghtml.html

Manning, E. (2016). 10 propositions for research-creation. In N. Colin & S. Sachsenmaier (Eds.), *Collaboration in performance practice: Premises, workings and failures* (pp. 133–141). Palgrave Macmillan.

Manning, E. (2021, January 23). *Post philosophies and the doing of inquiry Session 6 Erin Manning* [Video]. YouTube. https://youtu.be/GZHKK8hBLcU

Massumi, B. (2002). *Parables for the virtual: Movement, affect, sensation*. Duke University Press Books.

Massumi, B. (2015a). *Politics of affect*. Amsterdam University Press.

Massumi, B. (2015b). The supernormal animal. In R. Grusin (Ed.), *The nonhuman turn* (pp. 1–18). University of Minnesota Press.

Massumi, B. (2016). Working principles. In Senselab (Ed.), *The go-to how-to book of anarchiving*. lulu.com.

Pillow, W. S. (2020). Erotic power futures/relations that matter. *Departures in Critical Qualitative Research, 9*(2), 40–52. https://doi.org/10.1525/dcqr.2020.9.2.40

Richardson, L., & St. Pierre, E. A. (2005). Writing: A method of inquiry. In N. K. Denzin & Y. S. Lincoln (Eds.), *The Sage handbook of qualitative research* (pp. 959–978). Sage Publications.

Rosiek, J. L., Snyder, J., & Pratt, S. L. (2019). The new materialisms and indigenous theories of non-human agency: Making the case for respectful anti-colonial engagement. *Qualitative Inquiry, 26*(3–4), 331–346. https://doi.org/10.1177/1077800419830135

Seigworth, G. (2021, July 9). *What is affect theory?* [Video]. YouTube. https://www.youtube.com/watch?v=PuKIqF72Bwo

Smith, D. W. (2012). On the nature of concepts. *Philosophy Today, 56*(4), 393–403. https://doi.org/10.5840/philtoday20125642

Springgay, S., & Truman, S. E. (2017). On the need for methods beyond proceduralism: Speculative middles, (in)tensions, and response-ability in research. *Qualitative Inquiry, 24*(3), 203–214. https://doi.org/10.1177/1077800417704464

Springgay, S., & Truman, S. E. (2019). Research-creation walking methodologies and an unsettling of time. *International Review of Qualitative Research, 12*(1), 85–93. https://doi.org/10.1525/irqr.2019.12.1.85

St. Pierre, E. A. (2007). *Writing as method. The Blackwell encyclopedia of sociology.* https://doi.org/10.1002/9781405165518.wbeosw029

St. Pierre, E. A. (2016a). Deleuze and Guattari's language for new empirical inquiry. *Educational Philosophy and Theory, 49*(11), 1080–1089. https://doi.org/10.1080/00131857.2016.1151761

St. Pierre, E. A. (2016b). The empirical and the new empiricisms. *Cultural Studies ↔ Critical Methodologies, 16*(1), 111–124. https://doi.org/10.1177/1532708616636147

St. Pierre, E. A. (2017). Writing post-qualitative inquiry. *Qualitative Inquiry, 24*(9), 603–608. https://doi.org/10.1177/1077800417734567

St. Pierre, E. A. (2018). Post-qualitative inquiry in an ontology of immanence. *Qualitative Inquiry, 25*(1), 3–16. https://doi.org/10.1177/1077800418772634

St. Pierre, E. A. (2019). Post-qualitative inquiry, the refusal of method, and the risk of the new. *Qualitative Inquiry, 27*(1), 3–9. https://doi.org/10.1177/1077800419863005

St. Pierre, E. A. (2020a). *Post philosophies and the doing of inquiry Session 2 Bettie St. Pierre* [Video]. YouTube. https://youtu.be/wJxGcrytx6M

St. Pierre, E. A. (2020b). Why post-qualitative inquiry? *Qualitative Inquiry, 27*(2), 163–166. https://doi.org/10.1177/1077800420931142

Truman, S. E. (2022). *Feminist speculations and the practice of research-creation.* Routledge.

Vagle, M. D., & Hofsess, B. A. (2016). Entangling a post-reflexivity through post-intentional phenomenology. *Qualitative Inquiry, 22*(5), 334–344. https://doi.org/10.1177/1077800415615617

Whitehead, A. N. (2010). *Process and reality.* Amsterdam University Press. (Original work published 1929)

Wyatt, J. (2018). *Therapy, stand-up, and the gesture of writing: Towards creative-relational inquiry.* Routledge.

15 Re-searching research
Reflections on contributions to qualitative and post-qualitative research

Keith Tudor and Jonathan Wyatt

In this final chapter, we reflect on some themes that emerge from the chapters in this book, at least for us, that is, regarding the person of the researcher, and their positionality; method and methodology; language; and research and practice. Consistent with our own philosophies and styles, we do so in the form of a dialogue—with each other and the texts.

Connecting

KEITH: I think the first thing I want to say is: 'Whew! We made it!'

JONATHAN: Yes, we've got there/here. It's been over two years in the making/doing, from when we first mooted the idea to now, when it's all but done. It's never felt a drudge; it's required regular attention, but it's been stimulating in different ways as the process of the collection coming together has gone through its different stages.

KEITH: I agree. It's been a pleasure. Although we've never met in person, and in some ways don't—or didn't—know each other that well, it's been a very positive experience, mainly because it's been really easy to work with you, so tēnā koe, thank you for that.

JONATHAN: Likewise. Me too. I'm on a train heading north to Edinburgh. I have the chapters printed beside me, with time. The broken-down train ahead of us on the line is delaying me, allowing me to dwell with this, with our contributors. It's good to be here. It's been good to be here with you on this book's journey.

KEITH: I wonder if it would be good to start with how we met and how we came to come up with the idea of editing this book?

JONATHAN: One version of this—there are always a number of stories to tell, of course, and this is today's story—is how we were first in touch when I wrote to you in 2020 with the idea I might visit New Zealand and wondering if there was scope for spending some time with you at AUT (Auckland University of Technology). I'd known about you and your work for some time through my involvement in our counsellor education programme here and your presence on course reading lists. We had an exchange of emails and a meeting on Zoom, where I think you mooted

DOI: 10.4324/9781003280859-16

Re-searching research 209

the idea of an edited collection about psychotherapy research. So, I blame you! I don't remember, though, where this idea had come from for you and whether you'd been thinking about it for a while or if it arose in the course of our conversation. What's your recollection? What's your story of how we met and how the idea arose?

KEITH: I agree about your point about multiple stories. In the book on co-creative transactional analysis I wrote with my friend Graeme Summers (Tudor & Summers, 2014), as we came to write what was going to be the introduction, we realised that we didn't and couldn't agree on when or where we'd first met! Rather than getting into a fight about it and as we are constructivists, we decided to write two separate introductions (Summers, 2014; Tudor, 2014), which I think work really well and set the scene for the dialogic nature of that book. Your point reminds of that and invites our present dialogue. My memory is that I was talking to a colleague and friend, Rose Cameron, about areas of common interest, including humour, and she mentioned you and your interest in the subject (Wyatt, 2019), and the fact that you'd done some stand-up (Wyatt, 2016). A student of mine had just completed a dissertation on the topic (Ciurlionis, 2021), and I was interested to meet you. I actually can't remember who initiated the contact, but I do remember that, when we met online, there was a sense of mutual interest(s), and a sense of the equal meeting of like minds.

JONATHAN: I remember those links now. I'd lost them.

KEITH: When we met, I do remember being interested in the fact that you are professor of qualitative inquiry (I had assumed it would be of psychotherapy and/or counselling), and being curious about that—which I guess brings us to say more about ourselves and our motivation(s) to put this book together.

Positioning ourselves

JONATHAN: Another day, another writing space. I'm here in my office in Edinburgh. It's early August 2022, a cool mid-summer's morning—for now: the weather changes rapidly here—and the city is beginning to come alive as the Fringe events begin. It's the first in-person Fringe since 2019, its happening around me familiar yet strange ('Is this really here? Should it be?'). I haven't quite adjusted to how the city feels, the university campus around me taken over by pop-up venues, my building accommodating temporary event administration offices, classrooms in other buildings converted into theatres, the squares, parks, and pavements teeming with visitors. I haven't booked to see any shows—in 2019 I attended two or three a week—which indicates my continuing wariness. By lunchtime I'll hear around me the nearby shows' music begin. I can hear musicians warming up now as I write: an electric guitarist then a trumpeter then a drummer then a singer. By next week I'll be able to time my afternoons by which number in which performance is coming through my window.

210 *Keith Tudor and Jonathan Wyatt*

JONATHAN: All of which is a way to begin positioning myself in writing these reflections with you: as committed to bringing the personal (however defined, however boundaried) onto the page; to foregrounding the process of writing; and to writing *together*.

JONATHAN: I could add: I have been a therapist. I am a therapist. Being a therapist is part of who I am, but I am not seeing clients. For some time, my investments have been as a writer and researcher, and I am as much a client as I am a therapist. I'm more a researcher who does (or has done) psychotherapy than a psychotherapist who does research, and have been for some years, hence the 'qualitative inquiry' in my title.

KEITH: Thanks for that, Jonathan. Even though as I write this, it's a few weeks later (at the end of September 2022), I am with you in your office and having a real sense of the sight and sounds of your surroundings. I am writing in my office, which is in a sleepout on my property in a village in West Auckland, with a lovely and comforting view of the Manukau harbour. The only sounds I can hear (apart from my tapping of the keyboard) are the birds: kererū, kōtare, koukou, tūī. They remind me of place (living here in Aotearoa New Zealand) and of language—of birds and of tangata whenua (people of the land).

JONATHAN: … in my imagination I can hear those bird sounds and the sounds of their names as you read them to me…

KEITH: This brings me to my first position and positionality: that of an immigrant to this country and thus tauiwi (new bones). In this I acknowledge Māori as tangata whenua and, specifically, kei te whenua o Te Kawerau a Maki māua kainga nāianei (our house sits on the land of Te Kawerau a Maki, who are the local iwi or tribe). I also acknowledge and honour Te Tiriti o Waitangi (the Treaty of Waitangi), the founding document of our bicultural nation (for discussion of which, see Tudor, 2021).

KEITH: I am also with you in your wariness. The reason I am writing right now is because I've turned down an invitation for dinner with my son and his partner because I have a slight cough and am wary of passing anything on, something that wouldn't have crossed my mind two years ago. It's a stark and very personal reminder of living in a post-COVID-19 world.

KEITH: With regard to some of my other positions, I have—with your encouragement, thank you—included them in my own contribution to this volume (Tudor, 2023) so won't repeat them here.

JONATHAN: I notice how your writing about being an immigrant, and your acknowledging of the owners of the land, Te Kawerau a Maki, stills me. Talking with you over these months I have been aware of where you are in the world (the early morning meetings have been a regular reminder) but, on our screens, except when the light is shining through your window and it's light where you are on spring and summer evenings, I have not considered the specifics of the land, less so its politics. This is what has stilled me. I am reminded I, too, am an immigrant, having moved to Scotland from southern England nine years ago. I am reminded of this most days, as I move through my adopted city. There's a politics to this too.

KEITH: In terms of the book itself and my interest to work with you on this project, I have, for some time, been concerned about a) the privileging of quantitative research models in psychology and psychotherapy; b) the dominance of empiricism as the only 'scientific' method, such that 'evidence-based practice' becomes an assumed and largely unquestioned code for 'empirically supported practice and treatments'; c) the undue and largely unquestioned influence of psychology and, specifically, of clinical psychology in health care and practice at the exclusion of psychotherapy; and d) the passivity of some psychotherapists whereby they don't care about this or assert themselves—theoretically, politically, professionally, or personally. So, meeting you, with a strong interest in and experience of research and a background in psychotherapy, seemed like a good opportunity to promote qualitative research in psychotherapy.

JONATHAN: I share those interests and concerns. Since coming to Edinburgh in 2013, I have taught our core postgraduate research course, *Between Counselling and Research 1* (University of Edinburgh, 2022) (to which Fiona Murray refers in her chapter in this volume) with Fiona and others. The course takes students through an argument for qualitative research, making the onto-epistemological and political case for such approaches along the lines you outline. It's an immersive, sometimes exhilarating, sometimes troubling, experience for students, for whom in most cases positivist research has been the norm, the only approach they have previously encountered. The course is immersive for those of us teaching it too, ten Wednesday mornings between September and November—intense, exciting, demanding. The idea for this book, and talking with you about it, picked up on this kind of energy.

Method and methodology

KEITH: My first reflection about the research encompassed in this volume is that it represents a good range of the qualitative research that's undertaken in the field of psychotherapy with, as we planned, a focus on critical perspectives, such as the psychosocial (Fang et al., 2023), feminism (le Couteur, 2023), critical race theory (Charura & Clyburn, 2023), talanoa (Ioane & Tapu Tu'itahi, 2023), and queer theory (Thompson & Harris, 2023), but also critical perspectives within research methodologies and methods, i.e., grounded theory (Day, 2023), and (if I may) heuristic (Tudor, 2023), and, further, post-qualitative research (Murray, 2023), and reflexivity in research (Serra Undurraga, 2023). I am also delighted at the creativity of other chapters, especially those on poetic inquiry (Green, 2023) and your own on collaborative inquiry (Speedy & Wyatt, 2023), regarding which I want to acknowledge not only your own work in this area but also your support of others in developing creativity in qualitative research.

JONATHAN: Thank you. I appreciate this range across the chapters you refer to as well; and I like how there is the critical in the creative and the creative in the critical.

KEITH: Some chapters emphasise methodology or the theory of method more than others, and address issues of ontology, including a post-humanistic approach to this (Murray; Serra Undurraga); epistemology, including andragogy (le Couteur); and, in terms of method, as you say, the dialogical (Ioane & Tapu Tu'itahi; le Couteur; Speedy & Wyatt).

JONATHAN: I'm interested in how distinctions between terms such as methodology and method (and ontology and epistemology) become blurred at times, whether implicitly or explicitly. Murray's chapter goes further, explaining how post-qualitative inquiry discards methodology altogether, seeking instead 'to experiment, speculate, and imagine something new' (p. 193). Your chapter on critical heuristics makes the point that heuristics is—or can be considered as—both methodology and method; you offer the term *approach* (p. 118; my emphasis). It reminds me how Craig Gingrich-Philbrook (2005, p. 298) describes autoethnography not as methodology or method, or even an approach, but as 'a broad orientation towards scholarship', which seems to fit the ways of conceptualising research in a number of the contributions to this volume.

KEITH: I love the idea that autoethnography—and, indeed, other methodologies—are *approaches* to their subject. It reminds me of the shift in person-centred psychology from a focus on the client and, later, on the person, to the approach as 'a way of being' (Rogers, 1980). Wood (1996) writes about this as a 'psychological posture' (p. 169). Perhaps we should or could be thinking about research as a way of enquiry that involves a psychological posture? If so, this could be elaborated methodologically, and with regard to the researcher's posture, which, in turn, links back to positionality.

JONATHAN: In introducing grounded theory, Day draws attention to how the terms 'research' and 'methodology' in psychotherapy elicit contrasting responses, the former being seen as creative and generous and the latter, 'by contrast, can be received with a hiss' (p. 133), perceived as constraining and detached. The politics of and in methodology—of and in research, of and in psychotherapy—are present through the chapters, with different aspects, different takes, foregrounded more in some than others.

KEITH: I appreciate your clarification of this—and, at the same time, feel my critical energy rising. Why do people have such a problem with and antipathy to methodology? It's simply the 'ology' (the study) of method! Just as axiology is the study of axia (value or ethics), ontology is the study of the ontic (being), and epistemology is the study of episteme (knowledge), so methodology is the study of method. It's not rocket science—which, of course, would be roukétology!

Language

JONATHAN: Your coining of roukétology (which I think you should make something of) takes us into saying something about contributors' playfulness with language.

KEITH: It's one of the things that I've particularly enjoyed: from Liz (Bondi's) troubling of the concept of the case; through Trish (Thompson's) and Daniel (Harris') use of the term fossicking as a way of describing the sense of discovery and turning over; and Emma (Green's) advocacy of poetry and poetical thinking as helping researchers 'flex outside and around more established ways of thinking' (p. 163); to Fiona (Murray's) use of meta-mouring to developing creative-relational inquiry, and of co-conspirators to describe students.

JONATHAN: Yes to that. There's a playfulness throughout—with language, with form, with style, with voice: a playfulness that accompanies and enhances the seriousness, a playful seriousness, a serious play. We, too, have had some playful/serious exchanges about the differences between inquiry and enquiry. I think I proposed 'inquiry' as an alternative, less loaded, term to 'research' to one contributor and you suggested 'enquiry' as a carrying a lighter, less formal, less heavy set of associations to 'inquiry'. Is that right?

KEITH: Yes, indeed—and I am delighted to have had the opportunity to say that explicitly in my own contribution to this book. In British and New Zealand English, there is a distinction between 'enquiry' as more questioning and facilitative, as in therapeutic enquiry; as distinct from 'inquiry' being more formal and legalistic, as in a government 'inquiry'. American English does not make the same distinction. I think that most authors and researchers don't consider, or at least make, the distinction.

Research and practice

KEITH: While the book is focused on the theory of research, the contributions provide many examples from practice—from therapy (Bondi, 2023; Thompson & Harris, 2023), from education (Murray, 2023), and an analysis of a specific social policy (le Couteur, 2023)—as well some guidelines for or invitations to good practice (Charura & Clyburn, 2023; Ioane & Tapu Tu'itahi, 2023; Thompson & Harris, 2023). Drawing on Richardson and St. Pierre (2005), Liz (Bondi) makes the point that researching close to practice 'brings the internal experience of practitioners firmly into view' (p. 11). Interestingly, Liz goes on to link this to writing as, she argues, practitioners 'are therefore likely to use writing as a method of enquiry' (p. 10). Kerry (Thomas-Anttila) and Margot (Solomon) also comment on the tendency of psychotherapists to ponder and reflect and that that 'facilitates the writing process' (p. 20), in their case, a hermeneutic one. They also usefully quote Ogden (2006), who writes that 'writing, after all, is a form of thinking' (p. 1072), something to which I very much relate.

JONATHAN: Me too. It's a way of coming to know, to '[touch] the mystery, delicately, with the tips of the words' (Cixous, cited in Jenson, 1991, p. 134). In some chapters, the attention given to the research process and the researcher(s)—the foregrounding, even, of each of these—struck me: how chapters focus on the *doing* of research, so to speak, and how present, in some, the researchers are on the page. For some, the research process is, or includes, writing, as you mention, alone (Bondi, 2023; Helps, 2023) or together (Speedy & Wyatt, 2023; Thompson & Harris, 2023). In other chapters there is the foregrounding of the dialogic—dialogue as a method, perhaps (Fang et al., 2023). Authors are present to us as readers and to each other, and argue for the researcher's presence in the research (Ioane & Tapu Tu'itahi, 2023; Serra Undurraga, 2023; Tudor, 2023; etc.)…

KEITH: … yes; and this dialogic approach is represented in practice in a number of collaborations: between colleagues (Charura & Clyburn; Fang et al.; Ioane & Tapu Tu'itahi; Speedy & Wyatt; Thomas-Anttila & Solomon), and between a therapist and ex client (Thompson & Harris).

KEITH: Overall, and not surprisingly, there is an emphasis on the subjective—or, more accurately, subjectivities—on lived experience, albeit writ broad (Thomas-Anttila & Solomon in particular, but also Helps; Speedy & Wyatt; and Tudor); and on dialogue (Fang et al.; Speedy & Wyatt; Thompson & Harris). In the main, I think we and the contributors have encouraged what Charmaz (2016) refers to as 'methodological self-consciousness' (p. 3), which, as le Couteur (2023) observes, involves 'a committed, ethical stance to the recognition of multiple power differentials' (p. 65)…

JONATHAN: … and/or, as Serra Undurraga writes, 'to interrogate *how* [we] are relating when being reflexive and what that relating is *producing*' (p. 34). These observations about lived experience, subjectivities, and reflexivities bring ethics into view. Authors are alert to a range of issues: to the importance of attending to ethical implications from the outset of a research project (Charura & Clyburn; Ioane & Tapu Tu'itahi; Tudor); to the insufficiency of institutional ethics procedures when 'researching from within therapeutic practice' (Helps, p. 155); to the ethical importance of reflexivity/reflexivities (le Couteur; Serra Undurraga); and to the need, in the case of psychosocial research, to be committed to 'an ethic of disillusionment' (Fang et al., p. 55). Bondi and Helps each draw attention to the dynamics of therapists seeking consent from clients, Helps offering a series of questions for the therapist-autoethnographer to bear in mind, e.g., 'How will you explain that you are writing about them? How might asking for this permission change the way that the work unfolds?'; and Bondi noting, more directly, how the process of discussing consent means 'the purpose of the [psychotherapy] is irrevocably changed' (Bondi, p. 11).

Re-searching research 215

KEITH: One of the surprises in the contributions for me was not only, where relevant, the ethical issues with regard to client/case material, but also to the therapist's own autobiographical material (Bondi, 2023).

JONATHAN: Yes, and this offers a caution, perhaps, about what it means to put our lives on the page—for both current and future clients, and others in our lives?

JONATHAN: It's noticeable how some authors used fictional devices in their chapters, e.g., Liz (Bondi's) 'Jessica' and Fiona (Murray's) composite 'co-conspirator' student, or, in Helps' case, using other strategies of 'making more anonymous' (Helps, 2023, p. 156). I'm reminded of Peter Clough's (2002) claims for the truths such fictions allow.

KEITH: I wonder about this. I remember reading a book on various 'conditions' written by a person-centred colleague based on case studies, and then being astonished when I realised that it—in all, some 14 volumes, —was entirely based on 'fictitious dialogue' (Bryant-Jefferies, 2022). I think this is a problem as, at least in this case, the publications appear, at least, to serve to prove the theory, rather than the other way around.

JONATHAN: I'm with you in how you respond to that example. The use of fiction sounds contrived and dissatisfying. I think it's about purpose, for sure. For me, it's also about how it's written, how fully an author inhabits the character. Clough (2002) is committed to the 'search for the articulation of a persuasive voice' (p. 68), and that's my sense of what contributors here have found. The fictions they create are more than mere devices. They belong; they feel alive.

KEITH: One more observation about this connection between research and practice: notwithstanding what I think is a good result of contributions of psychotherapy research informed and illustrated by practice, I think we both noticed during the production of the book (from commissioning the chapters, through reading drafts, to final revisions), some colleagues tended to default to practice as distinct from research…

JONATHAN: … which, as I think about it now, isn't surprising given the strong echoes between the experience of psychotherapy practice and the approaches to research offered in this volume; practice in some sense is itself research. Bondi and Fewell (2016) argue for approaches to psychotherapy research, like the therapeutic encounter, '[honour] and [foster] lived experiences of being and struggling to be in relationship to ourselves and others' (p. 7). That distinction we've been holding in mind is blurred at times, even as we (all) worked to maintain the collection's focus on research.

Ending

JONATHAN: Bringing our discussion to a close with these connections between research and practice feels fitting, given the hopes for this book we articulated at the outset. It's now October. The Fringe—which, earlier in our exchanges here, was about to begin—is well over; and my train made it back to Edinburgh, despite delays. It's mid-Autumn; our clocks are about to go back an hour and it will become darker, earlier. You and I are soon to send this chapter, along with the other 14 chapters, to the publisher. We are finishing. Although there is plenty more to say about these chapters, and many other ways we could articulate the complex, engaging, important work they do, this seems a good place for us to stop; or, at least, pause.

KEITH: I agree. I'm glad your train paused only, in the scheme of things, relatively briefly, and started again to continue to carry you to your destination. This, I suggest, is a good metaphor for this book which, I hope, offers a pause in the practice of practitioners and students to consider and study—the 'ology'—of our method, however we define that.

JONATHAN: Thank you. Maybe we'll get to meet in person sometime. I hope so.

KEITH: Me too.

References

Bondi, L. (2023). Into the thick of it: Troubling case studies and researching close to therapeutic practice. In K. Tudor & J. Wyatt (Eds.), *Qualitative research approaches for psychotherapy: Reflexivity, methodology, and criticality* (pp. 3–14). Routledge.

Bondi, L., & Fewell, J. (Eds.). (2016). *Practitioner research in counselling and psychotherapy: The power of examples*. Palgrave.

Bryant-Jefferies, R. (2022). *Books published*. https://richardbj.co.uk/books

Charmaz, K. (2016). The power of constructivist grounded theory for critical inquiry. *Qualitative Inquiry, 23*(1), 34–45. https://doi.org/10.1177/1077800416657105

Charura, D., & Clyburn, S. (2023). Critical race theory: A methodology for research in psychotherapy. In K. Tudor & J. Wyatt (Eds.), *Qualitative research approaches for psychotherapy: Reflexivity, methodology, and criticality* (pp. 72–86). Routledge.

Ciurlionis, C. (2021). *In defence of a manic defence: A therapist's experience of humour in psychotherapy* [Master's dissertation, Auckland University of Technology]. Tuwhera Open Access Theses & Dissertations. https://openrepository.aut.ac.nz/handle/10292/14499

Clough, P. (2002). *Narratives and fictions in educational research*. Oxford University Press.

Day, E. (2023). Keeping it real: Grounded theory for a profession on the brink. In K. Tudor & J. Wyatt (Eds.), *Qualitative research approaches for psychotherapy: Reflexivity, methodology, and criticality* (pp. 133–148). Routledge.

Fang, N., Pirrie, A., & Redman, P. (2023). A psychosocial coming into play: Researching authenticity in therapy, the academy, and friendship. In K. Tudor & J. Wyatt (Eds.), *Qualitative research approaches for psychotherapy: Reflexivity, methodology, and criticality* (pp. 45–57). Routledge.

Gingrich-Philbrook, C. (2005). Autoethnography's family values: Easy access to compulsory experiences. *Text and Performance Quarterly, 25*(4), 297–314. https://doi.org/10.1080/10462930500362445

Green, E. (2023). (Re)searching poetically: Poetic inquiry in psychotherapy. In K. Tudor & J. Wyatt (Eds.), *Qualitative research approaches for psychotherapy: Reflexivity, methodology, and criticality* (pp. 163–175). Routledge.

Re-searching research   217

Helps, S. (2023). Researching from the inside: Using autoethnography to produce ethical research from within psychotherapy practice. In K. Tudor & J. Wyatt (Eds.), *Qualitative research approaches for psychotherapy: Reflexivity, methodology, and criticality* (pp. 149–162). Routledge.

Ioane, J., & Tapu Tu'itahi, A. (2023). Pasifika research methodologies and psychotherapy. In K. Tudor & J. Wyatt (Eds.), *Qualitative research approaches for psychotherapy: Reflexivity, methodology, and criticality* (pp. 87–101). Routledge.

Jenson, D. (Ed.). (1991). *Coming to writing and other essays (Hélène Cixous)*. Harvard University Press.

le Couteur, E. (2023). Feminist research in psychotherapy: The strange case of the United Kingdom's 'hostile environment' policy. In K. Tudor & J. Wyatt (Eds.), *Qualitative research approaches for psychotherapy: Reflexivity, methodology, and criticality* (pp. 58–71). Routledge.

Murray, F. (2023). From post-qualitative inquiry towards creative-relational inquiry in (and beyond) the education/training of therapists. In K. Tudor & J. Wyatt (Eds.), *Qualitative research approaches for psychotherapy: Reflexivity, methodology, and criticality* (pp. xx–xx). Routledge.

Ogden, T. H. (2006). On teaching psychoanalysis. *International Journal of Psychoanalysis*, *87*(4), 1069–1085. https://doi.org/10.1516/D6D1-TGVX-A4F0-JECB

Richardson, L., & St. Pierre, E. A. (2005). Writing: A method of inquiry. In N. K. Denzin & Y. S. Lincoln (Eds.), *Handbook of qualitative research* (3rd ed., pp. 959–978). Sage.

Rogers, C. R. (1980). *A way of being*. Constable.

Serra Undurraga, J. K. A. (2023). Using performative meta-reflexivity in psychotherapy research. In K. Tudor & J. Wyatt (Eds.), *Qualitative research approaches for psychotherapy: Reflexivity, methodology, and criticality* (pp. 31–44). Routledge.

Speedy, J., & Wyatt, J. (2023). Putting ourselves in the picture: Phototherapy, collaborative writing, and psychotherapy research. In K. Tudor & J. Wyatt (Eds.), *Qualitative research approaches for psychotherapy: Reflexivity, methodology, and criticality* (pp. 176–192). Routledge.

Summers, G. (2014). Introduction. In K. Tudor & G. Summers, *Co-creative transactional analysis: Papers, dialogues, responses, and developments* (pp. xxxi–xxxviii). Karnac Books.

Thomas-Anttila, K., & Solomon, M. (2023). Hermeneutic phenomenology: Exploring and making meaning of lived experience in psychotherapy research. In K. Tudor & J. Wyatt (Eds.), *Qualitative research approaches for psychotherapy: Reflexivity, methodology, and criticality* (pp. 15–30). Routledge.

Thompson, T., & Harris, D. X. (2023). Queering psychotherapy research: Collaborative autoethnography and fossicking. In K. Tudor & J. Wyatt (Eds.), *Qualitative research approaches for psychotherapy: Reflexivity, methodology, and criticality* (pp. 102–114). Routledge.

Tudor, K. (2014). Introduction. In K. Tudor & G. Summers, *Co-creative transactional analysis: Papers, dialogues, responses, and developments* (pp. xix–xxix). Karnac Books.

Tudor, K. (2021). Tūtira mai ahau. In K. Tudor, *20/20 vision, 2020*. Tuwhera Open Access Books. https://ojs.aut.ac.nz/tuwhera-open-monographs/catalog/book/6

Tudor, K. (2023). Critical heuristics in psychotherapy research: From 'I-who-feels' to 'We-who-care—and act'. In K. Tudor & J. Wyatt (Eds.), *Qualitative research approaches for psychotherapy: Reflexivity, methodology, and criticality* (pp. 115–132). Routledge.

Tudor, K., & Summers, G. (2014). *Co-creative transactional analysis: Papers, dialogues, responses, and developments*. Karnac Books.

218   *Keith Tudor and Jonathan Wyatt*

University of Edinburgh. (2022). *Postgraduate course: Between counselling and research 1: Approaches, issues and debates (L12) (CNST12007).* http://www.drps.ed.ac.uk/19-20/dpt/cxcnst12007.htm

Wood, J. K. (1996). The person-centered approach: Towards an understanding of its implications. In R. Hutterer, G. Pawlowsky, P. F. Schmid, & R. Stipsits (Eds.), *Client-centered and experiential psychotherapy: A paradigm in motion* (pp. 163–181). Peter Lang.

Wyatt, J. (2016). *Stand-up: Therapy on legs* [Video]. YouTube. https://www.youtube.com/watch?v=JmyBaeP_rqw

Wyatt, J. (2019). *Therapy, stand-up, and the gesture of writing: Towards creative-relational inquiry.* Routledge.

Index

Aafjes-van Doorn, K. 103, 113
Academy of American Poets, 163, 173
Adams, T. E. 157, 160
Ahmed, S. 103, 113
Ahmed, S. A. 134, 147
Akhtar, S. 24, 28
Alexander, E. 163, 173
Allen, R. L. 59, 68
Altman, N. 49, 56
American Psychological Association 80, 83
American Psychology Association Division 32 (Humanistic Psychology) Task Force 119, 129
Anae, M. S. 90, 92, 93, 99
Anandavalli, S. 78, 83
andragogy
Andrew, S. 154, 160
Andrews, K. 74, 83
Anthias, F. 59, 61, 68
Archer, M. **32**, 43
anti-discriminatory practice 59, 74
authenticity, inquiry into 45–57
Applebaum, B. 59, 68
Arthur, N. 118, 129
artistic concentration 172
assemblages 37–38, 43
Auckland University of Technology 13, 88, 127, 129, 143, 208
authenticity 45–56, 65, 95, 97, 99, 110; in pedagogical relations 51–54; in therapeutic encounters 48–51
autoethnography 149–160; collaborative 102–113; critical 103; within a methodological landscape 150–152; within psychotherapy 158–160

Bager-Charleson, S. 2
Barad, K. 34, 35, 36, 37, 39, 43, 194, 197, 205

Baraitser, L. 47, 50, 56
Barbour, K. 67, 68
Barnes, M. 176, 191
Barrineau, P. 119, 129
Beazley, P. 159, 160
Beck, G. 115, 129
being: and knowing 63–65; ness 15; there 15; a way of 28, 166, 212; -with 15, 23
Békés, V. 103, 113
Bemak, F. P. 63, 64, 69
Benjamin, J. 35, 43
Bennett, J. 190, 191
Berke, J. 176, 191
Bion, W. R. 21, 26, 29, **32**, 43
Birchard, T. 16, 129
Birks, M. 135, 139, 140, 141, 142, 147
Blackburn, S. 79, 83
Blakely, K. 68
Blyton, E. 188, 191
Bochner, A. 151, 160
Boell, S. K. 19, 29
Boldt, G. 203, 205
Bollas, C. 9, 13
Bondi, L. 4, 5, 13, 40, 44, 155, 160, 197, 205, 213, 214, 215, 216
Bonilla-Silva, E. 76, 83
Bowie, A. 166, 173
Bozarth, J. 119, 129
Brady, I. 164, 173
Braidotti, R. 195, 205
Braun, V. 65, 68
Breen, K. 76, 83
Brenman Pick, I. 49, 50, 51
Breuer, J. 6, 14
Bridges, N. A. 11, 13
Bridgman, P. 125, 129
Brinkmann, S. 141, 148
Browne, K. 102, 113
Bryant, A. 78, 83

220 *Index*

Bryant-Jefferies, R. 215, 216
Buber, M. 121, 129
Butler, J. 37, 44, 46, 56

Caelli, K. 16, 29
Caputo, J. D. 165, 173
Carroll, R. 7, 13
case: history(ies) 6, 7, 8, 11; study(ies) 3, 6, 7, 8, 11, 12, 13, 215; a/the 4, 5, 6, 7, 213
Casey, A. 119, 130
Cecez-Kecmanovic, D. 19, 29
Centre for Creative-Relational Inquiry 1, 197
Chang, H. 151, 160
Chantler, K. 62, 67, 69
Charmaz, K. 138, 139, 140, 141, 142, 143, 145, 147, 214, 216
Charura, D. 73, 79, 83, 211, 213, 214, 216
Chimera, C. 153, 160
Chu, C. 94, 100
Chung, R. C. 63, 64, 69
Ciurlionis, C. 209, 216
Clark, K. B. 77, 83
Clark, M. K. 77, 83
Clough, P. 215, 215
Clyburn, S. 211, 213, 214, 216
collaborative writing 103, 104, 105, 106, 108, 111, 112, 113, 176–191
Cobb-Roberts, D. 151, 160
Cohen, M. Z. 16, 29
Conley, D. 73, 83
conditionality and narrative truth 172
consent, informed 11
Corbin, J. 139, 147
counselling 48, 51, 194–195
COVID-19 pandemic 46, 103, 106, 145, 146, 186, 194
creative-relational 102, 104, 113; anarchiving 200–201; inquiry 199–205, 213
Crenshaw, K. 64, 69
Creswell, J. W. 115, 125, 129
critical: autoethnography 103; frameworks 63–65; heuristics 115–129; participatory action 80–81; perspectives in research 211; race theory 72, 75–77, as methodology for research 77–82; reflexivity 32, 58, 65–66; whiteness 74
Crowther, S. 22, 29
Cummins, A-M. 46, 56

D'Arcy, C. 61, 69
D'Arrigo-Patrick, J. 75, 83

Dahlstrom, D. 27, 29
Dalal, F. 50, 56
Dasein, 15, 17, 24, 165
data: analysis 19, 26–28, 78, 95, 140, 141, 151, 171, as dwelling and reverie 171; being-with, 15; collection 19, 94, 121, 138, 141; creating poetry from the 171; dialoguing with the 121–122; engaging with 30; the ground of the 135, 136, 137; interpreting 16; literature as 19; and method 138, 139, 140, 141–142, 145–146; and methodology 94–95, 121, 122, 157; sovereignty 82, 121; stories from 22–25; themes in 21–22; a way of being with the 28
Davis, J. 79, 83
Day, E. 134, 145–147, 211, 216
de Andrade, M. 200, 206
de Saxe, J. 65, 69
description, thick 3, 7–8
Deleuze, G. 37, 44, 193, 196, 200, 202–204, 206
Delgado, R. 75, 76, 80, 83
Denzin, N. K. 1, 2, 150, 152, 160, 201, 202, 206
DeVance Taliaferro, J. 78, 79, 83
dialogue 52, 53, 106, 112, 121–122, 137, 141, 142, 146, 208–216; self- 121, 122
Dilthey, W. 166, 173
disciplinary 46, 47
discipline(s) 54, 65, 127, 128, 133, 166
discourse 33, 37, 47, 49, 50, 53, 63, 78, 104, 134, 139, 177; immigration 60–62
discovery and surprise 172
discriminatory practice 60, 76
Diversi, M. 151, 161, 190, 191
Djuraskovic, I. 118, 129
Dodgson, J. E. 65, 69
Domingue, B. 73, 83
Doucet, A. **32**, 44
Douglass, B. 115, 117, 118, 119, 129
Dove, R. 170, 173
Dreyfus, H. 15, 17, 29
Dryden, W. 115, 129,
duo-ethnographies 151, 153
Dunne, J. 8, 13
Dunphy, K. 137, 147
Dupuis, C. 63, 65, 69

Edwards, J. 152, 160
Eisner, E. W. 125, 126, 129
Ellis, C. 151, 155, 160
Embleton Tudor, L. 117, 129

Index 221

enquiry: heuristic *see* heuristic enquiry; inductive, 140; and inquiry 120–121, 213; ontological, 133, 135; self-search 123; writing as a method of 10, 213
epistemology 36, 137, 151, 194, 198, 199, 212; ethico-onto- 38–39; onto- 36, 194, 197, 198; of transcendence 125
Esnard, T. 151, 160
Espin, M. O. 67, 69
Etchebarne, A. 72, 83
Etherington, K. 31, **32**, 44
ethical: agenda 58; boundaries 98; institutional 154; methods 191; non-monogamy 210; position(ing) 65–66, 75, 214; pitfalls 134; principles, 80; procedural 154, 155, 159; requirements 11, 134; research 149–160; responsibility 39; stance, 65, 66
ethics 154–157, 214; approval 11, 19
Eysenck, H. J. 73, 84
experience: embodied 34, 172; expanding 124–125; learning from 26–28; lived 15–28, 50, 53, 54, 76, 77, 78, 81, 82, 123, 159, 165, 169–171, 214

fa'afaletui 95–96
Fang, A. 46, 56
Fang, N. 57, 211, 214, 216
Farin, I. 18, 29
Faulkner, S. 163, 172, 173
feminism 63
feminist: agenda 58; approaches, 58, 63, 67; researcher(s) 62, 63, 68; thought 65; work 63 *see also* research, feminist
Ferendo, F. J. 119, 129
Ferguson, J. M. 102, 113
Fernández-Giménez, M. E. 171, 173
Fewell, J. 4, 13, 40, 43, 155, 160, 197, 205, 215, 216
Fine, M. 78, 81, 84
Finlay, L. 31, 44, 115, 118, 129
Fischmann, T. 116, 130
Fish, J. N. 103, 114
Flyvbjerg, B. 8, 13
Forber-Pratt, A. J. 154, 160
Forrester, J. 6, 13
fossicking 112–113
Foucault, M. 6, 13, 107, 114
Fox, R. 153, 160
Fraenkel, J. 90, 100
Francis, J. 128, 132
Franklin, R. 185, 191
Freeman, M. 163, 166, 169, 170, 173
Freire, P. 59, 69,

Freud, S. 3, 5–8, 10, 11, 13, 14
Frosh, S. 45, 46, 52, 56, 57
Fua, S. J. 94, 100, 101
Fussell, E. 76, 84

Gadamer, H-G. 16, 18, 19, 29, 165–168, 170, 173, 174
Gale, K. 103, 114, 177, 178, 190, 191, 200, 206
Garfinkel, H. 150, 161
Garner, S. 74, 84
Gendlin, E. **32**, 44
Geertz, C. 8, 14
Gill, R. 195, 206
Gingrich-Philbrook, C. 212, 216
Giovazolias, T. 79, 84
Glaser, B. 137–140, 142, 146, 147
Goffman, E. 150, 161
Goodman, L. A. 64, 69
Gordon, C. 80, 81, 85
Gordon, P. 4, 14
Graham, L. 73, 84
Gray, B. 66, 68, 69
Green, E. 163, 171, 174, 211, 213, 216
Green, M. J. 73, 74, 84
Greene, G. 6, 7, 14
Greenhalgh, T. 155, 161
Grennell, N. 117, 128, 129
Grennell-Hawke (Ngai Tahu, Ngai Mutunga), N. 118, 129
Griffiths, M. 60, 61, 69
Grinter, C. 154, 155, 162
Grondin, J. 166, 174
Grosz, S. 12, 14
grounded theory 78, 133–147; constructivist 139; examples 143–146; indicators of quality in 142; methods and tenets of 140–142
Grünbein, D. 171, 173, 174
Grzanka, P. R. 72, 84
Guattari, F. 37, 44, 193, 196, 202–204, 206
Guba, E. G. 125, 130
Gunew, S. 73, 74, 84
Guttorm, H. 193, 206

Haertl, K. 119, 130
Halapua, S. 91, 100
Halberstam, J. J. 102, 107, 108, 114
Hammond, M. 117, 130
Haraway, D. J. 39, 44, 185, 192, 202, 204, 206
Harding, S. **32**, 44
Harris, A. M. 102–106, 114

222 *Index*

Harris, D. X. 211, 213, 214, 217
Hart, M. 62, 69
Health Research Council of New Zealand 96, 100
Heidegger, M. 15–21, 23–27, 29, 165, 166, 170, 174
Helps, S. L. 152, 155, 159, 161, 214, 215, 217
Henriksson, C. 169, 170, 174
hermeneutic: circle 20, 28, 170; phenomenology, 16–18, 19, 20, 163, 165, 169, 170
hermeneutics, 16, 17–18; of facticity 165, 166
heuristic: enquiry 115, 117, 120–121, **124**, 127, 128; method 122, 124, 126; methodology 122; *see also* research, heuristic
heuristics 115–116, 117–118, 121, 122; critical 115–129; as methodology and method 119–122; and phenomenology, 119; and validity 125
Herrnstein, R. J. 73, 84
Herron, W. G. 153, 161
Hiles, D. 124, 130
Hill, J. 117, 118, 128, 130
Hipolito-Delgado, C. P. 78, 84
Hirshfield, J. 172, 174
Hofsess, B. A. 202, 207
Hogan, A. J. 134, 148
Holman Jones, S. 102, 103, 105, 114, 151, 161
Hopton, J. 59, 69
"hostile environment" (immigration) policy 60–62; implications for research 62
Howell, K. E. 78, 84
Hudson, M. 126, 130
Hughes, C. 153, 161
Hugman, R. 78, 84
Hurren, W. 173, 174
Husserl, E. 16, 17, 29, 165, 174

Immigration Act 2014 60, 69
Immigration Act 2016 60, 69
immigration policy *see* "hostile environment"
androcentric narratives in 60–62
Inwood, M. 21, 29
Ioane, J. 85, 87, 88, 94, 97, 100, 211–214, 217
inquiry: autoethnographic 41–42, 151; collaborative 81, 176–191; creative-relational 199–205; heuristic 119, 121,

125; poetic 163–173; poetry as 169–171; post-qualitative 193–199; psychosocial 45, 46, 48, 52, 56, as queer 46–47; self-search 122, 123, *124*
interpretation 18, 20, 21, 22, 24, 25, 95, 139, 142, 150, 166; the fore-structure of 20–22; psychosocial 54; of texts 18; of values 97

Jackman, M. C. 102, 114
Jackson, A. Y. 194, 196, 197, 206
Jenson, D. 214, 217
Jeris, L. 75, 79, 84

Ka'ili, T. O. 90, 91, 100
Kächele, H. 17, 29
Kaiser, W. C. 166, 174
kakala 94–95
Kanai, A. 195, 206
Karagiannis, E. 62, 70
Keating, F. 72, 84
Kidman, J. 94, 100
Kilian, A. 98, 100
Kinsella, E. A. 63, 64, 66, 71
Kirsch, G. 191, 192
Klein, E. 17, 29
knowledge systems *122*, 123, *124*
Knowles, M. S. 58, 69
Kohan, W. 197, 206
Kong, T. S. 102, 114
Kukatai, T. 121, 130
Kumar, S. 119, 130
Künkel, F. 123, 130
Kvale, S. 121, 130, 141, 148

Ladson-Billings, G. 81, 84
Lago, C. 73, 79, 83, 84
Langford, M. 186, 192
language 55, 93, 117–122, 166, 167, 168, 169–170, 172, 199, 213; and the other 165; poetic 164, 167, 168, 170, 171, 172; the power of 167; shared 141
Lapoujade, D. 200, 206
Lapping, C. 46, 57
Lather, P. 64, 69, 125, 130, 193, 206
Latour, B. 4, 14
Laverty, S. M. 165, 166, 174
Law, J. 165, 174
Layton, L. 45, 49, 55, 57
le Couteur, E. 211–214, 217
Leavy, P. 171, 173, 174
Lee, S. 139, 147, 148
Leggo, C. 163, 174
Leuzinger-Bohleber, M. 116, 130

Levinas, E. 61, 63, 68, 69, 165
Liberty. 60, 70
Lien, M. E. 165, 174
Lincoln, Y. S. 1, 2, 125, 130
Lipsky, M. 60, 70
literature: in constructivist grounded theory 140; hermeneutic 19; review(s) 118, 121, **124**; view(s) 121, **124**
lived experience 15–28, 50, 53, 54, 76, 77, 78, 81, 82, 123, 159, 165, 169–171, 214; and nearness of 164, 168–169
Lizzio-Wilson, M. 59, 70
Loewenthal, D. 115, 116, 130, 131
Lorås, L. 153, 161
Lucini, G. 143, 148
Lui, D. 90, 100
luva (report and dissemination) 94

MacLure, M. 149, 161
Maharaj, A. S. 72, 73, 84
Mālie (evaluation) 94, 95
Malone, K. 200, 206
Mankowski, E. 64, 71
Manning, E. 195, 197–201, 206
Massumi, B. 194, 200, 202, 206
Maté, G. 110, 114
Mazzei, L. A. 196, 197, 206
McBeath, A. 2
McCaffrey, G. 18, 29
McCann, M. 117, 118, 130
McDowell, T. 75, 79, 84
McLeod, J. 7, 11, 14, 78, 81, 84, 85, 115, 117, 130, 161
McNamee, S. 157, 161
McNay, L. **32**, 44
McNiff, S. 104, 114
Meekums, B. 153, 161
Meents, J. 119, 130
Merchant, A. 49, 57
Merleau-Ponty, M. 9, 14, 165
Merry, T. 115, 130
Mertens, D. 64, 70
metamouring: with co-conspirators 203–204; of practice 204–205; with theory 201–203
meta-reflexivity, performative 31–43; examples of 39–42
method *see* research method, talanoa
methodology *see* research methodology, talanoa, teu le vā
Michaels, A. 163, 174
Miller, R. M. 80, 85
Mills, J. 139, 140–142, 147

Milosz, C. 164, 174
Ministry for Pacific Peoples 89, 100
Moodley, R. 73, 82, 85
Moran, D. 16, 29
Moreira, C. 151, 161, 191
Mort, L. 60, 70
Moules, N. 16, 18, 19, 29, 70
Moustakas, C. 115–122, 124–131
Munn, Z. 118, 131
Murphy, P. 53, 57
Murray, C. 73, 84
Murray, F. 211–213, 215, 217
Murris, K. 200, 206

Nabobo-Baba, U. 91, 100
Nagayama, H. 80, 81, 85
narrative(s): 63, 64, 109, 145, 146; approach 78–79; androcentric 60–62; counter- 58; counter-cultural 63, 77; disruptions 105; heteronormative 106, 110; truth 172; visual 187
Nash, C. J. 102, 113
Nehamas, A. 53, 57
Newnes, C. 74, 85
Norris, J. 70, 151, 162
Nowell, L. S. 65, 70
Nowicka, M. 66, 70

O'Hara, M. 115, 131
Ogden, T. H. 28, 29, 213, 217
ontic 136, 137, 212
ontological 15, 17, 35, 177; assumptions 66, 79; claims 67, 68; enquiry 133, 135; foundations 142; and the ontic, 136; orientation 137; position(s) 78, 79; power grab 68; shifts 199, 202; stance 144; turn 165, 193, 198, 199; units 35
Orbach, S. 9, 12, 14
Orloff, A. S. 64, 70
Osborne, J. W. 145, 148
Oulanova, O. 76, 85
Owen, D. S. 73, 74, 85
Ozertugrul, E. 119, 122, 128, 131

Paquin, J. D. 80, 85
Parini, J. 171, 172, 174
Parsons, M. 98, 100
Pasifika Caucus of the New Zealand Association for Research in Education 92
Pasifika people 89–90, 94; values of 90, 95; worldview 94; *see also* research; research methodologies
Patton, M. Q. 118, 131

224 *Index*

phenomenology, hermeneutic 16–18, 19, 20, 163, 165, 169, 170; and differences with psychotherapy 15; and relevance for psychotherapy research 15–16
phototherapy 176–191
Pies, R. 11, 14
Pillow, W. S. 31, **32**, 34, 44, 207
Pirrie, A. 45, 57, 216
poetic inquiry 163–173
poetry: as inquiry 169–171; as (re)presentation 169–171
Polanyi, M. 22, 30, 119, 125, 128, 131
Polden, J. 11, 14
Polkinghorne, D. 119, 131
Polwart, K. 53, 57
Pomare, P. 73, 85
Ponterotto, J. G. 63, 70, 81, 85
positioning 79; ourselves (the editors) 209–211; social 31, **33**
post-humanism and reflexivity 34–37
post-qualitative inquiry 193–199
Poth, C. N. 115, 125, 129
Powell, K. 197, 205
Prendergast, M. 163, 174
presence 5, 7, 9, 11, 12, 126, 186, 189; bringing to 111–112; lingering 117; researcher 150, 214
Pring, R. 79, 85
Proctor, G. 63, 70
psychosocial 45–56
psychotherapy: profession 74, 80, 82; training 26, 59, 78
Punch, K. 79, 85

quality: appraisal tool 65; felt 45; indicators of 134, 138; 142, 143, 157; of the research relationship 99
queering psychotherapy research 102–113

Råbu, M. 153, 161
racism 73–75
Randeria, S. 62, 70
Rawicki, J. 151, 160
realism, contextual 126–128
Redman, P. 45, 47, 57
Reeve, K. 61, 70
reflexivity 31, 34–37, 38, 138, 140, 142, 150, 157, 173; critical 58, 65–66; embodied 125; as genealogy 34; the use of 31, *33; see also* meta-reflexivity
reflexivities 31, 34–38; productive *32*, 38–39; as ways of relating *32*
Reis, S. 61, 70
Reynolds, V. 59, 70

research: case study 3, 7.8; emotions in 66–68; feminist 58–68; hermeneutic 19–20; heuristic 115–128; Pasifika 91–96, 97–99; phenomenological 115, 119; queering 102–113; as a way of enquiry 212
research methods(s): challenges to 76; Indigenous 88; and methodology 211–212; participatory approaches to 78; Pasifika 91–96; qualitative, 1, 150; queer 112; queering 107–109; in psychotherapy 109–111
research methodology(ies) 16, 63, 81, 137, 170, 211; decolonising 82; Pasifika 91–96; scavenger 102–107; and psychotherapy 87–99
Richard Saltoun Gallery 178, 187, 192
Richardson, L. 10, 14, 100, 170, 171, 174, 190, 192, 205, 207, 213, 217
rigour 146, 171–173, 197
Rober, P. 153, 161
Robinson, M. 56, 57
Rogers, C. R. 119, 126, 128, 131, 212, 217
Romanyshyn, R. D. 171, 174
Rorty, R. 47, 57
Rose, N. 153, 161
Rose, T. 116, 131
Rosenblatt, P. C. 153, 161
Rosiek, J. L. 199, 207
Rossatto, C. A. 59, 68
Russell, S. T. 102, 114
Rustin, M. 4, 14
Ryan, L. 66, 70
Ryle, G. 8, 14

Saevi, T. 19, 25, 30, 169, 170, 174
Saini, A. 73, 74, 85
Salmond, A. 93, 100
Salter, L. 152, 159, 161, 162
Saville Young, L. 52, 57
Sawyer, R. D. 151, 162
Schmid, P. F. 125, 131
Schulz, C. 119, 131
Schuster, M. 166, 175
Schutz, A. 169, 175
Schwandt, T. A. 115, 131
Sedgwick, E. K. 189, 192
Seigworth, G. 203, 207
Sela-Smith, S. 119–124, 127, 128, 131
self: -consciousness, methodological 140, 142, 214; -dialogue 121, 122; -enquiry 115; -inquiry 122; researcher- 151; -search 121, 122, 123, *124*, 127; and

society 122–123; -transformation 123, 128
Semmler, P. L. 79, 85
Serra Undurraga, J. K. A. 31, **32**, 34–36, 39, 44, 211, 212, 214, 217
Shaed, D. L. 77, 86
Shantall, T. 119, 131
Sheehan, T. 15, 30
Shiff, T. 64, 70
Shinozaki, K. 65, 70
Shklarski, L. 103, 114
Siddique, S. 153, 162
Silipa, S. R. 90, 100
Silva, M. 166, 174
Silverman, H. J. 166, 175
Simon, G. 151, 154, 155, 157, 162
Sitkowski, S. 153, 161
Smith, D. W. 196, 200, 207
Smith, J. A. 78, 85
Smith, K. 81, 85
Smith, L. T. 97, 101
Smythe, E. A. 171, 175
Social Scientists Against the Hostile Environment 61, 71
Solomon, M. 18, 21, 22, 26, 30, 174, 213, 214, 217
Solórzano, D. G. 76, 80, 81, 85
Souba, W. 117, 131
Speciale, M. 153, 162
Speedy, J. 153, 156, 162, 176, 178, 186, 188, 190–192, 211, 212, 214, 217
Spence, D. 16, 29, 30, 171, 174, 175
Spence, J. 176, 178, 186, 187, 189, 190, 192
Sperry, L. 11, 14
Spinelli, E. 120, 131
Spong, S. 78, 85
Springgay, S. 199, 202, 207
St. Pierre, E. A. 10, 14, 193–196, 198, 199, 202, 205–207, 213, 217
Staemmler, F.-M. 133, 148
Stanley, L. 63, 68, 71
Stanley, P. 151, 162
Stark, M. 121, 131
Stefancic, J. 75, 76, 80, 83
Stein, C. 64, 71
Stevens, C. 115, 116, 131
Stirling, F. J. 152, 162
stories, crafting, 22–25
Stough, L. M. 139, 147, 148
Strauss, A. 137–139, 142, 146, 147,
student(s): as co-conspirators 196–199, 200, 203, 216, 216 *see also* metamouring

Su, C. 75, 85
subjectivities 38, 41, 58, 214; con-ceptualisations of **33**; and reflexivity **33**
Sultan, N. 116, 118, 119, 121, 122, 124, 125, 128, 132
Summerfield, D. 62, 71
Summers, G. 209, 217
Sumner, F. C. 77, 86

Taft, J. 127, 132
Tajfel, H. 59, 71
talanoa 91–92, 95, 98
Tamas, S. 177, 192
Tamasese, K. 88, 95, 96, 99, 101
Tapu Tu'itahi, A. 88, 93, 96, 101, 211–214, 217
Tate, D. L. 167, 168, 170, 175
Tate, W. F., IV. 81, 84
Taufe'ulungaki, A. 94, 101
Taylor, J. 121, 130
Tecun, A. 91, 101
teu le vā 92–93
Thaman, K. H. 94, 101
Thambinathan, V. 63, 64, 66, 71
theory: critical race 75–77; grounded 78, 133–147; race 72, 75–77; *see also* auto-ethnography; hermeneutics; heuristics
therapists: education/training of 193–205
the Unassuming Geeks 178, 192
Thomas-Anttila, K. 18, 22, 30, 145–147, 213, 214, 217
Thompson, T. 103, 105, 106, 114, 211, 213, 214, 217
Thomsen, S. 89, 90, 101
Thornberg, R. 138, 139, 142, 143, 147
Tillman, L. C. 79, 86
Tillman-Healy, L. 191, 192
toli (data collection) 94
Tolich, M. 151, 162
Totton, N. 117, 132
Tracy, S. J. 157, 162
transformation 65, 122, 123, 172–173; self-123, 128; social 128–129
Truman, S. E. 199, 202, 207
Tuagalu, I. 91, 93, 101
Tuck, E. 64, 71
Tudor, K. 116–118, 121, 126, 128, 129, 132, 154, 155, 162, 209–211, 214, 217
tui (data analysis) 94, 95, 96
Tunufa'i, L. 91, 101
Turkle, S. 144, 148
Turner, J. C. 59, 71
Tuson, J. 144, 145, 148

226 *Index*

University of Edinburgh. 194, 195, 211, 218
University of Otago. 96, 101

the vā 90–91
Vagle, M. D. 202, 207
Vaioleti, T. M. 91, 101
validation 96, 119; consensual 125–126
van Manen, M. 15, 16, 18, 19, 28, 30
Vass, G. 151, 162
Vessey, D. 167, 175
Vila, P. 150, 162
Viljoen, B. 143, 144, 148
Vincent, A. 171, 175

Wachtel, P. L. 79, 86
Waitoki, W. 88, 101
Wampold, B. E. 134, 148
Ward, K. 138, 139, 141, 148
Waters, R. 78, 85
Watson, M. 118, 132
White, M. 109, 114
Whitehead, A. N. 199–201, 204, 207
Whitt, M. S. 59, 71
Wilber, K. 122–124, 127, 132
Wilcox, M. M. 75, 86
Wilder, C. S. 73, 86
Wilkinson, S. **32**, 44
Williams, C. B. 79, 85
Williams, N. 46, 56

Williams, N. F. 119, 132.
Williams, R. L. 77, 86
Winnicott, D. W. 5–7, 14, 49, 50, 54, 55, 57
Winter, D. 115, 130
Winter, L. A. 81, 85, 86
Wise, S. 63, 68, 71
Wittgenstein, L. 55, 57
Wood, J. K. 212, 218
Woolf, V. 127, 132
Woolgar, S. 4, 14
Wortham, S. 59, 71
writing: autoethnographies 152; collaborative 176–191; phenomenologically 25–26; from within psychotherapeutic practice 153; for publication; and rewriting 20, 28
Wyatt, J. 103, 104, 114, 155, 162, 176, 177, 186, 190–193, 200, 203, 205–207, 209, 211, 212, 214, 217, 218

Xiao, Y. 118, 132

Yalom, I. 102, 103, 106, 109, 110, 112, 114, 176, 192
Yang, K. W. 64, 71
Yeo, C. 60, 61, 69
Yosso, T. J. 76, 80, 81, 85

Zembylas, M. 59, 71

Printed in the United States
by Baker & Taylor Publisher Services